T0369497

RADAR MAN

A Personal History of Stealth

Edward Lovick, Jr.

iUniverse, Inc.
New York   Bloomington

Radar Man
A Personal History of Stealth

iUniverse books may be ordered through booksellers or by contacting:

iUniverse
1663 Liberty Drive
Bloomington, IN 47403
www.iuniverse.com
1-800-Authors (1-800-288-4677)

ISBN: 978-1-4502-4802-0 (pbk)
ISBN: 978-1-4502-4804-4 (cloth)
ISBN: 978-1-4502-4803-7 (ebk)

Printed in the United States of America

iUniverse rev. date: 10/5/10

Dedication

I wholeheartedly dedicate this book to my best friend, Sherre, who encouraged me, supported me, and advised me. She did a great amount of work for me. She did not want to be known as my co-author, but I think of her as that, and much more. She is very much more. We are happily married.

While experiencing a sense of euphoria that lasted until after I began writing, I could not resist the temptation to write a bit of "deathless poetry," so here it is.

> *There are some books beside my bed*
> *Books that I have not yet read*
> *Some days or nights I'll read them through*
> *And then decide what next to do!*
>
> *There is a book within my head*
> *A book not ready to be read*
> *Because it's not quite fully writ*
> *My love and I will finish it.*
>
> *And let the entire world behold*
> *True tales of actions somewhat bold*
> *Because we had to "break the mold"*
> *Stories that are growing old.*
>
> *When we've finished what we've begun*
> *We'll hope no damage has been done*
> *No parts or pieces gone astray*
> *And that the smoke will clear away!*
>
> *Then she and I may gladly say*
> *We had great fun along the way!*

Contents

Preface

The year 1954 was a high point for the United States during the Cold War era. The United States and the Soviet Union teetered on the brink of nuclear devastation. Each nation fearfully suspected that the other might be plotting a military first strike. "Mutually Assured Destruction," MAD, seemed to be on everyone's mind.

America's hope for national security relied solely upon aerial reconnaissance, the ability to observe and gather reliable information about an enemy's strategic and tactical abilities, and from this attempt to predict his most probable actions. This was America's only plausible course of action for preventing nuclear war!

The need for an aircraft that could fly over Soviet territory and return with reliable information was starkly critical. The recently formed Central Intelligence Agency (the CIA) was given the task of obtaining the needed intelligence as quickly as possible, but no aircraft that could perform the required flights were available. A new one had to be designed and built immediately.

Dr. Richard M. Bissell, Jr., the CIA Director's choice to acquire a new aircraft, and Lockheed's most famous aircraft designer, Clarence Leonard "Kelly" Johnson, quickly began the design and construction of the U-2 aircraft that was expected to accomplish the needed reconnaissance.

Despite the opinions of the CIA's consultants that there was little chance that the new aircraft would be detected, the first U-2 aircraft was flown near Soviet Union borders in 1956. It immediately was detected and followed by Soviet radars, causing dismay and alarm.

President Eisenhower bravely but cautiously allowed the CIA to conduct a few flights over Soviet territory but was forced to limit them severely, requiring his personal approval for every flight.

Dr. Bissell and Kelly Johnson, out of desperation to buy time, allowed an attempt by CIA advisors to reduce the U-2 probability of detection, but to no avail.

That is where I came in.

Kelly Johnson invited me to join his "Skunk Works" in 1957. Luther Duncan MacDonald, Kelly's manager in charge of stealth technology, who knew of my extensive antenna and radar experience, recommended me. My first assignment was to help the CIA try to make the U-2 aircraft sufficiently "stealthy" to fly over Soviet Union territory, photograph anything of military interest, and fly out undetected.

Immediately after my work on the U-2, I began work on what became the A-12 triple-sonic reconnaissance aircraft that evolved into the YF-12, the most lethal interceptor aircraft ever built, and finally, the SR-71 Blackbird, a very successful triple-sonic reconnaissance aircraft. I also worked on the D-21 triple-sonic drone that was the first low radar cross section programmed reconnaissance vehicle. I contributed to the design and testing of the F-117 Nighthawk, the most nearly undetectable aircraft ever built during my aerospace career. Before retiring in 1990, I participated in numerous research projects, including the possibility of an analog stealthy submarine boat.

I enjoyed very much the time I worked closely with Kelly. He spent most of his time working at Lockheed in Burbank, leading the designers of more than forty outstanding aircraft. His P-38 Lightning fighter was a vital contribution to our winning World War II.

During the Korean War, his P-80 jet-propelled fighter was an important part of our arsenal.

Later, during the Cold War, he was the creator of the U-2, the A-12, YF-12, SR-71, and the D-21 drone, all of which were extremely important to our national security. He was one of the best, if not the best, aircraft designers who ever lived.

Although it was not his intent, during all those forty-two years he labored in Burbank, his work resulted in great benefit to the City of Burbank in terms of jobs and income to the city.

I think it ironic that Burbank is the only city in the world whose airport is named after a clown!

There have been several books written about Clarence Leonard "Kelly" Johnson and his Lockheed Advanced Development Projects, the "Skunk Works," but I do not know of any that tell the stories of some of the people who made significant contributions to the great success of the Skunk Works, and who never received well-deserved credit. Possibly that was because the Skunk Works grew so rapidly that many of us were lost in the crowd.

When I began, I intended to write mostly about a few people with whom I worked or consulted for or with. Part of my plan was to describe events in my life that I believe had relevance to my becoming an engineer and in my evolving into a physicist.

Also, I hoped to tell young people, especially young ladies, that science and engineering can be fun. Certainly, being a member of the Skunk Works was for me.

Since I have few personal records and some of the published material may be colored by ego, at first I decided to restrict my writings mainly to that which I could remember. I realized that I would not be perfectly accurate in my writing, so I decided to allow several opportunities for corrections. Have fun finding them!

However, as my writing progressed I realized that I needed to refer to whatever source material I could find to, at least, define the chronology of events.

Sometimes I was surprised that suddenly I could remember people or events that previously I could not. Also I have noticed that some events in which I participated or was well aware of actually were not described accurately in writings, perhaps because of "typographical errors," faulty memories, or dispersion of information to preserve a high level of secrecy.

Most of the people I will mention were Lockheed employees. All were people with whom I had significant experiences. If I describe an event and fail to credit a certain person, or persons, it most likely will be because my memory may not be good enough.

Sherre and I have copies of most of the references mentioned in the text. I apologize for the fact that many of them are old and may be out of print or difficult to obtain. However, we have obtained some material that was produced after the time we could have used it, but which perhaps can help in understanding some of the writings.

Presumably, if anyone cares, historians may correct oversights or errors.

I believe that it is important to learn as much as you can because you never know when the knowledge might be useful, important, or fun.

The most important subjects that I studied were English, Latin, mathematics, physics, and chemistry in high school and the latter three in university. While in university, I earned an aircraft pilot's license.

Postgraduate study included mathematics, computer programming, electromagnetic theory and practice, oceanography, marine acoustics, nuclear physics, and several medical courses.

Just for fun, after age eighty, I studied advanced music theory and played trombone in a seventeen-piece college jazz band.

I believe that young ladies have not been treated fairly when science and technology have been involved. I know from experience with my first wife (deceased), my two daughters, and with my wife, Sherre, that females can do very well with mathematics, science, and technology in general. In many cases, they may out-perform males. There are many examples in history.[*][1][2][3][4]

There were several young ladies who worked in the Skunk Works doing engineering important to our efforts to reduce the radar cross section (RCS) of several aircraft.

Lisa Brey Randolph was a designer of low RCS components.

Sheree Ervin Clark and Gale Wiechman contributed to the Have Blue RCS testing and data processing.

Marian Schuarte Blasek worked in RCS reduction materials development.

Patricia Y. Ames Urie worked with me on an infrared proposal. I also was impressed that she knew about and how to use Smith Charts.

Sherre Lynn Lilley Lovick, known then as Sherre Love, did important engineering in RCS reduction of an experimental stealthy U.S. Navy

---

[*] Nuclear physicist Maria Goeppert Mayer, Professor of Physics, University of Chicago and University of California, San Diego, Nobel Prize 1963 (ref. 1); Physicist Marie Sklodowska Curie, who discovered polonium and radium and won a Nobel prize for physics and one for chemistry (ref. 2); Lise Meitner, a German atomic physicist who discovered nuclear fission, and was denied a Nobel Prize, most probably because she was female (ref. 3); Grace Hopper, Admiral, U.S. Navy, a pioneer computer programmer; Anita Borg, PhD in computer science from New York University, a well-known pioneer computer programmer; Cecilia Payne-Gaposchkin, a famous pioneer astronomer; Lord Byron's daughter, Ada, expressed early notions about computer programming (ref. 4).

landing craft, the "Sea Shadow." She also became an infrared physics expert.

Let me make a suggestion—"Go, girl, go!"

Perhaps some ladies may wonder whether or not male engineers or scientists would be compatible husbands. My own experience lets me believe that, if the people involved have similar interests and can communicate well, they can have a wonderful life together. What can they talk about? "You'd Be Surprised!" [†]

[†] That is the title of a song written by Irving Berlin in 1919. It was sung by "Wee Bonnie Baker" with Orrin Tucker's Orchestra and recorded by Columbia Records (Columbia 1040).

Acknowledgments

We thank Stephen Justice for his generous help in finding factual material and encouragement toward finishing our self-appointed task. His interest and enthusiasm were inspiring.

Duane Halpape contributed much information and news about people we knew. He was very helpful in locating or accounting for former co-workers. He was modest about his own accomplishments.

Luther Duncan MacDonald, who was a mentor and friend, was a very important person in my life as well as in many of his Lockheed endeavors. He was in charge of all of the Skunk Works efforts to reduce radar reflections from several Lockheed aircraft. Mac was an excellent manager as well as a scientist. It was a privilege and a pleasure to work with him.

Francis Michael Ash was an important member of the Lockheed Burbank antenna laboratory and the Lockheed Burbank Advanced Development Projects group. He helped greatly in refreshing my memories of several of his significant accomplishments.

James M. Herron also was an important member of the Lockheed Burbank Advanced Development Projects group. He gave me memories of his many accomplishments and the pleasures of working with him.

Dr. Paul Suhler gave me important historical information that reminded me of events I did not remember clearly.

Arthur Casale and I had many rewarding discussions and exchanges of information. He is a book author, a professional aerial photographer, and very well could be an expert journalist.

Mrs. Annie Jacobsen, a well-known author, journalist, and television interview personality, who also is a family friend, was important in the early development of this book.

Introduction

My memories of my experiences in acquiring technical knowledge and a measure of competence are pleasant. From a very young age, I enjoyed learning about scientific and technical subjects.

I was fortunate that my parents were sympathetic, understanding, and helpful. They devoted as much time, energy, and money as they could spare to guiding and teaching me, my brother Robert, and my sisters Virginia and Hazel.

Although I enjoyed a career that lasted almost fifty years, for me the last thirty-two were the best, because I was a member of Kelly Johnson's Lockheed Advanced Development Projects, the Skunk Works.

I had a lot of fun as an engineering physicist in the Skunk Works. The challenges of trying to hide aircraft from radar seemed barely surmountable at times. The hours out testing in the deserts were long, but my work was fulfilling.

My colleagues and I believed, and we still do, that our work was vital to the safety of the United States, and perhaps the world, during the Cold War era.

Please refer to my Web site, www.edtheradarman.com, for further references, illustrations, and discussions that were not included in this book. In some cases, the definitions of terms or presentation of illustrations were not included in the book if they were found to be available on the Internet.

Curious Beginnings

A Glimpse into the Future

It was late in the afternoon of a gray and gloomy day in 1958. The sky was featureless and light, but very wet snow spattered the windshields of our twin-engined aircraft as we began our entry over the Atomic Energy Commission's bomb-cratered territory on our way to "Paradise Ranch," a secret CIA base in Area 51, north of Las Vegas, Nevada.

Pilot Bobby Schumacher in the left seat called for clearance and identified us as "Broken Bow."

The voice from the ground sounded like a high fidelity broadcasting station—not like ordinary aircraft radio. I wondered about what would happen if we had called in as "Ho Bo"!

As we approached a notch in the terrain, the snow increased in intensity, and the sky seemed darker. We experienced moderate turbulence as we cleared the gap, and I, in the co-pilot seat, got a glimpse of our destination.

The snow on our windshield seemed to swirl counterclockwise as Bobby entered a gentle descending right-hand turn toward Watertown's runway in Area 51. We aligned with the runway center line while the wipers scrubbed the snow from our view. The wheels rumbled softly as he made his usual perfect landing.

We taxied into the hangar area, shut down, checked in, and he closed our flight plan. After attending a briefing about our coming night's testing activities, I had early dinner in the small mess hall.

While under the soothing influence of a hot chocolate drink, my thoughts drifted to my seemingly long and somewhat erratic journey through time to this place.

I was born in 1919 in the small town of California, Missouri. While that was not much of an event for the locals, it allows me to say, with tongue in cheek, that I am a native of California. Some twenty-two years later I became a long-time resident of the state of California. I began employment in California in 1941, retired there in 1990, and still live in California.

My father and his parents emigrated from England and arrived in the United States from Canada. He became a naturalized citizen of the United States and was proud of that fact.

My mother was descended from several generations of American citizens. She was proud of her membership in The Daughters of the American Revolution.

While she was a young lady working as a bank teller in the village of Thebes, Illinois, my mother met my father, who was working as a heavy machine operator for a railroad. After their marriage, they were moved from place to place as my father's job assignments required.

My mother seemed to have considerable business mathematics skill, and she was a very accomplished pianist. She also had a sense of humor and occasionally said, "A little nonsense now and then is relished by the best of men."

On the other hand, my father seemed much more interested in mechanical activities—designing, building, and repairing things. I believe that I inherited a wee bit of each of their characteristics.

My brother, Robert, two years my junior, also shared similar genes. Our two sisters, Virginia and Hazel, had very different interests and abilities.

While I was a child, I always was inquisitive and frequently was building and trying things. "Curiosity" may have killed a cat, but it did not get me!

In the 1920s, our family settled into Falls City, Nebraska, a small town in the Midwest where my father was based at a major railroad maintenance facility. The population was about five thousands during the time that we lived there.

I am the in the exact center of my schoolroom photograph, taken when I was about ten years old.

Falls City, Nebraska Classroom

I never was fond of winter weather, but my mother made me laugh when she'd say, "The wind blew and the snow snew."

When the 1929 market crash occurred, although my family had little money, we were not impacted severely.

My father, I believe, was grateful to have a job even though being an occasional train wreck investigator was, at times, gruesome and stressful. My parents had no investments in that stock market, so, in that sense, we were fortunate. All the time that I was dependent upon my father and his livelihood, he had a job, and as far as I know, we never were in danger of being without food or clothing.

My parents never owned the homes we lived in because my father always expected to be relocated, but we always had a good place to live. We knew there were many people suffering for lack of food and a lack of income.

Sheltered from these hardships, I was free to enjoy my boyhood interests.

When I was about ten years old, I wanted very much to become a Boy Scout. As soon as I could, after I became twelve years old, I joined and was made a member of the Beaver Patrol. My father took the job of scoutmaster and our troop settled into a real log cabin on the shore of

Stanton's "Lake" that actually was a small pond formed by damming a small stream. Some parts of it were barely a foot deep.

During my scouting experience I learned a great deal about being able to take care of myself and others. My favorite merit badge was for First Aid. I learned to do very intricate bandaging, and I thought that was a great accomplishment. Also, I incinerated many mud-encased potatoes in camp fires!

Sometime while I was earning advancements in the Scouts, I decided to build a canoe. Our father bought a large collection of wooden barrel parts and some canvas and gave them to Bob and me. We used halves of barrel ends to form the ends of the canoe. The ribs were made from the wooden rings that held barrel staves together. After we covered the frame with canvas, we painted it white to waterproof it.

Bob and I built the canoe in the basement of our home. We had to carry it to Stanton's Lake to row around in it.

The municipal swimming pool was adjacent to Stanton's Lake. It was called Crystal Beach. There were no crystals or beaches near it as far as I could see! It was a conventional large rectangular concrete bowl.

I decided to make a diving helmet to go down in the deep end of the pool. My brother helped me convert a steel pail (we called it a bucket) into the helmet. We cut a large hole in the side of the bucket and installed a glass window. We installed an automobile tire valve in the bottom that allowed an air hose to be attached. As my younger brother, Bob was "volunteered" by me to pump the air in by using a bicycle tire pump while I did the test dive.

When we finished it we took it to the Crystal Beach pool, and I tried a dive. The dive actually was more of a slow sinking, but it did not progress very far. Almost as soon as I sank below the surface, the tar holding the window gave way and great leaks appeared, nearly filling the helmet before I could get out. We considered that a failure and abandoned the project.

Our Boy Scout careers ended rather abruptly when a company bought the land upon which the Scout cabin was built. As nearly as I can remember, the company's name was Sonken and Galamba.

Every Boy Scout aspires to attain the Eagle rank. Because of the loss of our cabin and the breakup of our troop, Bob and I did not become Eagle Scouts. Although we were disappointed, it did not affect our lives significantly because already we had experienced most of the benefits.

There were several adults, other than my parents, who influenced my adult life and to whom I am most grateful.

One was a medical doctor neighbor who took me at about age twelve to see a movie of the dissection of a cadaver. Later in life, I took several medical school classes for a while because of the interest I acquired as a boy. However, I decided that I liked being a physicist/engineer better. I still have my medical class notes and library, and I like to read medical material as a hobby.

Airplanes—an Early Love

Sometime in the mid-1970s preliminary design engineer Dick Scherrer came into my office in Bldg. 311 to discuss a problem. He had been trying to design an aircraft that would be nearly impossible for certain radars to detect. He described the requirements that he hoped to satisfy and some of the difficulties he encountered. At that time, the computer program at Lockheed could not calculate radar energy reflections from curved or warped surfaces correctly, so it seemed best to avoid them.

I showed him some charts of backscattering from triangular metal cylinders that we had recorded in 1958. They revealed that if the flat surfaces were large compared to wavelength and tilted, almost all the energy would be reflected away and not return toward the radar. That information helped him solve his problem.

The next time I saw Dick, he had a drawing of a large test fixture that could be used to validate the calculated RCS predictions of his aircraft design. Aircraft preliminary design engineer Ed Baldwin, who was well known for his sense of humor, nicknamed the test fixture design "The Hopeless Diamond." He said that he doubted that it could be made to fly.

As young boys, our major interests were minor sports, Boy Scout activities, and carving, then building model airplanes. Robert and I whittled many pieces of scrap wood into what we thought were reasonable facsimiles of real aircraft whose pictures we saw while browsing magazines in a local drug store.

Our first house in Falls City was near the lower end of a fairly long sloping area. A large building at the upper end served as a garage and my father's workshop. He had a good supply of wood scraps and boards that Bob and I were allowed to use for our pleasure. We were privileged to use some of his tools—if we put them back where they belonged.

Bob and I decided to make a biplane using the family coaster wagon. We used wooden boards to support sheets of corrugated box paper wings.

I tried to fly it down the concrete sidewalk next to our yard. As I gained speed, the wind in my face distracted me so that I had difficulty steering to avoid the fence along my left side and the drainage ditch along my right. The cardboard upper wings collapsed and fell on my head, and pieces continued to be shed as I wobbled from side to side. It did not fly, but it was fun! I do not remember who picked up all of the pieces along the flight path.

After I was about twelve years old, I became involved with building model airplanes. Both my brother and I built kits of various kinds that we could buy cheaply. Some of the aircraft we built supposedly were models of real aircraft. Actually they were very simple and had rather crude, angular airfoils.

Later on, in the middle 1970s, when I saw the first sketches of the aircraft that finally became the F-117 Nighthawk, I knew that rather crude airfoils could be made to fly.

As soon as we were able to get more money together, Robert and I bought better kits to build more accurate models of aircraft.

I remember one particular model very well. I spent my entire savings for a kit to build a flying scaled model of a "GEE BEE Sportster." I had seen a photograph of the plane in a catalog of the Cleveland Model Airplane and Supply Company, in an unusual yellow and black paint scheme. I liked it because it looked like a hornet.

The Granville Brothers built several different racing airplanes during the 1930s. They were very dangerous things. They were high speed, extremely high-powered, very radical shapes. They truly were not only very different, they were very unstable. Possibly it was because their center of gravity shifted too far aft of the center of lift of the wings as their fuel was burned, a very dangerous condition. They responded extremely quickly to their controls. Only the most skillful pilots could fly them. Jimmy Doolittle, who later led the carrier-launched B-25 raid on Tokyo, won the 1932 Thompson Air Race trophy flying a Gee Bee. At least three pilots who tried to fly them were killed. They seem to have been rather deadly airplanes.

After I had spent considerable time carefully building my GB Sportster model, I tried to make it fly. It was powered by twisted rubber bands inside the body and was supposed to "Rise Off Ground" (ROG) and fly, but it never did. It always would just taxi around and flutter, and not do anything significant. We referred to it in less than terms of endearment as "the ruptured duck." Finally, I decided that I would try to fly it at least once.

We had moved to a different house that was across the street from a large school ground. The town water tower, that may have been a hundred feet tall, stood on one corner of the schoolyard. It was equipped with an enclosed ladder that went up to a catwalk near the top. The lower ten feet or more of the ladder was folded up so I could not use it.

Since I could not get onto the ladder to go up, I took my model in hand and climbed up the bracing structure, which was a difficult thing to do with the airplane in one hand. When I was partway up the structure, a bee got into my hair and buzzed around quite a bit. Finally I swatted it, but it stung me on my head. Fortunately, I did not let go of my airplane or the structure. I decided to go up onto the catwalk.

Finally, when I got to the catwalk level, I wound up the rubber band motor. The fuselage creaked alarmingly as I put all the tension in the rubber bands that I dared to. Then, after I satisfied myself that it would not stand any more, I reached over the ledge of the protective railing around the catwalk and launched the airplane.

It went forward for a short distance, pitched straight up, reversed direction in a "hammer-head" stall, and then went straight down to the ground and smashed to bits. All my savings went with it!

In 2004, Sherre and I visited Falls City and attended the Falls City High School reunion. There were a number of representatives from the classes, ranging from the 1930s up to some of last year's graduates.

Three of the four homes I had lived in still were there. The water tower had been removed. But at its remaining foundations was a scaled model and memorial of the tower that had inspired the American artist John Phillip Falter to create his unique bird's-eye view of the world from the catwalk.

John Phillip Falter, local Falls City boy and cousin of my boyhood friend John Charles Falter, was a contemporary and rival to Norman Rockwell. He depicted Falls City's business shopping area (with some artistic license) on the cover of the December 21, 1946, *Saturday Evening Post* magazine.

Edward Lovick, Jr.

First Flight in an Aircraft

Our parents were very supportive of our young interest in airplanes. In those days "barnstorming" pilots would fly about the country, land in open fields near small towns to the great excitement of the local children, and sell brief rides. The first real aircraft that I saw—and touched the lower starboard wing of—was a Curtiss JN-4D, a World War I "Jenny" trainer.

I do not know how they were able to provide the money, but my parents treated my brother Bob and me to a ride in a Ford Tri-Motor. That convinced me that I wanted more to do with airplanes.

I rode again in a Ford Tri-Motor aircraft, together with my wife Sherre, in 2003 during the Oshkosh, Wisconsin, Experimental Aircraft Association (EAA) event, more than seventy years later. She rode in the co-pilot seat.

My First Rocket Experience

When I was about fourteen or fifteen years old, two of my neighborhood friends, Bob Goldsmith and Bob Kimmel, helped me to perform my first rocket experiment.

Has anyone noticed that I seemed to have been surrounded by Bobs? I actually knew "Tom" Davies and "Dick" Richard Gist, but it was much later that I finally met Harry. ("Every Tom, Dick, and Harry" was a common expression meaning "almost every man.")

I decided to make a small rocket. I soldered a metal cone made from a tin can onto another can to make the rocket body. My soldering "iron" was borrowed from my father. It was a large slug of copper about three inches long and one inch in diameter mounted on a long shaft of steel, with a wooden handle. I heated it by using a gasoline-fueled blowtorch.

Bob Goldsmith and I asked Bob Kimmel to "obtain" several shotgun shells from his father's gun supplies. Then we removed the powder and installed it inside the rocket. We inserted about six feet of some dynamite fuse that I had bought from a local hardware store into the rocket. It was held in place, together with the powder, by some mud.

When it was ready, we set it on the driveway next to my parents' house. I lighted the fuse and we watched it take off in a huge cloud of black smoke, go about twenty feet up, and clatter back down onto the driveway.

Then we noticed a large dark gray streak up the white side of the house! Luckily, I was able to wash it off before my parents could find out.

More than thirty years later, I studied a short course in rocket propulsion at the University of California at Los Angeles (UCLA).

Early Radio Experiments

During one of our occasional moves around town, my brother Bob and I discovered some very interesting items. We were accustomed to exploring alleys in search of discarded bottles, scrap metal, or anything else that the local junkman would buy. That special day we found some radio parts!

That was the beginning of my life-long fun with electromagnetic science.

One thing that attracted me was a vacuum tube socket that was made of clear glass. It was a nice-looking thing. I have no idea whatever happened to it, but that started me becoming inquisitive about radio equipment.

At first we had no idea what treasures they were. They were obsolete, but to us they were new, and still operable. One of our neighbors was an active amateur radio operator who had no desire to keep those parts.

We became acquainted, and he gave us an old book that described how to build radio receivers using 1920s technology, "crystal sets." In those days a crystal set was most practical for us because vacuum tubes, as they had progressed to by that time, still were quite expensive, especially for us who had no income except for what we could get from selling junk.

We read the book and started trying to build whatever we saw. Of course, Bob and I had no inkling that we were learning primitive, obsolescent ideas and methods, so we set about attempting to duplicate some of them. Our ambition became—build a working crystal set!

More than thirty years later, a succinct bit of history was published in the February 1969 issue of the *Microwave Journal:*

> **A VERY SHORT HISTORY OF**
> **MICROWAVE SEMICONDUCTORS**
> **MARION E. HINES,** *Vice President*
> *Technical Director, Microwave Products Group*

Microwave Associates, Inc., Burlington, Mass.

PREHISTORIC ERA
a. Galena crystal and catwhisker detect wireless broadcasts. Thousands of crystal sets sold to 12-year old boys.

W.W. II ERA
b. Crystal set improved by 12-year old boys, now grown up. Radar born. Microwave age begins.
c. North, Waltz, Torrey discover and mostly explain parametric negative-resistance effects in semi-conductor diode. Everybody forgets whole thing.

The remark "Everybody forgets whole thing" actually referred to the fact that the urgency of other World War II activities caused research of semiconductors to be considered not essential to the war efforts. Vacuum tube technology was predominant.

We built workbenches in the basement of our house and began acquiring various things to work on. We lived in a large house that had a rather large basement with a concrete floor and concrete block walls, so there was ample working space.

We acquired insulated copper wire and all the other items we needed and constructed our first radio receiver. I do not remember how we were able to get such things as what was called "magnet wire"; perhaps our neighbor gave us some or told us how and where to buy it. Magnet wire was copper wire that was insulated either with enamel or wrappings of fine green silk thread. "Bell wire" was made for wiring low-voltage door bells. It was 18 gauge copper wire and usually had two layers of paraffin-soaked threads wound around it for insulation.

I was happy to wind my own inductors—coils of wire wound around oatmeal cartons—monstrous things by today's standards.

Bob and I began experimenting with whatever we could find in the radio science. But we had difficulty in making a crystal detector, or a crystal rectifier. Our friend had given us several detector units that were small lumps of galena (crystalline lead sulfide) partially encased in a short cylinder of lead.

The secret, or trick, to making a detector was to find a sensitive spot by touching the crystal with a thin copper alloy wire. The little wire was known as a "cat whisker." We tried many times before one success.

Our father, of course, knew of our interest in this sort of thing. He was able to get a lump of galena about the size of his fist, and gave it to us.

We proceeded to chip away and make pieces of it, trying to find a sensitive spot, as it was called, to detect radio signals. That, for us, was advanced technology. Probably it was described in the book the neighbor had given us.

We were able to make a simple crystal set that worked. The nearest radio stations were about a hundred miles away. We were happy to receive signals from Kansas City, Missouri and Omaha, Nebraska.

All the pieces of equipment that we dealt with were quite large compared to modern components, but since the wavelengths of the signals that we were interested in were a hundred or more feet long, the components were almost infinitesimal in comparison. Therefore their size had no significant impact on the system's performance.

My appreciation and understanding of scale, or component size compared to wavelength, increased throughout my career in airborne antenna and radar design, and ultimately, radar cross section reduction.*

---

* Radar Cross Section is a measure of the power reflected back to a radar receiver from a target. It is expressed and displayed in terms of decibels referenced to the power that would be reflected from a perfect reflector of one square meter area. A one-square meter RCS is defined as zero decibels. RCS data is notated as dBsm. For example, "minus ten dBsm" means "1/10 square meter of reflecting area."

Formation of Young Engineers

For the next few years, we progressed until we could, and did, design and build radio receivers, low-powered transmitters, and audio sound systems utilizing vacuum tubes. We built receivers to listen to 2 MHz and higher frequencies. They were called "short wave" receivers because they responded to wavelengths that were shorter than those used by the commercial broadcasting stations.

Then we decided to earn money by repairing other people's equipment, mostly radio receivers.

I designed several pieces of test equipment that we built and enjoyed using. During this time I became aware of the "Golden Ratio"[5] as a factor in artistic design that I tried to utilize while designing our test equipment.

I have a test set that I built more than seventy years ago. It allowed us as radio servicemen to do on-site testing. It still may work, although some parts are missing.

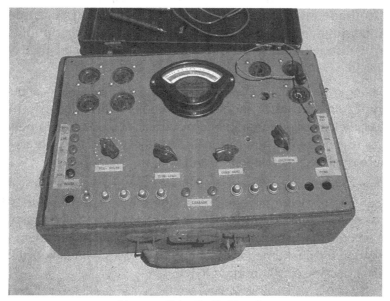

Vacuum Tube Radio Test Set

The test equipment served us well, enabling us to do simple repairs of radios for neighbors. We started getting a small amount of business repairing radio receivers for individuals and local stores. We never made much money, but the experience later became valuable, and this gave us some spending money that we used to buy electronic parts.

Sometimes we were able to buy parts from supply stores in Kansas City, Missouri. Since our father was a railroad employee, he could get us passes to ride in the trains. My brother and I would save all our money until we had four or five dollars, and my father would get us passes. We would go to Kansas City and walk from the railroad station to the supply stores, Burstein-Applebee, or McGee Radio.

We would look at all the wonderful things they had for sale, very carefully select what we could afford, skip lunch because that cost money, and walk back the mile to the train station. We were very happy to buy bits and pieces to work or play with, and we gradually accumulated a fairly large amount of parts and supplies.

Those activities helped us to earn some money so we could help pay for going to the University of Nebraska later.

At age eighteen, I wrote an article for a technical trade magazine describing signal generators that could change frequency continuously over a narrow range and repeat that performance over and over again to allow the response of a radio receiver to be displayed on the screen of a "cathode-ray oscilloscope" (CRO) so that tuning adjustments could be done quickly and accurately. That was my first published work.[6] Subsequently I wrote several more short articles that were published.

During my high school years, I spent a lot of time in the local public library reading technical and scientific books and periodicals. I was particularly interested in radio and electronic subjects and in general physics. I did not realize how fortunate I was that a small town library had so much good technical literature and books.

I learned that while vacuum tubes[7] were some of the most prevalent components of electronic equipment, there were gas-filled tubes for special applications.[8] Some of them contained carefully measured small amounts of neon, argon, or mercury vapor. I studied them and understood the phenomenon of ionization of gases, a bit of knowledge that later became very important to me.

Also I became familiar with the theory of electron emission from hot metallic bodies because it was so important to understanding how to use vacuum (electron) tubes in circuits. This knowledge also was very useful later in my career while solving a design problem critical to the OXCART aircraft.

My high school teachers gave me important education, and although it may not seem fair to most of them, I remember several because of my perception of their influence upon my later life.

Mr. John S. Boswell was my high school physics and chemistry teacher. He let me repair several instruments in his physics laboratory. He also gave me good grades.

Mr. Ralph W. Sympson was my very valuable high school Latin instructor. He looked like he could have been a Roman Centurion, and sometimes I thought that he thought he was because of the way he would wield a yardstick as a pointer!

I was not alone in my high regard for these teachers. The Friday, July 2, 2004, edition of *The Falls City Journal* newspaper that reported events related to the 2004 alumni dinner refers to both the Ralph W. Sympson and the John S. Boswell Scholarship funds.

My favorite high school mathematics teacher was Grace Myers. She was a gracious lady of whom I was a bit afraid when I first attended her class. I had heard, "If you make a mistake, she will throw the book at you." It took me a while to realize that I would not have to dodge a real book! She gave me my first taste of calculus.

My first experience as a "sound engineer" came about while I still was in high school as a result of building a complete set of sound amplifying equipment.

One of our neighbors was the head of the music department in our high school. He also was the leader of our town concert band. He let me operate my sound system for announcements and singers during the band's Saturday Evening Summer Concerts on the west lawn of the courthouse square.

Many years later, I began operating sound systems and serving as musical director for several Sunday afternoon jazz music clubs in Southern California.

Piano was the first instrument I tried to play. My mother was such an accomplished pianist that passing neighbors would stop to listen when the windows were open. She gave me several lessons. However, that was an exercise in futility because I did not learn to play the piano very well. I was more interested in electronic technology. Then I thought of a way to combine the two. I would build an electronic piano so that I could practice in private.

I made two discoveries in a local furniture store. They had several very old radio receivers that had been stored for many years, and they had an old upright piano that they wanted to discard. I was able to buy several old radios for fifty cents each and the old piano for several dollars.

They delivered them to our home and carried the piano downstairs to my basement work area! I do not remember what happened to the radios, but I recall the fate of the piano.

I took the piano apart. All I wanted was the keyboard, the "action," and the "lyre" or "harp" that carried the strings. My intent was to make a piano whose sound would be suppressed because there was no sounding board. Then I could pick up the vibration of the strings electronically by making a capacitor under each string with a piece of metal soldered to a machine screw in a wooden frame, pick up the sound, send it through a small amplifier to some headphones so I could practice, and play the piano and no one else would hear it.

My brother helped me partially disassemble it by removing the keyboard and the action. Many years later I learned that the actions in Steinway grand pianos used fifty-four parts per key, for a total of 4,752 parts for each piano! If my piano had been a Steinway grand, I might not have had the time or the inclination to add the electronics!

I made a fixture to test my concept of a way to produce an electrical stimulus for an amplifier that I could use to operate a head set. It consisted of a wooden frame upon which a steel wire was stretched. The wire and a flat piece of metal (a washer) soldered to a machine screw through the base served as the two terminals of a small capacitor. When the metal "string" was disturbed, the capacitance varied and the result was a changing voltage that drove an amplifier.

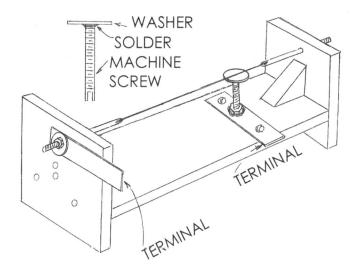

Electronic Piano Test Fixture

I do not remember why I abandoned that project. I did have a crude but workable pickup system so I could hear the sound, and hardly anyone else could hear it. The remains of the piano were discarded. I do not remember what happened to the piano case, but we may have burned it in the furnace, because in those days we had a wood or coal-burning furnace to heat the house.

I had an early attraction to pranks. My mother liked to say, "A little nonsense now and then is relished by the best of men."

I still remember a particular company that I admired, Johnson-Smith in Racine, Wisconsin. I knew about it as a teenager. Although I never bought anything, I got a catalog from them and I really liked what I saw. It had prank products like itching powder, and soap that would turn you green. One thing I really wanted but never got was a teaspoon made of Wood's Metal.

Wood's Metal is a metallic alloy that melts at the relatively low temperature of 160 degrees Fahrenheit. After stirring a cup of hot coffee, for example, all that might come out would be a stump! I do not know if it would be dangerous to drink the stuff, but that could be startling. I do not think anyone would drink coffee if it appeared to dissolve a spoon.

Would that be fun to have? You could say to someone "I have to warn you, that coffee is pretty strong—see, I told you!" I would like to try that on Sherre's father. (It would not work—he is too smart. He is a nuclear physicist.)

I believe that harmless pranks can be important for stimulating creative thinking.

In my senior year's high school yearbook, I received the caption beside my picture, "Almost to all things could he turn his hands." I was branded a "Jack of all trades" at an early age! I suspect that Bob Goldsmith's sister, Charlotte, was the author of that comment.

My brother Bob and I hoped to attend a university to obtain electrical engineering degrees. As things transpired, we both were able, with considerable sacrifice by our parents and part-time jobs, to attend two years at the University of Nebraska. Bob later finished the course there and obtained his E.E. degree.

After I had graduated from high school, Mr. Harvey Hinz and I worked for a local Montgomery Ward's store where he taught me to service and repair refrigeration equipment. I became quite familiar with the aromas of sulfur dioxide and ammonia! We also serviced and repaired radios and other appliances. Harvey was a licensed amateur radio operator who built most of his own equipment.

While I was employed by Montgomery Ward, I had an interesting experience delivering a battery-powered radio receiver.

Sometimes during the delivery it seemed that I had gone astray because as I approached the ends of several successively smaller country dirt roads I could not find the customer's house.

Finally the last road ended on an upslope of ground and I could see that, farther on, the ground sloped down to the West bank of the Missouri river. I decided to look around before leaving and, fortunately, saw a short cylindrical pipe with a conical cap protruding up in a large, grass-covered area on the highest part of the land. It appeared to be a vent pipe for something, so I walked past it downhill and found the entrance to a cave in the hillside.

The customer was at home, and so I was invited into it. The owners had finished several rooms in the hillside so that they looked very neat and comfortable. They had installed false studding and probably drywall to form rooms that were much like an ordinary home of those days. I installed the receiver and instructed them about operating it and then left.

Sometimes I have wondered what it must be like to live in a cave.

One of my part-time jobs while I was attending university was working in a photography laboratory processing film, printing, and restoring old photographs. I was able to do the jobs because, while still in high school, I had learned to take and process photographs and to make enlargements.

My "professional" photographic career consisted of selling to the *Omaha Bee News* newspaper one picture of a local "Indian Princess" standing in a field of very tall corn!

My favorite camera at that time was an Argus C-3 model. I also had an Argus enlarger that was a perfect complement to the camera. I have not seen an enlarger like it since I left home to work for Lockheed but I have three of the cameras.

I still was very interested in airplanes. In 1937, I had written to Lockheed in faraway California asking for a job. They had replied saying that, at that time, they were not hiring. I liked to think that it may have been because I was in Nebraska and they did not want to pay my way out.

One difficult decision I had to make was whether to build a radio-controlled model airplane or save the money for school. I decided to do the latter.

During the year before I went to university, I became aware of a federal government program to train civilians to become aircraft pilots. I almost volunteered but decided that I wanted an engineering degree instead.

I became interested in a school for airplane mechanics. I was able to go to Kansas City, Missouri, for six weeks, to a school to learn the techniques that they employed in those days to do various aircraft structural repairs. I got to see many old airplanes and work on a few of them making parts.

One day I was startled when I saw someone remove part of the fabric covering on the left side lower wing of a very old biplane, possibly a Jenny, and watched as dried tree leaves fell out! I suppose that the pilot had made a pass too close to a tree, put a patch over the hole after he landed, and just continued to fly. That was quite common in those days.

I never did try to qualify as a real mechanic, but one thing that I learned to do was rivet, and later on at Lockheed that was of some value. I had to make a fuel tank as a graduation project. I hand formed aluminum parts and then riveted them together. And as far as I know, it did not leak!

I continued to work odd jobs until Bob and I entered the University of Nebraska in the fall of 1939.

Very early in my first semester, I inadvertently created a minor incident that later became a source of amusement for Bob and me.

After a very brief investigation of some laboratory facilities, I went to the dean's office and told him that the radio laboratory was an obsolete mess (or words to that effect)! Of course he was surprised that a freshman would do that. He also knew very well that it was true.

Years later my brother, who had become a good friend of Dean Edison, told me about the laughter that event caused! Science can be fun, at least for some people!

Sometime later the laboratory and the curriculum greatly were improved just in time for World War II. By that time, I was long gone.

Lockheed at Last!

In 1941, before the United States entered World War II, there already was the beginning of a buildup in developing and manufacturing aircraft.

During summer vacation, after my second year in university, I discovered that Lockheed was hiring technical people. They advertised in Nebraska newspapers for workers. I applied immediately, and after what seemed a long time, was offered a job.

I borrowed a few dollars from my brother Bob to go by railway to Burbank in sunny California. I arrived in Los Angeles Union Station in early November and stayed overnight in a nearby hotel in a room next to a busy, noisy elevator shaft. Early the next day I went by bus to the Lockheed employment office in Burbank and signed in.

They had people helping to find lodging, so I was set up quickly.

I was surprised to learn that I had been hired by the Vega Airplane Company, a subsidiary of the Lockheed Aircraft Corporation. However, to me at least, I was an employee of the real Lockheed.

I remember being impressed as I first arrived at the Lockheed employment offices, passing a large parking area in which I saw more airplanes together than I had ever seen before. They were twin-engine "Hudson" bombers, each missing their left side propeller.

The British, for whom the aircraft were manufactured, preferred countra-rotating propellers on twin-engine aircraft to minimize gyroscopic and inherent "p-factor" yaw with the resultant left-turning tendencies. Lockheed engineers had designed them for two identical engines and propellers, so that was a change in progress. From early times until even today most propellers turned clockwise when viewed from the pilot's seat.

My first job assignment was not what I had expected. I was asked to work in the template-making department because I could work trigonometric problems, use my analytical geometry, and a "slide rule." My university transcript showed that I had received a grade of 100 percent in trigonometry. My analytical geometry grade was not quite that high.

As an interesting side note, I hope, Englishman William Oughtred introduced the "x" symbol to denote multiplication in 1631 and he invented the slide rule, probably in 1641. Also, he may have introduced the decimal point.

I still have a 1941 mathematics textbook, written by Raymond W. Dull,[9] in which an entire chapter of twenty-six pages is devoted to the use of slide rules.

As a template designer, I developed flat metal patterns to define how three-dimensional parts could be made from flat sheets of metal.

My supervisor and mentor was a gentleman named Spencer Wick. I liked him, and I think he liked me. He gave me interesting assignments and encouraged me to do ever more complicated things. Under his aegis, I did my first, and only, spot welding. It was not quite science, but it was fun as sparks flew!

While I was in the template department, I met several people who would help me later. My supervisors and I got along much better than many seemed to do with their bosses.

Fifteen years later, I was an engineer and Spencer was a shop foreman in the Advanced Development Projects (ADP), the renowned "Skunk Works."

For a while I enjoyed making the templates that were flat metal patterns used to guide machines that cut aluminum sheets that were bent, twisted, and drilled into aircraft parts. But after several months, I decided to move on, so I arranged to go to an engineering group.

Radio and Radar Installation

While I was in college, I had decided that I did not want to do engineering drawing for a living. And as my father occasionally remarked, "By Gum," I did not. But it turned out that after I transferred from the template department, I was assigned as a draftsman to a group who designed the radio and inter-com installations for the aircraft being designed at the moment.

I met two gentlemen who were excellent engineers and later, excellent engineering managers.

Luther Duncan "Mac" MacDonald was the engineer in charge of the group. Mac was very highly regarded and respected not only for his technical ability but also for his friendliness. He was, however, more of a scientist than an engineer—if such a distinction can be made.

He later served as a very important member of Kelly Johnson's famous Skunk Works. I enjoyed the privilege and pleasure of working with him in the Skunk Works.

Dallas Burger was his second in command. He was my immediate supervisor. Later he became Project Engineer for Lockheed's F-104 Starfighter.

After a few not very successful attempts at drawing installations of radio and other electronic equipment, Mac very kindly decided that I was more likely to succeed at designing electric circuits and schematics, and so my work changed and indirectly led to my becoming a RADAR EXPERT!

While I was employed in the template department I worked during the "swing" shift, four PM to midnight. When I joined Mac's group I worked during the day shift, and that allowed me to attend school in the evenings.

Lockheed's upper management was very active in promoting continuing education and had arranged to provide technical courses for anyone who wanted to participate. I attended several courses in-house as well at UCLA and the California Institute of Technology (CALTECH) in Pasadena.

Under Lockheed sponsorship in the evenings after work, I studied microwave theory and participated in laboratory work at CALTECH. During that time, I lived in Burbank on Victory Boulevard almost in line with and near the south end of Runway 17 of Lockheed Air Terminal.

To attend classes, I had to ride my bicycle up hill to the Burbank Library, where I hid it under some bushes. I rode a street railroad Red Car to Glendale and transferred to a bus that went near CALTECH. After school, I had to catch the last bus at almost midnight from Pasadena to Glendale and then ride the Red Car back to Burbank to retrieve my bicycle. It was downhill from there back to my rented room.

I completed a course in microwave theory at CALTECH, taught by visiting professor Hugh Skilling, Acting Chair of Stanford University's Electrical Engineering Department.

After the course, I knew the theoretical properties of hollow metallic tubes used to guide microwaves, so I was ready, willing, and able to become an expert. That was part of the fun of science and engineering.

My big chance came early in a discussion about how to support the waveguides for a radar installation being designed for a bomber aircraft. The waveguides were hollow metal tubes of rectangular cross section that carried radar waves. That was the first time Lockheed had had the opportunity to include radar in an aircraft, so there were unresolved questions.

I simply said there was no problem about clamping bare waveguides to metal structure using simple metal clamps. My reputation as a "Radar Expert," at least for a time, was made! A little knowledge may be a dangerous thing, but I escaped that time!

A most enjoyable outcome of that event was that I was allowed to participate in a limited way in the actual installation of the first radar. I liked what I saw and did in an experimental shop.

While I was in Mac's group, I wrote an article about directional characteristics of aircraft antenna patterns.[10] Ultimately it was published in the July 1943 issue of *Aero Digest* magazine.

Years later Mac remembered me, and that led to a great change in my career.

B-17 Bomber Aircraft

In 1942, Lockheed-Vega was doing subcontracted fabrication and assembly work for the Boeing Aircraft Company in the push to produce B-17 bomber aircraft. There was a lot of noise in the factories. Rivet guns caused most of it. It sounded like war movies were being filmed in the main assembly areas.

A group of people in the experimental shop were working to install liquid-cooled Allison engines in a B-17E bomber aircraft designated XB-38. I heard that someone had laid a large number of round rivet heads along the upper part of the leading edge of one wing, as a joke.

Apparently this happened just before a high-level manager was supposed to come in for an inspection of the assembly. He was very upset about how that looked. They were trying to keep that surface as smooth as possible for aerodynamic performance, and it looked like some riveters had made a huge mistake.

I have seen humorous instructions on drawings. I remember a set of instructions starting with "draw to 0.001 inch," "mill to 0.01 inch," and, finally, "beat to fit." I assume that "beat to fit" needs no explanation!

"Skin and tin" on electrical drawings meant "remove the insulation from the ends of bundled strands of wires, twist them together, and then 'tin' them by actually melting solder on them." The solder would stiffen the wires to facilitate insertion into terminals in connectors so that secure connections more easily could be made.

The aluminum "skin" on B-17 aircraft was very thin, perhaps only 0.02 inch, or two hundredths of an inch thick. We referred to the skin as, "Oh—too thin!" Its basic function was to carry part of the mechanical loads imposed upon the fuselage structure. The major part of the structure of the airplane was inside, and it was not pressurized.

The skin was pretty much a replacement for cloth. I do not remember seeing any puncture holes in aircraft in the factory. The reason they made it so thin was to reduce weight because they needed to fly up to 25,000 feet or higher, hopefully to evade anti-aircraft fire. Near the end of the war, they were trying to get to 35,000 feet in other aircraft. Early in the war, some British fighters were able to fly even higher for very short times.

They had electrically heated flying suits in the B-17s. I had one that I obtained years later as war surplus.

Thirty-two volt DC electrical systems were standard in the aircraft, and that was not practical for home use. The suits actually were like a sort of super version of "red flannel" underwear, except that they were gray and infested by heater wires. The crewmen also wore heavy leather jackets and padded, quilted pants over their uniforms, in addition to boots and gloves.

I did some very minor work on B-17 electrical design. One day while I was climbing out of a B-17 in the factory, a plug that stuck out from a radio rack caught and tore one of my pants' pockets. So I wrote an Engineering Change Order (an E.O.) specifying a right angle plug instead of a straight one. That was my B-17 design contribution!

While I was in Mac's group, a Lockheed PV-1 or -2 aircraft had trouble landing. It ran out of runway, crashed through the fence at the south end of Runway 17, bounced over railroad tracks and a street, and settled in the Valhalla cemetery.

I suppose the crew was all right, but a desperate hunt began when it was discovered that the radar had come out of the airplane's nose. The radar was secret, and so a swarm of people converged on the cemetery, frantically picking up pieces of the radar amongst the cemetery's occupants.

Years later I sometimes spent part of my lunch time in that cemetery, practicing playing my trumpet. Some guy walking by said, "You might as well quit. They're already dead!" (Actually, that did not happen—but it might have!) I do not remember awakening anyone.

Sometime while I was a member of Mac's group, I became involved in establishing a small technical library for the entire engineering staff. I do not remember much about it except for two things: working part-time after hours selecting a few books from Lockheed's book store and that the lady in charge was Mrs. Eastman. I do not remember knowing her first name, but I was sensitive to her last name because my brother was working for Eastman Kodak in Rochester, New York, doing research and development on proximity fuses in shells for naval anti-aircraft guns. Even selecting books can be fun!

While I was doing my library work, I became aware of a small group working nearby that was designing, building, and using electronic testing equipment. I could not resist asking for a job in that group—so I did.

Electronic Test Equipment Group

My interview with the man in charge of the electrical and electronic design activities was not memorable, but it was sufficient. It happened during a Friday afternoon. He suggested that I design a simple, low-frequency audio amplifier and submit it to him. I was delighted! I could do that!

I went back to my rented room and set to work. I had done this kind of design before while in high school, so probably I snickered a bit as I consulted my vacuum tube handbook to select a typical amplifier tube.

During the weekend I laid out, in great detail, all aspects of the design using equations and graphical solutions. I went into detail as much as I could without overdoing it, I hoped. I knew the amplifier would work as predicted because I had done similar designs.

As early as I could the next Monday morning, I presented my homework to Mr. Robert E. Rawlins, Jr. and was delighted to hear that he was very impressed. Shortly thereafter I was transferred into Bob Rawlins's group. Soon we became friends.

A year later, he gave me a new task that ultimately led to very fortunate consequences for me.

My first assignment in my new group was to design and supervise the construction of a "shaker motor," a device that could be attached to an aircraft structure and literally shake it at controlled rates and amounts to determine whether or not dangerous flexures or vibrations could occur.

That was a delightful assignment. It gave me a chance to do something different.

The design requirements were simple. I could utilize existing pieces of equipment. I could utilize any materials that I needed, if they were available. That was during early 1942. The World War II era was a time of severe material shortages.

The shaker motor was required to supply one hundred pounds of peak force, at a maximum amplitude of one half of an inch when the armature current was thirty amperes.

A power supply was available that could deliver direct current, required to energize the magnetic field in my design. An audio frequency signal generator and a powerful audio amplifier were set aside for me to use with the shaker motor.

I proceeded with the design of a "linear motor" that was, in essence, a modified dynamic loudspeaker. Instead of a coil of wire moving in the strong magnetic field generated by an electromagnet driving a conical paper piston to move air, my design dispensed with the conical piston and simply provided a threaded rod supported by a flat three-branched phosphor bronze spring to allow mechanical attachment to test specimens.

During my design process I used my college textbooks that were written using physicist's terminology (metric) rather than engineer's language (English).

This caused some confusion for Virginias Junias Braun, an engineer who was asked to critique my design. I did considerable translation for him. That was fun with science and engineering!

Although he may not have been convinced, he agreed that my design probably would work. Both he and I greatly were relieved when the finished article actually performed as was required!

More than twenty years later I saw that shaker motor in a Lockheed Rye Canyon laboratory, far from its original Burbank location in the early 1940s.

After my initial success I was given other interesting assignments. I learned about the use of strain gauges applied to many different situations, measuring strains, vibration amplitudes, and frequencies. I learned to design various strain gauge circuit arrangements and to install them on test specimens.

Sometimes I participated in the design of specialized automated test equipment. I became familiar with electro-mechanical servo systems design.

During my time in L. D. MacDonald's group, I had studied a course on transient response of disturbed systems with emphasis on vibration and damping of the resultant motions, so I was prepared to work in the vibrations group. I also had studied servomechanisms theory and that helped me to participate in the design and building of some test equipment.

There were times when I was involved in physical testing, such as the time I thought that I might shake the tails off a twin tailed PV-1 bomber!

During a frequency sweep, I encountered a resonance that caused surprisingly large motions of both vertical tail members. Quickly I reduced the driver strength and hoped no one had noticed! There was no damage except to my composure. In those days, there was great interest in controlling tail flutter of several different aircraft, and we were involved in many tests.

A different kind of testing was more exciting than interesting. After several of our group had installed strain gauges, accelerometers, and who knows what else, we watched as a twin engine bomber, possibly a PV-1, was dropped several feet, inside a hangar, to test the landing gear strength. The area around the testing position was surrounded by walls of baled hay to absorb any flying pieces that might result.

Our instrumentation was employed to determine structural stresses and as it turned out, the bursting strength of at least one Oleo shock absorber strut.

Several tests were performed, each at a greater drop distance, until some damage occurred. It was expensive and somewhat dangerous but, at the time, it was the best we could do. And it was fun.

Our group worked in Plant 1, a building complex next to the Burbank airport. There was a row of two-story buildings, a gap, and another row of two-story buildings. There was an elevated catwalk connecting the two rows of buildings, part of which was close to a guard station. The back building ground floor was where the research and development group built and tested things. Engineering was on the second floor, where there was a large drafting room.

I believe Lockheed was one of the first companies to utilize three-phase fluorescent lighting systems. There were three separate fluorescent bulbs in each light fixture, and the power would time cycle among them to minimize flicker, reducing draftsmen's eye strain.

The engineering drafting room was quite large and had exposed trusswork supporting the roof. One of the main horizontal beams was decorated by a cartoon of Kilroy, a fictional character popular during early World War II. Army veterans will remember Kilroy.[*]

The front building had administrative offices, and much later, a computer department in the lower level.

From the start and throughout my career, I had good relationships at Lockheed. I do not remember any bad times at Lockheed, except perhaps when one of my bicycle tires exploded. Lockheed helped me acquire a bicycle in times when rubber was rationed. The tires were made of either recycled or synthetic rubber, war-time materials that were of poor quality.

I had convinced a guard to let me park my bicycle under his guard station. The station was at street level, and under ground level there was another set of buildings. After work one day, as I went to retrieve my bicycle, the guard told me there had been an explosion. One of my tires had blown. I walked the bicycle home that day.

Immediately after the Japanese attack on Pearl Harbor on December 7, 1941, there was fear that they could and would attack the United States mainland and Lockheed would be a major target.

Very early in 1942, all the Lockheed factory buildings were camouflaged by covering them with fabric supported by wire netting on a network of steel framework held up by steel poles. Artificial trees, shrubbery, and fake buildings of various shapes, colors, and sizes to resemble urban neighborhoods were installed on top of the fabric.

Green lawns and agriculture plantings were painted to blend into the general appearance of that part of the valley.

Streets, alleys, and other details were simulated by painting on the fabric. Even the airport runways were disguised to look like part of the neighborhoods.

During daytime, the underside of the netting appeared light gray with patches of dark gray scattered about. We quickly became accustomed to the shade and ignored it.

Crash Investigation at NOTS

While I was working in the vibrations group, my experience stream took another fortunate turn. I do not know why, but I, a technician, was included in a small team sent to the Naval Ordnance Test Station, Inyokern,

---

[*]   "Kilroy was here."

California (now the Naval Air Weapons Station, China Lake, California), to investigate an aircraft crash in the China Lake area.

The pilot, Navy Lieutenant John Murray Armitage, for whom Armitage Field at the Naval Air Weapons Station is named, was killed in the accident. Lt. Armitage was flying a low altitude rocket-firing test when his aircraft suddenly nosed down and hit the ground.

Firing large rockets from aircraft was a capability that was just being developed, and it was dangerous. However, the rocket work at Inyokern/ China Lake was very significant. The firing techniques developed there were used to sink several Japanese ships during the war.

We were flown there in a single-tailed PB4Y-2 "Privateer," the Navy version of the twin-tailed B-24 "Liberator" bomber. I remember wondering if the navigator had made a mistake. I did not know that the Navy would go so far away from oceans!

Investigation revealed that the trim tab on the port side elevator had been dislodged and deflected upward by the turbulent rocket exhaust, causing the elevator to deflect downward and force the aircraft to nose down.

The tab had been disconnected from its control cable and was fastened in neutral by means of a flat piece of aluminum that was held in place by self-tapping sheet metal screws. The rocket exhaust apparently deflected the tab and tore loose the patch that wedged in the space between the tab and the elevator and kept the tab deflected upward.

That was the first time I saw a wrecked aircraft up close. I became interested in rocket firing development, and I liked the military courtesy and commitment I saw there.

Naval Ordnance Test Station, Inyokern

In early 1943, I left Lockheed and became a civil service employee of the Navy in NOTS, Inyokern.

I spent about sixteen months working at NOTS/NAWS (Naval Air Weapons Station) helping to do airborne rocket launch tests on several aircraft.

I was hired to do instrumentation of aircraft structures and interpretation of measured data. All of my work was involved in testing the effects of rocket firing upon aircraft structures.

When I first arrived at NOTS, Inyokern, we were billeted at the Inyokern airport in Quonset huts that I considered rather primitive. After the occasional sandstorms, our beds were likely to be coated by dust.

Each day we commuted several miles to the entrance to the base at China Lake near Ridgecrest, California. Then we would drive along dirt roads to our office in a crude frame building. Sixty years later when I accompanied Sherre, who visited there for a conference, the base was so changed that I did not recognize any of it!

The Navy conducted ground tests and airborne firing tests, each involving small five-inch diameter or large eleven-inch diameter rockets. Of the rather large assortment of aircraft available, I instrumented only an F6-F fighter. Other rocket firing aircraft I remember were SB-2C Scout Bombers and F4-U Corsair fighters.

The F6-F was a great aircraft, but my favorite was the gull-winged F-4U,[11] the "Bent-Wing Bird," which I still think is beautiful. There can be beauty as well as excitement and fun in science and engineering.

The ground testing was done by hoisting rocket-equipped aircraft about fifty feet above ground and then firing the rockets by remote control through cables. Two large cranes were used to raise hawsers from which the aircraft were suspended.

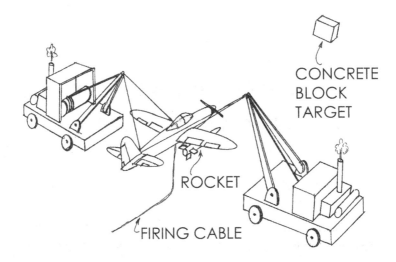

CONCRETE
BLOCK
TARGET

ROCKET

FIRING CABLE

NOTS Rocket Firing Ground Testing

The first time I heard a rocket firing I thought that it sounded like the sky was being ripped apart! It was great fun!

All the tests were conducted several miles away from the main base out in raw desert. The rockets were aimed at large concrete block targets.

Airborne tests originally were performed by flying instrumented rocket-equipped aircraft from the Inyokern airport out to the target area and back.

My field involvement was installation of strain gauges, accelerometers, and oscillograph recorders in aircraft. My office work was extracting information from crude graphical analog recordings.

That era was long before wire or tape recorders were available. By modern standards, our recorders were huge boxes that contained a row of galvanometers, each of which was operated by an individual amplifier.

The galvanometers were motor-like devices whose rotation was limited to a few degrees. Each galvanometer rotated a mirror that reflected a beam of light onto a strip of photosensitive paper that was pulled past them by motors in the container. The beams of light were deflected across the paper perpendicularly to the motion of the paper and so recorded a history of events.

After developing the paper, we frequently unrolled twenty or more feet of it on a hallway floor to read the data.

In early 1944, I was riding in a Navy PBJ, the Navy's version of the B-25 "Mitchell" bomber aircraft, flying from Burbank to NOTS. I remember very clearly that I was sitting in the navigator's station on the starboard side across a very narrow aisle from a large fuel tank.

While I was thinking about that tank, I happened to see out of a corner of my right eye a moving object crossing under us.

Quickly I looked out the window in time to see a very well streamlined low wing aircraft flying faster than any other I ever had seen. It disappeared under a cloud layer, and I did not see it again.

It might have been Lockheed's first jet fighter, Kelly Johnson's "Lulu Belle," the prototype of the P-80 aircraft. The white tip on the vertical tail of a production P-80 was a fiberglass cover over one of the antennas I would later design and develop.

In 1943, Kelly Johnson had assembled a small group of engineers and mechanics to design and build the first American jet-propelled aircraft that went into production.

They occupied a very ramshackled shelter whose walls were made of lumber salvaged from aircraft engine crates. It was covered by a rented circus tent. The project activities were concealed for security. They actually built the prototype aircraft inside that enclosure.

One day an engineer (possibly Irving Culver) answered the telephone saying, "Skonk works." Kelly heard him and did not like what he heard and almost fired him. (Kelly had a tendency to "fire" someone and then immediately order him or her to get back to work!)

At that time, there was a popular newspaper comic strip "Little Abner" that featured a character who "rendered" (boiled) skunks, old shoes, and other "ingredients" to make "kickapoo joy juice" in his "Skonk Works."

Eventually Kelly decided that he liked "Skunk Works" and he adopted it. A cartoon of a cute skunk became part of a Skunk Works logo that was painted on many Lockheed aircraft.

While we were based at the Inyokern Airport, several hair-raising events occurred.

One day, while I was on the Inyokern flight line, I saw an F-4U Corsair begin a take-off run with an eleven-inch diameter, ten feet long HVAR rocket suspended beneath the fuselage. Suddenly the A-frames supporting the rocket descended, dragging the rocket on the runway and creating a trail of sparks. I thought that rocket would explode, and apparently so did the pilot. He stopped and got out so quickly that I do not remember seeing him.

Navy Lt. David Carnahan, the bomb disposal officer, and his crew successfully recovered both the aircraft and the rocket. I sometimes wondered if he survived the war.

Another incident involved an SB-2C aircraft with a two-man crew. As I remember hearing about it, they had just fired a rocket when a gun camera mounted on the underside of the starboard wing came loose and hit and so severely damaged the rudder that the pilot ordered the gunner in the aft cockpit to bail out. During his attempt to get out, he deployed his parachute in his cockpit and could not leave.

I was in the lower level of the control tower and heard the pilot report the situation and say that he would return to base. I went outside to watch him return.

A large portion of the north end of the Inyokern Airport Runway 15 sloped so much that at touchdown near the threshold, aircraft rolled uphill. The difference was so great that even large aircraft such as a PB4Y-2 might not be seen immediately by an observer on the ground near the tower, as I was that day.

I saw the wounded aircraft approach and go down for landing. It seemed a long time after he disappeared until he rolled up over the crest. That pilot saved two people and an aircraft by flying skillfully a functionally rudderless aircraft.

Still another incident that I remember happened to a British Wing Commander flying an F-4U aircraft for a rocket-firing test. After he released the rocket, he reported that the engine had lost power and was vibrating severely, but he thought that he could get back to base.

After he landed and taxied in, it was discovered that nearly a foot of each of the three propeller blades was missing! It was obvious that the rocket had not been lowered below the propeller before it was launched. There was not much science or fun during these events, but there was enough excitement!

I was asked to instrument a rocket to be launched from an F6-F to determine how much time elapsed between the pilot's firing switch closure and the rocket firing.

Not wanting to resort to highly sophisticated technology (and having none available), I decided to fasten a narrow loop of thin insulated copper wire across the rocket nozzle so that when the exhaust burned the wire in two, a current fed to a recorder channel would be interrupted. By comparison of the timing signals to each recorder channel, we could determine the delay.

I installed the wire loop myself. Although it took little time to do it, as I faced the rocket nozzle it seemed to grow much larger! To our satisfaction, it worked.

One day an F6-F that I had instrumented with strain gauges took off headed for the firing range. As he circled from the Inyokern runway the pilot reported that, as soon as he armed it, the rocket had fired and appeared headed toward Ridgecrest. Panic ensued!

Meanwhile the pilot returned to base. After he got out of the aircraft, it was discovered that a bomb shackle that had held a five-inch diameter rocket had been torn off along with some minor wing structure and a large piece of wing skin.

Fortunately, the rocket was found in the desert safely away from Ridgecrest.

Rattlesnakes were a danger, especially while we worked at night. Frequently we worked at night because it was too hot during the day. We had to be very cautious about our environment because rattlesnakes seemed to be everywhere. Sidewinder tracks in the sand were common. We were issued flashlights that we used, even during daylight hours, to illuminate any space that we might need to reach into or look into. We were issued "Eisenhower" jackets and pith helmets to wear during daytime work.

Several men voluntarily searched for snakes while we did our work. Fortunately for me, I did not encounter one.

Well after midnight one cold night I learned to like REAL Navy coffee—hot, unsweetened, and black. It was a real spine straightener!

At meals usually there was a coffee pot set on each table. It was customary that the first person who reached for the pot served all others at that table. Especially at breakfast, there was a lot of nervous waiting for someone to get up!

There was a lot of "hangar flying" at mealtimes. One story I remember involved an SB-2C scout bomber crew practicing a carrier landing.

The Navy had a replica of a carrier deck laid out on desert soil so that pilots could land, take off, and maintain their combat readiness without getting wet.

Edward Lovick, Jr.

During one practice run, the pilot forgot to lower the landing gear. The gunner/bombardier, who sat in a cockpit aft of the pilot's, realized that the aircraft was too low at touchdown. He saw the doors of the empty bomb bay grind away and a river of sand come rushing through. He had just enough time to cover his face before he was engulfed. Almost as soon as the aircraft stopped sliding the pilot scrambled out and came around to check on the crewman and help him out of the sandy mess.

Several days before Christmas in 1943, we were moved into new Bachelor Officer's Quarters (BOQ) at China Lake.

I was billeted with an officer who worked on rocket solid fuel development and testing. I remember that he or his uniforms often released a faint sickly sweet odor. I spent as little time in our quarters as I could. The rooms were nice and comfortable. The club was very nice and the food was very good.

I was playing table tennis during a Christmas party when a little girl, perhaps six or seven years old, kept grabbing stray balls and running away with them. Finally I tried to get her to return them and looked up just in time to see the base commander, Captain Sherman Burroughs, looking down on us. I thought that I was in trouble, but he took charge of his daughter and led her away. I saw him very seldom and never had contact with him.

About this time, I heard about an incident that I was glad that I did not cause. A flight line crewman pulled and collapsed the nose wheel of Cmdr. John T. "Chick" Hayward's PBJ aircraft just before he was to fly it to a naval base near Washington, DC.

Hayward was the executive officer under Captain Sherman E. Burroughs. R. Adm., Ret. Hayward retired as a vice admiral[12] after serving as the twenty-first Chief of Naval Operations.

During my time working at NOTS, I associated with several pilots. We often ate at the same mess and got to know each other.

One day I got bitten by the flying bug. I was invited by a pilot to go to an airport in the Los Angeles area in a Navy version of a Beech "Staggerwing" (a Navy G-2).

The Torrance airport taxiway was so rough that I wondered whether the radio in the rack behind my head would bounce out.

During the flight he let me take the controls for a while, and that settled the issue for me. I decided to try to become a Navy pilot.

42

In the Navy

I took leave for several days and went to Los Angeles to enlist and apply for flight training. Several members of my Falls City High School class were aviators during World War II. Frank Elam, John Falter, and possibly Marvin Dunn were Navy pilots. Thomas Davies was an Army Air Force pilot. He flight tested B-29 bombers.

Early during the morning of the next day after I arrived, I found the Army Air Corps recruiting office and decided to take their entrance examination in case I had trouble with the Navy's exam. Before noon I finished what seemed to be easy tests, so I decided to go to the Navy office where I had an appointment for that afternoon.

I had at least two hours available before going to the Navy office, so I ate lunch and, while walking about until time to go, I saw a sign in a small storefront that invited me to "TAKE THE EDDY TEST."

Mostly out of curiosity and, having nothing else interesting to do, I entered and took the test. The Eddy[13] test was designed to identify men who could become Navy radio and/or radar maintenance technicians. Captain William Crawford Eddy was the founder of the Navy's school for training radio and radar maintenance technicians. The test seemed easy, and I promptly forgot about it. Later it turned out to have a very beneficial result for me: science, fun, and much more!

That afternoon, I took the Navy flight training tests and passed easily. The only part that I remember vividly was overhearing someone say, "That man has excellent night vision. He would be great with range-finders." What a shock! The worst thing I could imagine was submarine duty! Fortunately for me, it did not happen.

I never mentioned my Army Reserve Officers' Training Corps (ROTC) participation during my two years at the University of Nebraska because I thought that the Navy would not value it. Furthermore, I had no interest in staying in the Navy after the war.

After a short time, I received a letter informing me that the Navy had discontinued the flight-training program. During World War II it took eighteen months, or more, to become carrier qualified and combat ready.

Soon after that news, I was called to enter the Navy radio and radar technicians training program as a student. I was very disappointed by the closing of the pilot training program, but it turned out very well for me.

I was sent from Los Angeles to Camp Paul Jones in San Diego for an abbreviated introduction to boot camp. The Navy "cooks and bakers" school was located nearby, and we appreciated that!

After that I went by train to Chicago with a large group of men, including Edward Martin, who later became a very important member of Kelly Johnson's Advanced Development Projects,[14] the famous Lockheed Skunk Works. Ed and I became acquainted and later became friends and colleagues.

We went to Chicago for preliminary training that was mostly mathematics and electric and electronic circuit theory and practical laboratory work, all of which I already had done.

After study in Chicago, Ed went to Corpus Christi, Texas, to the aircraft radio and radar school.

I was sent to Gulfport, Mississippi, for more theory and work on actual ship-board radio, radar, sonar, IFF (Identification: Friend or Foe), and attack plotter systems. While there, I demonstrated my ability to diagnose equipment malfunctions quickly. That was a result of my radio repair experience.

After graduation, I was assigned to Navy Pier, Chicago, where I spent the rest of my naval career teaching electronics theory.

The Navy Pier facility was very well self-contained. There were living quarters, classrooms, laboratories, and mess halls. If the weather was too bad, one could carry on without difficulty.

My only wartime injury occurred on Navy Pier when I was hit in the back of one of my legs by a light wooden chair that someone threw into a passageway while I was walking to the mess hall. I was not even bruised! It seemed like the Marines and Navy sailors always were scuffling.

During World War II, Chicago justly was known as a great "liberty" city for all service personnel. I met Ellen Betty Lucille Alm, a Swedish-American girl, in Chicago. She was a hostess at a Stouffer's restaurant in "The Loop," an area in downtown Chicago encircled by elevated train tracks. Several of us liked to eat in that restaurant when we were off the base.

Lucille already had graduated from the University of Illinois in Champaign-Urbana and was waiting to take a teaching job in her hometown, Rockford, Illinois, ninety miles away.

We began dating regularly. After several months, we became engaged to be married. Shortly after that event, she accompanied her parents aboard the Swedish ship *Gripsholm* on its first civilian voyage after the war to visit their hometown in Sweden.

While she was away, I was discharged from the Navy in Lido Beach, New York, so I visited my brother in nearby Rochester, New York, and then went to meet Lucille in Rockford. I found a summer job in Rockford and got to know her family quite well.

I remember standing at a bus stop in Chicago's "Loop" with my brother Bob and his wife Dorothy, waiting for our younger sister Hazel to arrive. I was in uniform standing with my back to the bus stop when Hazel alighted, so I did not see her.

She told us that when she asked the bus driver to stop, he said that he would not stop for a woman who could recognize a sailor from behind! We were glad that she did, and that he did!

That was my Navy career. I did not do much flying until after I was out of the Navy. My first logbook shows some time as a civilian student while I was in the Navy in Gulfport, Mississippi. (It did not mention that I had "ground looped" a tail dragger aircraft. A ground loop is an involuntary maneuver caused by loss of control that results in an aircraft spinning around at least one time. It is most embarrassing!)

After I was discharged from the Navy I realized that Fortune had, indeed, smiled upon me. There were hordes of unemployed surplus aviators!

University of Illinois

My next endeavor was to enter a university to continue my education. To that end I applied to the University of California at Los Angeles, and the University of Illinois in Champaign-Urbana.

While I waited, hopefully, to be accepted by UCLA or Illinois, I worked in a Rockford machine shop from June to September 1946 and gained more hands-on experience in manufacturing.

There were thousands of returned service men and women, so competition for entry was quite intense. I preferred to go to UCLA, but in those days there were so many people trying to get into the colleges that I decided to take the first offer I got. The University of Illinois responded a few days before I received notice that UCLA had accepted me, so I went to Illinois, fully intending to return to California and Lockheed as soon as possible after I graduated. As usual, things worked out a bit differently, but much better than I expected.

In the fall, I entered the University of Illinois in Champaign-Urbana for my junior year. I lived for a short time in the men's gymnasium with a large group of men and then shared a room in a nearby house with a man whose name I cannot remember. He was a political science major, so we had nothing in common.

Meanwhile, Lucille taught school in Rockford, so I saw her only occasionally when I could drive my old automobile there. We planned to be married in June after school was out.

Lucille and I were married June 21, 1947, in Rockford. Navy Lt. Paul Brink, a friend from my time at NOTS, Inyokern, was our best man.

Almost immediately we drove across the country to Glendale, California, to live for the summer while I worked for the Northrop Aircraft Company in Hawthorne.

Lucille was not enthusiastic about living in California at that time. Several years later, she changed her mind about it after we had visited her parents in Illinois during Christmas time. She became ill with a cold and was quite happy to return to warm Southern California.

My summer work at Northrop was part of a program to develop a star tracker system to aid navigation in space. That was an early effort the outcome of which I never learned. Perhaps some of the results helped in the design of the star tracker system for the SR-71 aircraft. It was scientific fun while it lasted.

When Lucille and I returned to Illinois for my senior year at the university, we moved into a loft, with fancy furniture consisting of orange crates and suitcases on end covered by towels. But I was not living on cots in the mens' gymnasium like I was during my first year, and I had very good company!

While I was studying for my electrical engineering degree, Lucille worked as a research assistant in the home economics department.

In order to hasten my return to California, I obtained twice the normal course credits by passing proficiency examinations in addition to completing the regularly required credit courses.

One memory of my time at the University of Illinois is the "Great Scott!" connection. The General Electric Company had donated a large battle gray, brand new transformer that incorporated what was known as a Scott connection intended to convert single-phase power to two-phase power. The very large transformer divided alternating currents into 15 percent and 85 percent portions. It used silicone oil as a coolant.

Whenever we students connected equipment together for practice in high power problems in the laboratory, we were required to verify our connections before we applied power because it was dangerous to make errors.

Somehow my group connected the terminals backwards so that the 15 percent and 85 percent portions were interchanged, and that thing began really heating up. Soon the oil was boiling and smoke was rolling off it—I do not know if it was the paint or the oil burning. I thought that we had had it for sure! Fortunately we were able to disconnect it before damage occurred.

There was another event that I heard about that involved the respected Professor Marion Stanley Helm.

One day Professor Helm made the mistake of plugging a short cable into the power panel and dropping the other end, which hit the metal frame that supported the power panel and caused large, loud sparks.

He was seen trying to kick the cable away from the frame, only to fail several times. Finally he was able to unplug the cable, but not before several people saw him "perform." One of his fellow professors told us later in class about the incident. It seems that even the best of us make mistakes.

There was a building on the engineering campus that housed a small cyclotron facility. Cyclotrons were called "atom smashers" in those days. During cold winter weather, I passed through a hallway that allowed me to go from building to building without going outside. Each time I went through I expected to see a deadly bright blue beam crossing the passageway—but I never did. I had heard talk of people being injured by radiation in there, so my imagination sometimes worked too vigorously!

I had learned about cyclotron theory[15] during my study at Caltech before I went into the Navy so I had some appreciation of the possible dangers.

I still remember from my Caltech studies that a type 42 electron tube that was a common audio power amplifier tube used in radio receivers would work as a very high frequency magnetron oscillator if a suitable permanent magnet was brought near it. Also, I remember that an ordinary wooden two-by-four could guide microwaves, but poorly.

As part of my studies, I took flight training and got my pilot's license. The training in those days was more intense and thorough than it is today. For me, the most memorable events were the precision (accurate) spins. The examiner, perhaps my flight instructor Jesse Stonecipher, would specify the direction and number of rotations and the heading at recovery. That was fun, interesting, and exciting.

The aircraft that we flew were what now are called "tail draggers." Early in our training, we were taught to make "three point" landings. That is, we were supposed to contact earth with both main wheels and the tail wheel or a "skid" at the same time. Near the end of our training, we were introduced to "wheel" landings that required us to keep the tail up as long as we could. Now, since tricycle landing gears are so common, special training and an endorsement are required to be considered qualified to make three-point landings!

We also were taught to start the engines manually. "Hand propping" can be an exciting experience!

My final examination in flight training was a solo flight to two nearby airports and back. I left the University of Illinois airport and immediately encountered a strong headwind that slowed my progress and used fuel at an alarming rate.

As I approached my first scheduled stop, I did not see the airport. immediately because of snow on the ground. I checked my navigation data and decided that I must be near my destination. My fuel gauge was near empty, so I was anxious to find a place to land. I rolled the aircraft and looked down—the airport was almost directly below me!

I touched down carefully on what looked like a sheet of black ice, rolled onto a dry portion of the runway, and taxied to the fuel pumps before my fuel could run out.

The second leg of the flight was uneventful, but the last leg was quite different.

I took off just before sundown, and when it was becoming dark I realized that I had no cockpit lights, no flashlight, and no radio. The weather was excellent, so I could see trees, houses and their lights, and a railroad track that I followed back to the vicinity of the airport. Then I made my first night landing with the aid of airport lights.

I did not do anything with my license for a long time, but it was time well spent legitimately. I knew I was headed for the aerospace industry.

After graduation in June 1948, with my electrical engineering degree secured, my plan again was altered.

I received and accepted an offer on campus from the Douglas Aircraft Company in Santa Monica, California, because they offered me an aerospace engineering job and paid our travel expenses back to California, which was everything I wanted. I had no need to apply for employment at Lockheed in Burbank.

After we returned to California, we rented part of a house at 2530 Pearl Street in Santa Monica near the Douglas factory, and I went to work designing control circuitry for Nike missiles.

A short time later, I was assigned to work as a final checkout engineer in the factory.

After several missiles were manufactured and tested, I was sent to the White Sands Missile Range near Las Cruces, New Mexico, to participate in some test firing. My wife, Lucille, accompanied me.

We arrived at the base camp shortly after a spectacular event had occurred.

A few days before we arrived at the base, a large missile, perhaps a V-2, was launched from a pad a mile or so away, and instead of going where it should have, it seemed headed toward the base camp! Fortunately, the camp buildings were up a slope and well above the launch pad level. The range safety officer destroyed the missile short of the camp!

While I was there, we experienced telemetry failures due to attenuation of the 6 GHz radio signals by the ionized gases in the Nike rocket exhaust. Unfortunately for me, I was not involved in the effort to circumvent the plasma "blackout."

Before we left to return to Santa Monica, I watched another rocket launch failure.

I was inside a "block house" built for observation and control. It was a sturdy concrete building with very thick multi-pane glass windows. Launch controls, range safety instrumentation, and telemetry recorders, together with several people, were contained inside.

As I watched through a window, the motor of the very large rocket ignited and a huge flame issued. The rocket lifted only a few feet off the launch pad, then fell over on its side and disappeared in an enormous bonfire. The event took only a few minutes, but it ruined a whole day! Painful as it may be, failure sometimes may be part of the price of progress.

Return to Lockheed

Soon after returning to Douglas in Santa Monica, I received an unexpected call from my former boss and good friend, Bob Rawlins. His group had a new boss, Elvin O. Richter, an aerodynamicist. Bob said the former structural testing group was now involved in aerodynamic testing, and he thought I would find it interesting. The group designed and built special equipment to be used in testing aircraft both on the ground and in the air. He was aware of my stress and strain instrumentation experience at NOTS, which could be valuable to the group. He offered me a job. I liked Rawlins, so I did not need a reason to come back when he called in 1948, and I accepted.

I still remember that it was a November day that Lucille and I moved from the chill of Santa Monica to the soothing warmth of the San Fernando Valley. We rented a room in a house directly south of the main runway of the Lockheed Air Terminal, near where I had lived as a bachelor.

Bob Rawlins introduced me to our boss, Elvin O. "E. O." Richter. He informed Richter that I knew about a new and—at that time—fairly rare electronic circuit known as a "Phantastron."[16] [17]

I had learned about it during my Navy teaching career. Its value was that it allowed an extremely constant rate of deflection of a cathode ray tube fluorescent spot so that distances to targets could be measured and displayed much more accurately. It had been a significant radar circuit improvement.[18] I did not know why they had such an interest in this circuit. Obviously Rawlins already knew about the circuit. Perhaps they were considering incorporating it into an SCR-584 radar, the best and most famous radar in the WW II era. It was designed and prototyped at the MIT Radiation Laboratory. Lockheed had one available to them.

Its value to me was that it helped me to get a job that I liked.

Our group was housed in a building that was one of several separate but neighboring structures in Plant B. We had laboratory and office space on a mezzanine floor arranged around a wind tunnel facility that had been designed by Elvin O. Richter.

We used quarter-scale or smaller partial models instrumented to gather aerodynamic and structural data for various conditions, such as rate of roll, pitch, or yaw, rate of climb, accelerations, and vibration. Dropped from a P-38 aircraft, they could transmit data by radio telemetry during free flight.

Some models, aiding the design of the X-7 missile and possibly the F-104 aircraft, were launched by rocket boosters. These tests required vacuum tubes that could survive the acceleration of a rocket launch.

In our laboratory, we hung metal weights on strings and let them swing and hit candidate vacuum tubes while they were operating as audio amplifiers. The tubes that did not break or become noisy were accepted.

The models that I worked on were carried aloft under a P-38 aircraft left over from World War II and dropped from 10,000 feet or so. Then they would glide through mechanically programmed trajectories as they fell to Earth in the desert on Edwards Air Force Base, California. I believe that Anthony "Tony" LeVier flew at least one flight of the P-38 aircraft. There were two fifteen feet tall trailers sitting side by side out there in the desert, about thirty feet apart. The P-38 pilot flew low, rolled the airplane wings vertical, and flew the gap between the trailers. I could hardly believe it! I guessed it was Tony, because he had the greatest skill in the P-38.

It was before the days of good computer-controlled equipment, so the desired maneuvers were executed by means of electrically driven mechanical devices. Strain gauges, accelerometers, and gyroscopes, together with aneroid barometers to determine altitude, and differential pressure monitors to determine airspeed and rate of change of altitude, supplied information to the radio telemetry transmitters. Bob Rawlins led the electronic system design efforts. All the systems were analog.

Even in the digital age some analog technology might be useful. Its novelty can be fun, and it might even be a better, less expensive, or more reliable choice in some designs.

I modified several instruments that utilized gyroscopes and so I learned interesting facts about gyroscopes. For example:

P = S x T

The "**x**" in this equation indicates a vector cross-product, not an ordinary multiplication. In ordinary English, that equation might be, "The precession vector points in a direction perpendicular to the plane in which the spin vector and the torque vector are at right angles to each other"!

This simple vector equation is very useful for understanding gyroscopes, as well as what might occur if a pilot allows the tail of a tail dragger aircraft to lift too quickly during a take-off run. Too many pilots have experienced this left turning effect as they ran off a runway! The gyro rotor in this case would be the rapidly spinning propeller. The opposite effect could occur during landing.

Robert Fuller led the rocket launch and recovery group. Fuller devised a simple rocket launcher rack made from wooden two-by-fours, including the rails. After a rocket was placed in the rails, he would set fire to a ten-foot length of dynamite fuse and step back.

Fuller's model recovery method was simple—a small parachute was deployed to slow the models as they neared the ground. Then like lawn darts, their sharp, pointed noses stuck into the ground unless they hit a rock!

The drop testing supplemented wind tunnel aerodynamic data for the X-7 missile and F-104 aircraft.

The first time I saw drawings of the F-104 aircraft, I thought that someone had made a mistake—the wings drooped down! That was my introduction to "anhedral." Anhedral was necessary to prevent dangerous "Dutch roll" during landing. These models exposed me to some state-of-the-art low speed aerodynamic features.

One day in the laboratory during instrumentation, a model was resting on a bench with its sharp-pointed nose out into a passageway. I decided that the nose was too dangerous to be left unprotected.

I obtained a white rubber ball and painted part of it light blue. I added a white paper reinforcement ring over the blue area. Then I made a cluster of strings of various lengths and painted them red. Next, I inserted the strings into the ball opposite the blue area. Finally I pushed the iris of the ball onto the point of the model nose to make an eyeball that had "optic nerves" dangling out. It was better than a poke in the eye, I'd tell the curious.

Antenna Testing

After a short time doing electronic instrumentation design, fabrication, and use, I was given an assignment to measure the radiation patterns of a simple antenna installation in a test configuration.

Theoretical radiation patterns characteristic of two similar antennas connected together and spaced apart had been published in two references.[19] [20]

I was able to obtain a simple oscillator that produced the desired radio frequencies. Also, I was able to obtain a suitable receiver. Both items were from World War II military equipment surplus that was plentiful and inexpensive for several years.

I put the transmitter on the parapet of a nearby building and put the antenna to be tested and the receiver on a similar ledge on the roof of our building. A simple vertical wire was used as a non-directional transmitting antenna. The receiving antenna, a two-element array under test, was mounted on a "Lazy Susan." It was rotated by hand in ten-degree increments through 360 degrees for each frequency required. For each angular increment and each frequency, a signal strength meter indication on the receiver was recorded. The receiver actually was a form of voltmeter. I plotted each datum on polar coordinate graph paper. It was crude but adequate. That was our first antenna radiation pattern measurement facility.

Antenna radiation patterns were plotted on paper using rectangular or polar coordinates. They also were plotted as relative electric field strength data or relative logarithmic (decibel) data. The most common presentation was relative field strength on polar coordinates.

Decibel notation was invented by early-day telephone engineers as a practical mathematical aid to dealing with very large and very small numbers and combinations thereof. Although it may have appeared that some accuracy had been lost, the results were so useful that the notation has become standard. The decibel notation describes power ratios.

I had studied electromagnetic theory in special courses at Caltech, while in the U. S. Navy, and at the University of Illinois. I had calculated many antenna radiation patterns but never had measured actual antenna properties. That was my first experience in actual real antenna measurements.

My next assignment was to provide an antenna to be used to recover telemetry data from the falling models.

I designed and had our shop build a helical antenna mounted upon a World War II surplus aircraft machine gun mount so that it could be tilted and swiveled by remote control using signals from a tracking theodolite, a special telescope that was used to follow the models.

Telemetry Tracking Antenna

The reason for the helical design was that it would be able to receive the linearly polarized waves from the falling models regardless of their orientation.

About this time, late 1950 or early 1951, Lockheed acquired the assets of a simple antenna test facility from an East Coast company, Airborne Instruments Laboratory (AIL).

It was housed in a small building just safely west of the north end of the North-South Runway 17. It contained office space, equipment storage space, shop space, and measurement laboratory space—all in less than five hundred square feet of floor area!

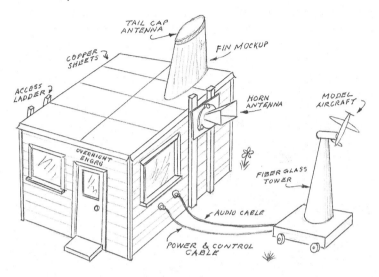

The First Lockheed Burbank Antenna Laboratory

The original antenna laboratory was crude. It had no relief facilities. A large mockup of an aircraft fuselage nose section was standing on end nearby. We called it "Hogan's Hogan," and it became our emergency facility that was used infrequently.

While there I worked on antennas for F-90, F-94, P-80, F-104, and the C-130 aircraft.

Almost all of our designs were flush with the aircraft's contours to minimize aerodynamic disturbances that cause drag. Some were well inside plastic enclosures, either radomes or radar windows.

The flat roof of the one-story building was covered by sheets of copper soldered together. It served as a "ground" (image) plane for mockups of antennas whose impedance characteristics were to be measured. Access to the roof was by way of a ladder attached to one side of the building.

Physicists and engineers think of and represent forces and actions in graphical or mathematical terms as entities that have magnitude and direction. Surveyors and navigators may specify locations similarly in terms of distances and direction.

Electrical and electronic engineers think of electric potential differences (voltages) as magnitudes and relative timing of sinusoidal functions (relative phase of currents) as graphical direction and they may call the results vectors, but a more acceptable terminology may be "phasors." Similar ideas apply to electric currents and ratios of potential differences and currents (i.e., impedance, or its reciprocal, admittance).

Impedance, in general, is a measure of how much stimulus is required to produce a result. The concept is valid for mechanical, electrical, acoustic, hydraulic, thermal, and perhaps other disciplines. To electrical engineers, it is the ratio of the potential difference, or voltage, impressed upon a circuit component to the current that flows in that component.

There may be complications that arise if the current and the voltage do not change in the same way as time progresses. That is, there may be phase differences to consider. The principal condition to be met is impedance matching to allow the maximum transfer of power from place to place. Sometimes the most desired result is to reduce or eliminate reflections that can cause reverberations that can interfere with the timing of events.

One of our most interesting and useful instruments was a "slotted line," used for low-frequency impedance measurements. Most of our work in that era involved communication, navigation, missile warning, or instrument landing antennas that utilized wavelengths greater than about two feet.

It was a heavy brass bar ten feet long that contained a coaxial transmission line. A movable carriage incorporating a tunable crystal or bolometer detector and a small probe antenna that traveled in a thin slot parallel to the transmission line inside enabled us to measure the relative electric field strength and the location of the maxima and minima of standing waves therein.

Standing waves are caused by waves of the same frequency traveling in different directions combining to increase or decrease amplitudes. The physical locations of maxima and minima do not move if the frequency does not change. They can be generated in a bathtub or swimming pool by timing carefully new wave impulses with existing waves.

The ratio of the maxima to the minima or Voltage Standing Wave Ratio (VSWR) and the location of at least one minimum allowed us to plot impedance data on a Smith Chart.*

---

*   Simple examples of its utility are shown in Appendix A.

Somewhat similar but smaller slotted lines utilizing hollow rectangular waveguides were used to measure impedances for higher frequencies.

All the measurement equipment was state of the art for the post-World War II era and in fact, was simple and easy to use. I still prefer that old-style equipment because modern instruments tend to obscure the physics involved.

Two valuable assets acquired at that time from AIL were engineers William R. "Bill" Martin and Raymond "Ray" Anderson. Bill had been hired by Lockheed to supervise the antenna laboratory and soon became my supervisor and good friend. Ray stayed for a few months and then left Lockheed.

Bill became my mentor as he helped me learn the intricacies of designing broad-band—wide frequency span—impedance matching networks to meet military specifications.

I enjoyed doing calculations using slide rules and Smith Charts, a special graph paper. Each network design was like solving a puzzle. We even had a circular slide rule version of a Smith Chart that was our most sophisticated computer!

Early in my career I became aware of the great power, and often ease, of the technique of using analogies to solve problems, to gain understanding in unfamiliar fields of science, or to explain situations. I have used analogies a great many times with much success.[21] [22] A very well-written account of the use of analogy by a very famous mathematical physicist was published in the book *The Making of the Electrical Age.*[23]

Also, I learned the great value of different kinds of special graph papers[24] and nomographs for quick and convenient solutions of problems.

Much later I would plot data on graph paper and then derive useful equations that I could enter into a programmable calculator.

Even after I learned to program computers, I continued to use graphical solutions to problems. For many design problems, graphical solutions are adequately accurate and may be much quicker.[†]

Familiarity with logarithms and logarithmic charting are very useful accomplishments.

---

† Analogies and graphical aids are further discussed in Appendix B.

Antenna Radiation Patterns

There was another interesting aspect to antenna performance measurements—the determination of directional sensitivity to receive energy or to project energy into space. The results were displayed graphically as "radiation patterns."

Our radiation pattern measurement facility utilized a fiberglass tower about six feet tall supported upon a wheeled platform that we rolled out of the office space each morning onto a grass-covered plot. We connected power, control, and data cables, and then mounted a scaled model of an aircraft that had scaled model antennas[‡] and tuned detectors installed onto the tower.

In our scaled model tests, only two scaling conditions were important. First, the model size needed to be scaled one to one inversely relative to frequency. For example, a 1/10th scale model must be illuminated by ten times the full-scale frequency. Second, the model's surface conductivity needed to be scaled inversely to the model scale. A 1/10th scale model's conductivity must be ten times that of the full-scale object.

We were able to test at scaled frequencies. The best conductivity scaling we could do was to use copper foil to cover the scaled models.

In all cases of radiation pattern measurement, we made the model antennas receive energy even though the real full-scale antenna might be used to radiate energy.

We took advantage of a fundamental theorem of electromagnetic theory—the Reciprocity Theorem,[25] [26] [27] which says, in effect, that the coupling between two simple antennas is independent of their function, whether or not one or the other sends or receives energy. This fortunate happenstance allowed great simplification of model installations.

Of course there were other factors to consider in real full-sized antennas, such as ability to handle high power and complicated feed structures that may incorporate directional couplers, circulators, or even gaseous switches. However, none of these factors applied to the simple communication, navigation, missile warning, instrument landing, beacon, or radar antennas that we were concerned about.

---

‡ A table on page 1368 of George Sinclair's 1948 IRE article lists the basic conditions required to make a geometrical scaled model of an electromagnetic system suitable for antenna or radar cross section measurements.

The model antennas were illuminated by energy radiated from simple antennas mounted on the outside of the building. The transmitted energy was modulated by periodically turning it on and off one thousand times per second. The receivers produced an audible 1000 Hz output, a tone about 5 percent flat of C two octaves above the frequency of concert middle C, the fortieth piano key counted from the left.

A control console and a polar recorder were inside the office. We could see the model on the tower through a window. The controls allowed us to rotate the tower and to spin the model mounted on the tower independently. Radiation patterns were plotted by our Scientific Atlanta Model 122B recorder in either linear or logarithmic (decibel) scales. Changing the tower angle changed the elevation angle relative to the model. Fixing the tower angle then turning the model through 360 degrees yielded a "conical" antenna pattern, a 360-degree pattern at a fixed elevation angle.

Our transmitting antennas were designed to radiate linearly polarized electromagnetic waves. Linear polarization means that the electric field force is exerted alternately in one direction or its opposite in space. For our purposes, we defined polarization as vertical or horizontal to correspond to real world conditions. Vertically polarized electric field forces oscillate up and down. The models were mounted with their wings vertical. Therefore, model world horizontal polarization was real world vertical polarization and vice versa.

Determination of the directivity of an antenna required mathematical integration of radiation patterns over all space for two orthogonal (perpendicular to each other) polarizations. To aid in accomplishing this, we rotated the transmitting antennas to change polarization.

When we first began measurements, integration was accomplished by determining the area of each of nineteen patterns per polarization (a total of thirty-eight) manually using a polar planimeter,[28] a mechanical device for measurement of areas of graphs. Each area was multiplied by the cosine of its elevation angle with respect to the model's horizontal plane and then the products for each polarization were added.

I wrote a memorandum entitled "Radiation Pattern Integration," dated April 17, 1952, describing the theoretical basis for the procedure and its application.[§]

---

§   Memo can be found at www.edtheradarman.com.

That procedure was time-consuming, error-prone, and tedious, so I decided to devise an easier and better way.

There was a veritable gold mine of surplus World War II electronic equipment available, so I was able to obtain a variable ratio transformer, an audio amplifier, and an indicator for an Earth Inductor Compass (EIC).

The model support tower utilized Selsyn transmitters that sent the model azimuth angle and tower elevation angle to Selsyn indicators in the recorder console. A Selsyn system[29] [30] is an electro-mechanical arrangement that allows a mechanical rotation to be transported from one place to another by magnetic effects of electric currents in a network of wires. The angles were displayed by analog dials similar to clock faces.

The variable ratio transformer resembled a small electric motor. When it was linked mechanically to the tower rotation Selsyn receiver in the recorder console, its output was made proportional to the sine or cosine of the angle through which the Selsyn generator in the model support tower rotated. That yielded the equivalent of elevation angle in real space.

The audio frequency signals from the model antennas, which were the amplitudes of signals received by the antennas at specific model and tower angles, were introduced into one winding of the variable ratio transformer that, in turn, sent voltages to an audio amplifier. The cosine-multiplied output voltages of the amplifier were sent to the Earth Inductor Compass (EIC) indicator.

The EIC was, in effect, an adding machine, adding its pointer rotation by amounts corresponding to the amplitude of the voltages that were proportional to the energy a model antenna received during each model rotation impressed upon its motor.¶

This system was a great improvement over our original procedure, but subsequently it was replaced by even better all-electronic equipment designed by Robert E. Rawlins, Jr., our boss.

¶   Appendix C describes how we would use the EIC set-up to derive antenna directivity.

Modern Antenna Laboratory

We moved into a new antenna development facility in Plant B during the winter of 1951–52, away from the airport and surrounded by unused space. Bill Martin and I shared an office in a nearby electronics laboratory. Bill headed the expanded Lockheed antenna laboratory.

Thomas "Tom" Hancock was the supervisor of a new antenna radiation pattern range facility that had been built in an open area outside our laboratory building. Later he became an engineering manager in Advanced Development Projects.

We did impedance match testing of antennas using mockups on the roof of the laboratory building or protruding out of second-story windows well above the ground. We would have a window removed, replace it with an antenna mounted on a metal-covered piece of plywood customized to fit the window frame—and keep most of the rain out!

During an unusually hot weather period, the air conditioning system used to cool the pattern range electronic equipment failed to cope with the heat load. I remembered my post-high school experience as a refrigeration service man, so I suggested that the condenser unit should be sprayed with water to increase its cooling ability. A quick test with a garden hose demonstrated that the scheme would work and a more sophisticated sprayer was installed.

Engineers were expected to wear business attire and ties. We were not allowed to do any shop work unless we were demonstrating a process or procedure. Sometimes there could be danger caused by conventional ties, so usually we wore clip-on bow ties.

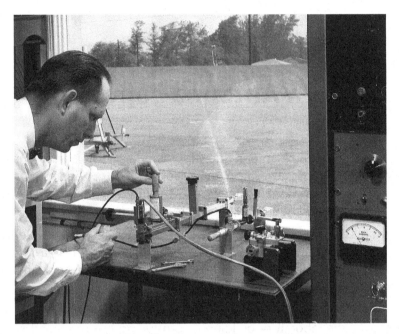

Ed in the Antenna Laboratory

Creative people tend to like harmless practical jokes, and the antenna group was no exception.

I used to have a fancy-looking drinking glass with engravings all around it, but in one place the engraving went all of the way through. It was called a "dribble glass." Irving "Bud" Alney, an antenna engineer at Lockheed who eventually became the manager of the group that developed the re-entry tiles for the Space Shuttle, was at our house for a party. I gave him the glass with water in it.

He started drinking out of it, and soon he was looking at his shirt, and then looking around to see if anyone had seen him. There were several engineers and their wives there whom we had told that this would happen.

Bud was embarrassed that he was getting his shirt wet and did not know why.

I do not know what happened to that glass. He may have taken it or thrown it away.

Bud had an accident with a bottle of catsup at someone else's house. He was slinging it around and the cap came off and he put a stripe of catsup around the kitchen. Oh dear, what an embarrassment!

A lady who served as a secretary for the entire electronics laboratory group had a desk near the door to our office.

One day, before lunch, I told her that if she continued to type so fast, she would burn out her typewriter. She smiled and continued to type.

During the lunch break while she was away I obtained some clear flexible plastic tubing and inserted it into the back of her machine. Then I arranged the tubing so that I thought that she could not see it going into our office.

After she returned from lunch she resumed her typing. I had obtained a cigarette that I lighted and then blew smoke into the tubing with the desired result! She nearly panicked but quickly realized what I had done—and who had done it. I had told Bill Martin about the trick beforehand and he thoroughly enjoyed it.

On another occasion Bill and I collaborated to cause a humorous incident.

There was an engineer who was testing a section of flexible waveguide to estimate its probable time before failure. He was sitting at a desk, busily engaged in working on something else, with his back to a partial wall while his test device that was mounted on a bench near another wall to his right was periodically bending and straightening the waveguide. The test generated noticeable sound for almost a week and was somewhat annoying.

One day after all the other people had left for the evening, Bill and I decided to do something about the noise.

I obtained some metal scraps from our model shop and put them into a metal wastebasket. Then I hid a small loudspeaker behind the tester and led some thin wires from it over the partial wall to a tape recorder.

Bill found a large thick sheet of aluminum, drilled a hole in one corner, and suspended it with a piece of rope above a workbench.

I stood in our office doorway so I could see the waveguide's motion and began shaking the wastebasket in circles in synchronism with the waveguide tester's action. Then I walked slowly toward the tape recorder's microphone and stopped for a second or two and poured the scraps into another metal trashcan. After a short pause Bill struck the aluminum sheet with a padded mallet and it rang like a Chinese gong.

The next day we alerted the people, except the victim, that they should watch him just after the customary ten o'clock coffee break.

Shortly after the appointed time, the noise from the tester became increasingly louder. At first he seemed to not notice it, but soon he looked at it and then tried to concentrate on his other work. As the noise grew louder he could not ignore it, so he tried to jump out of his chair, but hit his legs on the center drawer of the desk. He fell back into the chair that moved backward and hit the wall. Finally he was able to get out of the chair and rush over to his tester.

Just as he arrived there was a moment of silence and then the gong sounded—loud and clear!

Gentleman that he was, Knute Hoff graciously accepted the results and, in fact, enjoyed the joke. Mysteriously, the tape was erased.

Sometimes serendipity happens. Bill Martin was struggling to accomplish impedance matching of a high frequency beacon antenna. Without thinking, I said, "Let me show you how to do it." I picked up a nail from a workbench and went outside to the antenna and stuck the nail in it. We were startled when he measured an excellent impedance match!

Inadvertently, I had completed a connection that the machinist had not. With minor changes the job was finished. Bill gave me the small mockup antenna that I used as a desk ornament for several years.

We had a "screen room" in the electronics laboratory that was a building consisting of basic wall structures sufficient to hold up bronze window screening on all sides, the ceiling, and under a plywood floor enclosing a space.

Screen rooms were used to test electronic equipment, mostly radio receivers, in an interference-free environment and so their alternating current power supplies were filtered carefully as well. The screen room was dark inside unless a light was turned on. There was an office desk inside that engineers could use for their work. The room was not occupied most of the time.

My wife, Lucille, had inherited a 1920s-era fox stole (a fox fur scarf-like ornament) from her grandmother, but she had no desire to keep it. I brought it to work and hung it on a wall in the screen room so that, to see it, one had to enter the room.

I installed a small neon lamp in the fox's navel and connected it to some special electronic circuitry that caused the lamp to turn on and off periodically. The blinking belly button attracted a lot of attention!

After a while I took the stole back home and scared our dog with it. Shortly afterward he disposed of it.

There was some science involved in the blinker. It was part of a "relaxation oscillator."

The circuit utilized a capacitor connected in parallel with a neon-filled lamp. The lamp would not light (conduct) unless the potential difference (voltage) between its terminals was greater than about fifty volts so that, in effect, it was not in the circuit.

The capacitor was charged through a current limiting resistor until the voltage across it reached the "striking" voltage of the lamp, causing it to conduct and quickly drain the charge from the capacitor. That reduced the voltage across the lamp below its extinction voltage and it ceased to glow. The combination of the resistor and the capacitor determined how often the cycle would occur.

Now, almost sixty years later, modern solid state components, a 555 semi-conductor timer chip, a light emitting diode (LED), and a small battery can do the same performance with much smaller circuit components.

There was a cafeteria with a covered but open eating area near our office. I usually ate lunch there, but during a rainy day I took my lunch back to our office.

After eating, I had nothing urgent to do during the lunch time, so I decided to draw a cartoon of an "Aerial Engineer." "Aerial" was the British equivalent of the American word "antenna." I cleaned my white lunch plate, and using a black crayon, drew my "portrait" upon it. I then sprayed clear acrylic on it and took it home where I photographed it and then had a badge made. I still have the plate and the badge.

"Aerial Engineer" (Self Portrait circa 1952)

I heard a story about Hall Hibbard, Lockheed's Chief Engineer, who was crossing the country as a passenger in a Lockheed Constellation aircraft. He was sitting in the first class section. At less than half the speed of modern airliners, those trips took much longer than they do today. He decided to have some fun teasing a stewardess.

He threw a rivet up so that it hit the ceiling and then fell into the aisle. The stewardess heard an odd sound and went up the aisle to investigate. She saw the rivet, looked a little puzzled, then picked it up and went back to whatever she was doing.

Hall waited a few minutes and did it again. He repeated it several more times and the stewardess became quite worried. She took the rivets forward and showed them to the Captain.

It took him only a moment to realize that these were unused rivets. He went back into the cabin and quickly found the perpetrator, whom he recognized as Hall Hibbard!

In 1952, I was given an assignment to design and develop a Very High Frequency (VHF) communications antenna for the C-130 airplane, later named the Hercules.

Using a half-size mockup of the vertical tail fin, I utilized a horizontal slot from the leading edge aft almost to the rudder hinge as means to excite vertical currents on the surface of the metal fin. Although the later scaled model testing showed that the design was adequate, they never used it.

I believe that the engineers were reluctant to use fiberglass instead of metal in the tail. They still build C-130 aircraft, almost sixty years later, but without my design.

Scale Model Antenna Testing

I "designed" the first indoor anechoic chamber for Lockheed Burbank in 1953.

I converted a screen room that was a building consisting of basic wall structure sufficient to hold up bronze window screening on all sides, the ceiling, and under a plywood floor.

To control room reflections that were interfering with antenna tests, I had butcher paper sprayed with "Aquadag," a commercial product, a colloidal suspension of graphite in water. Then I had the paper suspended, using strings, about one foot away from the metal screen walls that served as reflecting planes in a crude form of a Salisbury Screen.[31]

In addition to antenna radiation pattern measurements, we also would measure impedance, which did not require rotating the model. We would use the largest model that was practical for impedance testing.

We had a fifty-foot tall wooden tower built to allow us to measure impedances of scaled model antennas installed in a one-tenth scale model of a Constellation aircraft. The model was about ten feet long.

We installed a plank as if it were a diving board part way up the tower. Bud Alney, my leaky water glass victim, and I used to crawl out on the plank to set out smaller scale models.

Sometimes I would modify test equipment to accommodate special circumstances. Bill Martin often was startled, but he always recovered.

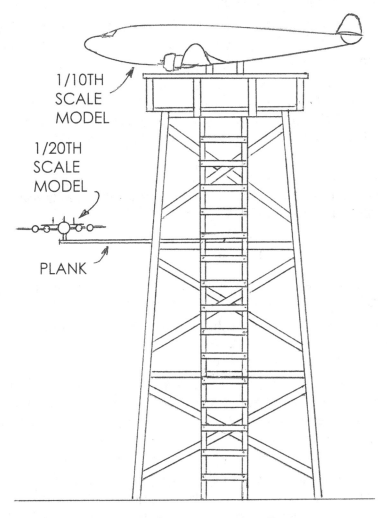

1/10TH SCALE MODEL

1/20TH SCALE MODEL

PLANK

Antenna Impedance Measurement Tower

Antenna technology involves several major attributes that need to be accomplished and verified by measurement. Efficiency, directivity, and power handling are some.

Others may be ease of manufacture, cost, maintainability, service life, time between failures, and obsolescence. We were mostly involved with the first three.

Efficiency, in a systems sense, means, "How well does an antenna transfer energy between a piece of equipment and free space, or vice versa?"

Energy can be lost through conversion to heat by resistance to current flow in or on conductive materials, and by internal friction in insulating materials.

Energy can be prevented from reaching a destination by being reflected by impedance mismatch.

Our antenna work was devoted almost exclusively to designing and developing antennas that were contained within the aircraft contours. I quickly developed the ability to visualize current flow on and near antennas on an aircraft's skin. That helped greatly in antenna design and, later, in understanding the state-of-the-art aspect of reducing radar reflectivity.

High frequency currents, such as antenna currents, do not involve electrons or any other charged particles moving at or near the speed of light, but only the tendency to move. Forces are due to moving electromagnetic fields. I sometimes have described this action as "the urge to surge."[32] The most appropriate analogy that I have to offer is that action indicated by collisions in a collection of elastic spheres[33] in that desktop exhibition device known as "Newton's Cradle."[34]

P-2V Antennas Field Testing

Sometimes we were involved in rather elaborate field tests. In 1953, we evaluated eight antennas that were installed on a large aircraft, a P-2V. L. D. MacDonald was the project engineer.

The plan was to fly eastward from our ground station transmitter at Edwards Air Force Base while the output of each of the eight receivers was recorded aboard the aircraft, and then to collect recordings again as the aircraft returned to our location. Several of these flights were performed so that several sets of data for different frequencies could be acquired.

In order to obtain accurate data, it was necessary to match each receiver's input impedance to the coaxial cables connecting them to their respective antennas.

I designed an impedance matching element and had our shop fabricate twenty-four of them, three for each receiver, packaged in eight separate containers. Each element of the impedance matching network was unusual. Turning a knob attached to a metal rotor inside a plastic tube that had metal patches, connected by wires on its outer surface, caused very large changes in reactance and allowed easy impedance matching.

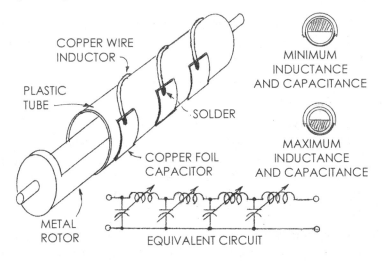

Impedance Matching Network Element

Calibration of each receiver in a laboratory consisted of adjusting each matching unit to cause maximum output as read on a meter in the receiver. This procedure was performed for several frequencies for each receiver and the settings of all the knobs were recorded for use during the flight tests.

A useful by-product of this calibration process was a procedure for measurement of the input impedance of active receivers.

All that was necessary was to replace a signal generator with a proper terminator on the input connector and then measure the impedance "looking backward" into the output connector. The result was the complex conjugate of the receiver's input impedance. This is an example of how scientific methods can simplify data collection.

The in-air tests were uneventful except for the heat and a sandstorm.

After the first day, I had the ground transmitter immersed in a barrel of oil to keep it from overheating.

We had begun the testing early in daylight one day while a sandstorm was well away from us. Part way through a flight we experienced trouble with our radar. During all of the test flights, we used a World War II SCR-584 military radar[35][36] to track the aircraft. It was an "S-Band" (3 GHz)* radar housed in a trailer.

The display was obscured by noise that, at first, we thought was caused by defective equipment.

When Gordon Riggs, our radar operator, opened the trailer door to go outside to inspect the antenna, I noticed that the wind was extremely strong. Then I realized that the receiver noise was caused by discharging of tribo-electrically charged sand particles when they hit our antenna. The sandstorm had come to us. Nevertheless, we were able to test every day but one.

While I was in the antenna laboratory I became a member of the Association of Old Crows, a group of engineers who were involved in design, development, and testing of active radar countermeasures. The Old Crows were started by Mel Jackson, who had been a U.S. Army Air Corps officer during World War II.

I also became involved in a training program for managers. Mr. Ernest R. Siefkin, an engineering middle manager, was my sponsor. After I had completed several seminar-type courses, I decided that engineering was more suitable for me, so I returned to the antenna laboratory.

Later in my career, I was glad that I was not a manager, and according to a *Daily News* article on December 17, 2006, titled "Climbing Up the Ladder, Do You Really Want to Go There?" I was not alone. Most of them did not seem to enjoy their work as much as I did mine. I saw men become managers and then disappear.

Dr. Tetsu Morita

During the summer of 1953, Dr. Tetsu Morita, who supervised Harvard University's antenna laboratory, became a visiting engineer in the Lockheed Burbank Antenna Laboratory. He was very well known and highly regarded in the antenna engineering community. It was an honor to have him as our guest.

---

* The meaning of "S Band" and other World War II military designations of frequency bands can be found in Appendix D.

He was escorted into our electronics laboratory by E. O. Richter, R. E. Rawlins, and W. R. Martin, all of whom were startled when he recognized me and I greeted him with "Hi, Tet!"

Tetsu, my brother, and I, had been undergraduate classmates at the University of Nebraska before World War II and knew each other quite well. My superiors were mollified.

He shared an office with Bill Martin and me, and we had many rewarding discussions.

One day he put down his slide rule, a ten-inch K&E "log-log Decitrig" model typical of the time, and said, "You guys can get results faster than I can calculate them. I'm going out in the lab and cut metal like you do!" And he did!

When he left at the end of the summer, we convened a luncheon and presented him "The Hacker Award of 1953"—a suitably mounted gold plated General Radio coaxial connector. He seemed very pleased. The last I knew about him was that he was working at the Stanford Research Institute in Stanford, California.

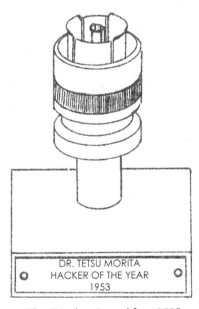

The "Hacker Award for 1953"

The Bornholm Incident

Sometime probably during the mid-1950s, Elvin O. Richter told me about a very strange incident that was reported to have occurred over the Baltic Sea along the German coast.

A radar station on the island of Bornholm[37] midway between the German coast and Sweden routinely was observing actions of Soviet Union aircraft flying along the German coast when radar echoes and all radio communication into and out of Western Europe rather suddenly were lost. The effect seemed to be caused by a light fog along the coast that was created by one or more Soviet aircraft.

He said that, although electromagnetic wave propagation seemed to be prevented by the fog, our American reconnaissance aircraft could detect radiation from sources inland from the fog. In effect, "They could see over the curtain."

Other "facts" that he reported were: the effect disappeared after sundown; small reddish brown spots were found on the handrails of an external stairway to the top of the radar tower; and the spots were thought to be red phosphorus. He also said that a faint "garlicky" odor in the air was reported. My interpretation of these reports was that possibly a slurry of white phosphorous[38] in water was sprayed into the air. White phosphorous[39] is highly reactive in air[40] but may have been inhibited by the water and the moisture in the air so that its reaction rate was greatly reduced, but was stimulated somewhat by ultraviolet radiation during daylight that essentially stopped at sundown.

This may have been an early manifestation of what much later was called the "Marburg effect." That seems to be a hint that Marburg College in Germany was involved in the development of the fog.

Conversion of white phosphorus to red by oxidation is a violent reaction, during which electrons may be free temporarily and therefore be influenced by the electric fields of passing waves. In other words, the fog may have been an attenuator of electromagnetic radiation. This subject was discussed in a *Los Angeles Times* article by Tel Sell on October 24, 1969, titled "Russ May Have Found New Way to Foil Radar."

Another possibility that I do not remember being mentioned was that hydrogen peroxide may have been sprayed into the air.[41] Its conversion to water vapor perhaps could have caused the reported effect and would not have left detectable evidence.

I am not aware of any attempt to investigate these reports. They may have been considered to be deliberate "disinformation"—it was the Cold War era. They were interesting, nevertheless.[†]

---

† In an August 10, 2003, *Aviation Week & Space Technology* article by Douglas Barrie titled "Russian Low-Observable Technology Research Detailed," several novel technologies are mentioned, including a plasma-field generating system named Marabu, for the Meteorit missile. There may be a follow-up article in the *Aviation Week* April 18, 2005, issue regarding the Meteorit.

AWACS and Kelly Johnson

During late 1956, I was in Washington, DC attending a meeting about a Request for Proposal (RFP) for an Airborne Warning and Control System (AWACS). My interest concerned potential antenna designs for such a system.

Mr. Henry Rempt, a Lockheed engineering manager, suggested a large antenna in a rotating streamlined radome mounted atop a Lockheed 1049 Super Constellation (or its Navy equivalent, the WV-2E) aircraft. The idea was very well received, and Lockheed subsequently was given a contract to develop it.

As a result of that meeting I was assigned the delightful task of developing an antenna to accommodate the search radar. The radar was to operate at the frequency of 425 MHz and radiate five-megawatt pulses of horizontally polarized waves.

I decided to utilize eight antenna elements in an array connected by large waveguides arranged in a "corporate feed" structure. Each element consisted essentially of continuations of the wide surfaces of the waveguides oriented vertically to support and guide horizontally polarized waves. The radiators were to be utilized to define the shape and support the plastic radome, thereby decreasing the weight and simplifying the design and fabrication of the whole assembly.[42]

There are four commonly used modalities, other than antenna-to-antenna in space, for transporting energy by electromagnetic waves from one place to another. Any or all of these configurations may be termed "transmission lines":

- A parallel wire construction;
- The common coaxial configuration;
- Hollow metal tubes that may be round, square, rectangular, or ridged in cross section; and
- "Printed circuit" waveguides.

In a corporate feed structure, all pathways are of equal length, resulting in equal delays or equal phase lags. This arrangement essentially is insensitive to frequency changes. I utilized a corporate feed structure for my antenna design.

If a hollow tubular waveguide is too small compared to a wavelength, it will not allow wave propagation. It is said to be "cut off." A familiar example of such action is the loss of AM radio signals in tunnels or even under roadway overpasses. Wavelengths of commercial broadcast AM radio waves range from approximately 600 feet to 1800 feet.

Later in my career, I used the phenomenon of cut-off in the design of the A-12 and the F-117 aircraft.

Rectangular waveguides usually are operated so that the electric fields exist between the wider surfaces of the tubing. I decided to arrange the waveguides so that the electric fields would be horizontal for the search radar.

I had a 1/20th scale model of the search antenna built for impedance matching and radiation pattern measurements.

1/20th Scale Model of AWACS Antenna

While the model was being fabricated, I had the pleasure of testing an S-Band co-ax to waveguide transition using a high-powered radar.

The coaxial portion of the transition was needed to allow mechanical rotation of the Airborne Warning and Control System (AWACS) antenna and its radome.

I arranged to have a horn antenna attached to a short piece of waveguide point straight up from the roof of our building so that the likelihood of interference with other tests or services was minimized. The tests were few, short, and successful. We were confident that the design could be scaled up in size to be used for the search radar antenna.

One pleasant afternoon in August of 1957 an event occurred that—although I did not realize it at the time—would change my career at Lockheed in ways I did not dream.

I was out on the Lockheed antenna range happily testing my latest creation, the 1/20th scale antenna for the AWACS rotodome airplane, when three gentlemen approached me. Two were well known to me as friends, but I did not recognize the third.

My boss, Bill Martin, introduced me to my former boss, "Mac" MacDonald, and C. L. "Kelly" Johnson. Mac, who was to become my next supervisor, was the person who recommended me to Kelly Johnson.

I had no idea who Kelly was, but I sensed that he was important.

After a short time conversing, during which Kelly asked me several technical questions, he asked me if I would like to join a small group to work on an interesting project. Kelly, head of the Advanced Development Projects, known informally as the Skunk Works, said the job might last six weeks or so. Thirty-two years later, I retired from that organization.

Although I had no inkling about what I was agreeing to, I decided immediately that it seemed like an interesting challenge and, because Mac and Bill were there, it must be important. It was.

Kelly was a technical genius, a great recruiter, excellent organizer, and a very able businessman of impeccable reputation in high places. He also was a man of action—as I soon found out.

It took a short time for the CIA to grant my security clearance. Meanwhile I finished the Rotodome antenna tests.

The impedance matching, radiation patterns, and the gain measurements using the 1/20th scale model antenna were very successful so we decided to send the model to the Naval Research Laboratory (NRL) in Washington, DC for verification of our data.

I proposed that we have the all-brass model gold plated to inhibit tarnishing and the idea was accepted. Somehow the plating thickness specified in the order was TEN times what I had intended. When my boss's boss, Elvin O. Richter, informed me of the error, I thought my Lockheed career was ended. It was not, and the antenna was beautiful!

I took the antenna to NRL and left it for them to test. After a short time, we were informed that their measurements agreed with ours. I proposed that the same waveguide assembly also could be used for the Identification-Friend or Foe (IFF) transponder by introducing waves polarized vertically (the electric fields between the narrow sides of the guides), thereby simplifying the total design.

The satisfaction was short-lived. The Navy chose an array of "half-wave dipole" antennas backed by a parabolic reflector for the search antenna. I believe that our antenna development contract was awarded to comply with directives against sole source procurement. The winning rotodome antenna was tested on a Boeing aircraft. Lockheed never built production rotodome aircraft.

Into the Skunk Works—the U-2

I started in the fall of 1957 to help modify the U-2 aircraft to make it less detectible by the Soviet Union forces. Our first task was to reduce the detection ability of the Soviet Union's S-Band radars, at that time considered to be the most likely to track the aircraft and guide missiles.

Before I became involved with the U-2 aircraft, I had no idea that there was a U-2. Also, I was not aware of efforts to make so-called stealthy aircraft before I was invited to join the Skunk Works. However, I had known that a friend from Navy days, Edward Martin, had gone somewhere but no one would (or could) tell me where he went.

After I joined the Skunk Works I discovered that Ed was the project engineer for the U-2. He was based at the Bakersfield airport in Oildale, California, at that time. He had a mournful-looking stuffed buzzard on a file cabinet in his office.

We had a rather large assembly area there where several U-2s were built. After the aircraft were built they were partially disassembled and sent by truck to a special place in Nevada called Area 51. There the aircraft were reassembled and test flown. Kelly nicknamed it "Paradise Ranch". He had a real working ranch in California.

The morning of my first day in the Skunk Works, I met two people who were destined to become major participants in our efforts.

Melvin Frederick George, Jr., an excellent chemist, and Perry Merlin Reedy, who also was an excellent chemist, certainly was well named.

Kelly chose Mel to lead a small group who would develop or test many of the materials the Skunk Works needed to do its jobs.

Mel enjoyed power boating with his wife, Georgia. Georgia once said to me that she had to marry Mel in order to keep her monogrammed towels!

Merlin, an excellent technician as well as a great source of chemical lore, was a perfect compliment to Mel. Merlin seemed to be possessed of total recall of all things chemical. He was a longtime president of the Burbank Orchid Society. He and his wife also fluently spoke Castilian Spanish.

Mel became liaison to materials suppliers and consultant to our "Customers," the Central Intelligence Agency (CIA) and the U.S. Air Force (USAF).

Mac called a meeting with Mel, Merlin, and me to define a program to help the CIA modify U-2 aircraft, and to select and obtain facilities and personnel to accomplish our task.

Kelly Johnson developed the U-2 aircraft under the aegis of the CIA's Dr. Richard M. Bissell Jr., heir to the Bissell carpet sweepers fortune. Mel slyly referred to him as "Mr. B."

Kelly informed us that we should modify a U-2 aircraft to reduce as much as we could the ability of S-band radars to detect it.

When the U-2 had been designed, it had been done so without any anti-radar treatment. There were no electronic countermeasures. It did have a missile warning system known as "Oscar Sierra" (pilots can translate that). The aircraft relied solely upon height for its stealthy aspects. It flew at about 70,000 feet. At the time that altitude put the aircraft just out of harm's way. Soviet surface-to-air-missiles (SAMs) could not travel that high. Furthermore, at that altitude the Soviet missiles could not have responded adequately in the rarified air to their own radar guidance systems. The U-2s were just barely safe.

In those early years of the Cold War and the space race, the Soviets were working feverishly on military technology, as were we and the British. The CIA knew that it was only a matter of time, perhaps two years, before Soviet missiles would be able to shoot down our reconnaissance aircraft. Four years later, Gary Powers, flying a U-2, would be shot down over Soviet territory.

Our meeting began with a briefing on the previous attempts to reduce the U-2 S-Band radar cross section. At this initial meeting, the discussions were solely about difficulties with a previous high-frequency coating design. Through time, I learned that in 1956[*] there had been some unsuccessful attempts to reduce the low frequency early warning radar reflectivity of the U-2 aircraft, hopefully to prevent the Soviet early warning radars from detecting it.

---

[*]   See Appendix E for various historians' accounts of these early tests.

There was a small group of engineers and physicists who were working in the Boston area for the CIA. Some of them worked for a company named the "Scientific Engineering Institute" (SEI) in an attempt to hide their real activities. Most of them came from Harvard University or the Air Force's Lincoln Laboratory that was run by the Massachusetts Institute of Technology (MIT).

The group of consultants proposed covering reflecting surfaces of the aircraft with a high frequency electromagnetic wave absorber, wherever it was feasible, with the hope of defeating the S-Band tracking radars. These included the fuselage and vertical tail surfaces. No attempt to cover critical aerodynamic surfaces was allowed. Kelly Johnson would not allow the coating to be more than one quarter of an inch thick for aerodynamic reasons, and its installed weight had to be as small as possible.

Some of the early attempts by the CIA people at designing an absorbing layer incorporated squares of highly conductive paint on Teledeltos (TD) resistive paper, an obsolete printing medium. It essentially was a conducting layer contained between two layers of porous paper. When it was used as a printing medium an electric current flowing through the paper burned (scorched) characters upon a light gray layer.

This may be known today as "R-C circuit analog" construction because it includes resistive elements (the TD paper substrate) and capacitive elements (the squares). The squares were expected to serve as capacitors that would tune the assemblies for best absorption. The concept was to build a reduced thickness Salisbury Screen.[†]

Two aircraft were treated using this scheme. The initial coverings using the CIA designs were performed under the direction of Mel George using materials supplied by SEI. The original installation covered essentially the entire fuselage and vertical tail.

It may seem strange to treat the fuselage and vertical tail and ignore the wings and horizontal tail assembly. But in fact the wings were not a serious concern because, when the aircraft was viewed from the side by a radar, they acted like mirrors that would reflect most of the energy away from the radar, whereas the fuselage had large amounts of area that would be reflecting energy back toward the radar.

The first CIA S-Band treatment consisted of a build-up of layers of fiberglass cloth, phenolic honeycomb, and TD paper with painted squares. A layer of fiberglass cloth was cemented to the aircraft skin.

---

† See Appendix F for information about Salisbury Screen design.

Phenolic honeycomb was bonded to the inner layer using an epoxy resin. Another thin layer of fiberglass was glued to the outer surface of the honeycomb. One aircraft then was coated by unmodified TD paper and the other was coated with TD paper imprinted with isolated squares of silver paint. An outer fiberglass layer was applied. Then it was painted light gray.

Development of experimental aircraft always has been difficult and dangerous. Accidents causing injuries and death were not uncommon. One such tragedy happened just a few months before I joined the Skunk Works.

Flight testing of a mostly-covered U-2 against S-Band radars was underway in the vicinity of Edwards North Base.

At an altitude of about 70,000 feet, or more than thirteen miles up, the U-2 overheated and suffered a hydraulic system failure. The aircraft became uncontrollable.

Test pilot Robert Sieker's helmet faceplate opened when his partial pressure suit inflated. He was battered about in the cockpit, and he lost consciousness before he could close it. At that height the air is too thin to breathe. At 50,000 feet the estimated effort to breathe is about fifty times that at sea level and more than three hundred times more difficult at 70,000 feet. Without artificial life support, a person will become unconscious in a few seconds and die soon thereafter from cerebral hypoxic anoxia and internal organ damage caused by release of gasses dissolved in body fluids.

The aircraft probably went into a flat spin. I heard speculation that after the aircraft had descended several thousands of feet, Sieker apparently regained partial consciousness and was able to escape from the cockpit. But he was hit by the spinning aircraft and killed. (He may have been thrown out.)

The plane crashed as a result of the radar-absorbing coating covering the entire fuselage. The aft fuselage structure, where the engine and exhaust pipe were located, had overheated.

As a result of Robert Sieker's fatal crash, Kelly volunteered to redesign the treatment using Lockheed personnel. That may be why I had been called in.

During World War II while I had served as an instructor in the Navy school for radio and radar technicians on Navy Pier in Chicago, I became quite familiar with the theory of Salisbury Screens.

I was asked to design a gentle S-Band electrical transition from the upper portion of the SEI absorbing coat to the metal skin of the fuselage while, simultaneously, exposing as much metal surface as possible to the cooling effects of the ambient air.

The SEI installation became informally code named "Thermos" because of thermal properties resembling those of an inside-out Thermos bottle. In addition to overheating the aircraft systems, heat was a structural hazard because aluminum weakens as its temperature increases.

My design approach was mechanical tapering and serration of the edges for reduction of radar wave reflections from the transition region. Kelly Johnson had decided that U-2 aerodynamic considerations restricted the coating thickness to one quarter of an inch so our transition materials would have to meet that requirement as well. Because weight was such a critical parameter it was necessary to use a low dielectric constant, low-density phenolic honeycomb material and compensate for the reduced spacing by incorporating special properties within the absorbing layer.

Early versions, circa World War II, of the Salisbury Screen were said to have utilized paint containing carbon (probably graphite) on a dielectric layer spaced one quarter of a wavelength from a metal surface. At 3 GHz, this would require a one-inch thick coating. I knew from my experiences in antenna theory that adding a capacitive nature to certain materials could increase their apparent electrical thickness so that it might be possible to reduce the material's physical thickness, or to improve on the performance of the SEI material within the same thickness.

Our design efforts in the fall of 1957 became concentrated in Building 82, an old hanger-like structure that the U-2 program had been utilizing. A combined chemistry and materials development laboratory was established. Our first "office," for Mac, Mel, Merlin, and me, literally was a janitor's closet! We used to say that we had to go outside to turn around!

We needed electromagnetic test facilities to verify our design concepts.

There was a large hanger at Edwards North Base that was used for testing and maintenance of U-2 aircraft. Several test flights were flown from there. It was isolated from the rest of Edwards AFB for security.

Our first measurements of absorber samples in waveguides and reflectivity of much larger samples were made in the hangar at Edwards. I designed a special sample holder to terminate an S-Band waveguide slotted line. The sample holder, a signal generator, a slotted waveguide standing-wave detector, and a VSWR indicator were required to conduct the measurements.

To save time, Mac and I borrowed the necessary test equipment from Bill Martin's antenna laboratory and began some measurements of candidate specimens made by Mel and Merlin. Bill and Ed Martin were not related nor did they know each other but, because of those two gentlemen, we were able to do these and many other measurements.

Incidentally, the fact that several people, Bill Martin, Charles F. Widell, and Frederick R. Zboril, knew what we had borrowed and possibly could surmise its use, caused some of us serious concern for the security of our efforts. However, apparently there was no violation of our unavoidable trust.

The Big Rumbling Cart

The quickest way to find the best coating transition design was to test full-scale specimens. During the late fall of 1957 and the early part of 1958, we did testing at Edwards North base using a rather strange looking contraption that we called "The Big Rumbling Cart"—because that was what it was!

The Big Rumbling Cart was designed to carry a number of instruments that we used to send and receive energy that was reflected off of the material that was on aircraft or the rotatable drums that we used to test candidate materials.

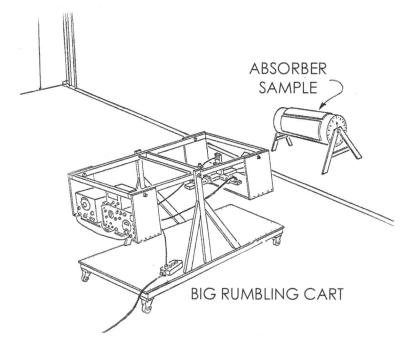

ABSORBER
SAMPLE

BIG RUMBLING CART

Big Rumbling Cart and Cylindrical Fixture

The Cart was constructed so that it could be moved easily, either on its own wheels on hangar or factory floors, or disassembled for shipment between sites. Frequently it was used to check the coatings on aircraft at Edwards North Base and occasionally in the factory at Unit 38 on the Bakersfield airport.

The equipment Cart had a balance-beam arrangement that supported two pivoted saddles, one at each end. One saddle supported a signal generator and a VSWR indicator, a form of voltmeter. The other saddle held the microwave bridge[‡] and horn antenna. Since S-Band waveguide components and horn antennas made of brass are quite heavy, there was little difficulty in arranging a balance. It allowed us to raise, lower, and tilt the horn antenna to point at the part of the aircraft of interest or at a coated barrel.

All these measurements were performed at close range, within the Fresnel region of the horn antenna, where the wave front was considerably curved. Even under these conditions, very useful coating design comparisons were made with the Big Rumbling Cart.

‡   Appendix G describes microwave bridges in more detail.

One 1957 test arrangement, in particular, deserves description. Several circular cylinders three feet in diameter and four feet long made of sheet aluminum with wooden ends were covered partially or completely with the same type of absorber that was (or was to be) used on aircraft. These cylinders were mounted, one at a time, on a portable support so they could be rotated about a horizontal axis. Lines corresponding to ten-degree increments of rotation were marked on the ends.

In the evenings after everyone else had gone, Mac, Mel, Merlin, and I would open the north door of the hangar partway and set the Cart just inside. Then, using the open door and the region outside in lieu of free space, the microwave bridge was nulled while the antenna was looking at the north sky. Next, a cylinder on its support was positioned so that the horn antenna was about three feet away from the cylindrical surface. After that the cylinder was rotated by ten-degree increments and the unbalance indication was recorded and plotted, point by point, on graph paper.

All the reflections from the absorbing treatment were compared to the reflection from a bare aluminum cylinder that provided the zero decibels of attenuation reference.

Mac, who was in charge of the whole crew, occasionally served as a person who would rotate the drums in ten-degree increments using the crude scales of angle marked on one end of each drum.

As a joke we put up a sign that read "Danger—Radioactivity." It was radioactivity in the sense that we used radio frequencies to illuminate the drum. I do not believe anyone took the sign seriously. At least we never had repercussions from it.

The drum tests provided the aircraft coating and transition design information that we needed. Our tapered edge design tests were successful. We were able to coat most of the fuselage but leave about the top quarter uncovered for cooling purposes. Since there was no thermal consequence to covering the vertical fin, our new design kept the vertical fin fully covered, which eliminated the need for any termination there.

We began to prepare for flight testing working in the hangar on Edwards North Base. Mel and his people covered the fuselage and vertical tail of two U-2 aircraft using the new Lockheed coverage design and transition materials.

The TD paper, supplied to us in secrecy by the Boston group, came in two conductivities, one approximately twice the other.

Mel and his group once again experienced difficulty installing some of the SEI material. The TD paper with the printed silver squares was very difficult to match to the contouring of the aircraft skin, especially doubly-curved surfaces.

One evening Mel and his group were putting large slabs of absorber on the vertical fin of a U-2. They started working late in the afternoon and then they went for a lunch break at about eight o'clock.

When they returned, they discovered that the stuff was peeling off the vertical fin—just falling off! What an uproar that caused! It turned out that someone had forgotten to put the hardener in the epoxy resin.

Mel decided that was not going to happen again, so he ordered that the hardener be tinted purple. It looked like grape juice. When it was mixed with the epoxy, the whole thing would be colored, and they would know that it was not going to fall off.

We occupied a motel in Boron, a little town just north of Edwards. We would go to a certain restaurant for breakfast, and then we would eat lunch out at the base. We would go back in the evening for dinner, usually at that same place.

One of the men in Mel's crew got one of the little breakfast jelly containers and put some purple epoxy into it. The next morning he took it into the restaurant and then, during breakfast, complained to a waitress that there was something wrong with his jelly. It was too hard.

The waitress took it and tested it and, sure enough, it was hard. The story I heard was that she took it back into the kitchen, pounded on it, and decided that it really was pretty hard. They tried boiling it, and that didn't work.

That is typical of a creative group. You have some "horseplay" of that nature, harmless but puzzling. I do not know when they told her, but finally she found out what it was.

As the flight tests progressed, we had observed inconsistencies between the expected and actual electrical properties of the SEI material. Because some of the flight tests indicated less absorption than we expected, some waveguide testing was performed by cooling the sample and slotted waveguide assembly to very low (-60 degrees F) temperatures approximating the air temperatures under flight conditions. However, this testing seemed inconclusive, and so it was discontinued.

We discovered that the conductivity of the TD paper varied so much from sample to sample that we had to replace it with several different materials made by Mel's group at Edwards North Base, and then later in our new Burbank facilities. Mel, Mac, and I worked cooperatively with the Boston group to manufacture special absorbing layer materials to be incorporated into the U-2 Salisbury Screen coatings.

A small group of ADP people directed by Mel and Merlin worked on the development of a continuous film that incorporated both energy storage (time delay to compensate for the reduced thickness of the assembly) and energy dissipation properties.

The films that were studied, developed, and tested were essentially thin Mylar or fiberglass cloth substrates coated with a paint-like layer of aluminum and graphite micro-flakes dispersed throughout a dielectric binder. The aluminum flakes were selected for a tendency, because of their shape, to form layers. Since the aluminum flakes were insulated from each other and were mostly parallel to each other (and parallel to the substrate), they formed myriad capacitors mutually interconnected so that their total effect was a large delay in a very thin film. As much as fifty times the delay in vacuum was accomplished. Graphite flakes were introduced to dissipate the wave energy. Some samples incorporated silver flakes as well as graphite to aid in controlling the dissipation.

Fortunately, I was able to make very good waveguide measurements at Edwards North Base of very small samples of our absorbers that we were expecting to put on the U-2.

The electrical testing of experimental samples was done initially using S-Band waveguide equipment. A sample of the surface film was inserted into a special holder and the assembly was used to terminate a waveguide slotted line. Then, the reflection coefficient was measured as a function of frequency and the results were translated into equivalent absorption. Typical results showed large attenuation (small backscatter) at the design frequency and more than 20 dB (less than 1 percent reflection) over bandwidths of the order of 28 percent.

For a design frequency of 3 GHz the 20 dB bandwidth would extend from 2.58 to 3.42 GHz.

Small Scale Model Testing

A small amount of experience with the Big Rumbling Cart and drums set-up convinced us, and Kelly Johnson, of the need for much more sophisticated facilities.

We continued to test in the hangar at Edwards North Base while Kelly had larger offices and electromagnetic laboratory space provided for us in the U-2 area in Bldg. 82 in Burbank.

While our test equipment and test samples were being moved to Burbank, Mac and I visited SEI's secret laboratory in Cambridge, Massachusetts, to observe their test facility and to discuss their results.

We traveled in a DC-7 aircraft. It was an overnight "red-eye" flight, having left Los Angeles about midnight. We and one other person were the only passengers, so Mac and I sat in the seats just aft of the cockpit doors and had good views of the engine cowlings, propellers, and wings. Our cruising altitude probably was between eighteen and twenty thousand feet.

As we approached the highest Rocky Mountains, we encountered rain and lightning. After a few minutes we saw bright blue haze over the cowlings and wings. There appeared to be bright blue rain blowing aft from the propellers.

Then we saw very bright blue streamers emerging from the "spinners," the streamline shells covering the propeller hubs. Propagating forward into the air, they appeared to be about an inch in diameter and about a foot long before a lightning flash occurred nearby and the entire display disappeared. The process repeated about every ten minutes for almost an hour.

The phenomenon was caused by tribo-electric charging of the aircraft[43] [44] [45] [46] [47] [48] by electric charges carried by impinging raindrops. It was essentially the same as "Saint Elmo's Fire" often experienced on ships at sea.

The light was recombination radiation, mostly from relaxing excited or ionized molecules of nitrogen in the air.

The only effect upon the aircraft might have been erosion of the propeller bearings due to the electric current flowing through the streamers. We hoped the airline used conductive grease in them!

I was quite frustrated because I had left my camera at home.

As we began our tour of SEI's facility, we entered a dimly lit warehouse building that reminded me of a coal mine such as I had seen in the Chicago Museum of Science and Industry. We were led to the one well-lighted area in which their test facility appeared.

It seemed quite remarkable. Whereas every backscatter range I ever have seen projected electromagnetic energy horizontally (nearly parallel to Earth's surface), theirs did so vertically.

It was as clever as it was unusual. Microwave energy was projected horizontally into a reflector shaped as half of an ellipse of revolution about a vertical axis. Small models were mounted horizontally at the focus of the reflector. Microwave energy that was not back scattered from the models was supposed to be reflected upward and out through a large hole in the roof of the building. The hole was covered by a thin translucent plastic dome. Because of the reflector's small size only very small models could be accommodated.

Whatever energy was reflected back from the test target was detected from the output of a "Magic Tee."[§] Backscatter from a metal sphere was used to define the equivalent backscattering area, or RCS, of the targets.

We had no information about how effective the reflector was at reducing interfering background reflections compared to absorber lined anechoic chambers, so we decided that we would prefer the latter.

Calibration of radar measurements is accomplished by comparison with reflections from targets whose reflectivity has been calculated and verified by comparisons among one another. Several such reflectors are available, but probably the most commonly used calibration target is a highly conducting sphere. Perhaps the next most used reflector is a triangle sided "corner reflector."

Unfortunately, SEI's facility could utilize only very small test items and so the results were fraught with uncertainty. The aircraft models that we saw were not well enough detailed to reveal more than gross scattering features. Apparently they were just beginning to learn to measure radar cross section.

Technical discussions with them dealt mostly with Salisbury Screen absorbers. Some discussion about construction and testing of these absorbers completed that first meeting. There seems to have been a fascination with the apparent simplicity of the Salisbury Screen technology.

Before we returned to Burbank, I visited a Harvard professor to discuss the mathematical theory of measuring specimens in a waveguide to make an effective absorber assembly, but after a short discussion, I realized that

---

§   Appendix G discusses the Magic Tee in more detail.

he would not be of much help. He was an expert in electromagnetic theory, but I seriously doubted that he had ever done any measurements of the kind we needed. We discussed the characterization of the so-called characteristic impedance of rectangular waveguides.

S. A. Schelkunoff described three different ways to define it.[49][50] Only one seemed promising for doing impedance matching, the essence of absorber design.

As far as I knew, he never had done any antenna work, whereas by that time I had been designing and supervising testing and development in the Lockheed antenna laboratory for about six years. I decided that I would go my own way, do my own design, do my own measurements, try the results, and see how they turned out.

On our way back, we visited William F. "Bill" Bahret's laboratory at Wright-Patterson AFB in Dayton, Ohio. They were deeply involved with testing fundamental shapes to verify calculated backscatter and were not equipped to test scaled models. At the end of our visit, we concluded that we would need to design and build our own facilities to test larger scale models to support our treatments' design processes.

I did the preliminary design specifications for the first backscatter anechoic chamber for RCS measurements in the Skunk Works to test our U-2 signature reduction materials concepts and aircraft scale models. It was built in the southeast corner of Building 82.

My original design specifications for the chamber called for a rectangular cavity twelve feet wide, twelve feet high, and thirty feet long in which the walls were parallel to each other, ceiling and floor were parallel, and the back end wall was perpendicular to the Poynting vector, the direction of propagation of the simulated radar waves.

The chamber frame was to be built in three sections that were bolted together. Each section would be framed like a house using wooden two-by-fours. The sections were to be lined with half-inch thick plywood for strength and rigidity. A remotely controlled rotator was to be built into the ceiling of the farthest-most section. Readily available absorbing material was to be added to all interior surfaces in such fashion that the sections easily could be unbolted for transportation to another site.

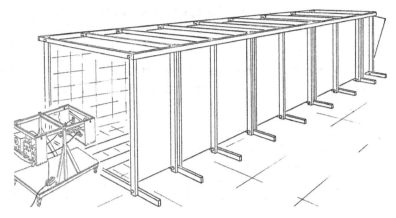

The Early Anechoic Chamber in Bldg. 82-B

One end of the chamber was to be open to accommodate the Big Rumbling Cart with the transmitting and receiving horn antennas on it. We would acquire a polar recorder from Bill Martin's laboratory to use in the chamber.

U-2 Infrared Sensor Calibration

During a lull in activities, Kelly assigned me the task of calibrating a U-2 infrared (IR) sensor. It was a very interesting experience sitting out in the desert at night, at Edwards North Base, in a U-2 aircraft. That was fun, but it didn't last very long.

The CIA wanted to analyze the exhaust from Soviet rockets to determine the kinds of chemicals that were being used as propellants. The instrument was enclosed in a tall, circular cylinder with a hemispherical cap mounted on top of a U-2. It was a scanning spectrograph that used a rock salt crystal prism that was rotated to yield a spectrum.

I utilized the planet Venus as one source of IR energy for calibration.

I used a borrowed "black body" simulator to confirm the calibration. It was a heated rectangular body that contained a spherical cavity that had a small, conical opening in one side through which infrared energy escaped. The size of the opening and the internal temperature determined the amount and the spectral distribution of the energy released. The German name for such a device is "hohlraum."

A black body is a theoretically perfect radiator or absorber of radiant energy of all wavelengths. Although such an entity cannot exist, it is a mathematical convenience and is useful for performance comparisons.[51] [52]

I made detailed calculations to predict the performance of the instrument by analyzing the effect of each component in its system. At one stage I needed to integrate the spectral response of several optical (infrared) filters.

I was able to accomplish this by weighing a rectangular piece of cardboard on a very sensitive chemical scale in Mel's laboratory and then repeating the procedure after I had plotted the relative spectral response as a graph on the cardboard and cut away the area outside the curve. The ratio of the two weights yielded the normalized integral that then was used to determine the performance of the sensor. The calculated performance agreed very well with the experimental results.

That was a demonstration that there may be more than one way to attack a problem.

Some interesting data relating decibel notation to astronomy are:

- The faintest star visible to "average" people is referred to as the sixth magnitude. This brightness may be called "tangential sensitivity" (TS).

A great many observations and measurements of the relative brightness of visible stars, the moon, and our sun have revealed the following:

- A change of one magnitude is equivalent to a change of 4 dB.
- Tangential sensitivity equals -24 dB.
- The moon is rated at +12.6 M or 50.4 dB, (74.4 dB brighter than TS).
- The sun is rated at 26 M or 104 dB, (128 dB brighter than TS).

I almost got to the point where I thought that I could fly a U-2! I sat in the cockpit with full electrical power on for several hours during several nights.

Early Anechoic Chamber Testing

When the anechoic chamber was finished, we moved the Big Rumbling Cart and the rest of our equipment from Edwards North Base to Building 82 in Burbank, and we began to learn to measure backscatter from small objects and scaled models, continued full-scale transition tests with drums, and began to conduct large sample testing of new Salisbury Screen lay-ups on two feet by two feet flat aluminum panels.

Just as the chamber was finished, Francis Michael "Mike" Ash and James "Jim" M. Herron joined our group. They were destined to be extremely valuable members. Together we devised and developed RCS test equipment and measurement techniques for the Skunk Works.

Our first measurements were of aircraft absorber mounted on aluminum-covered cylinders three feet in diameter and four feet long. After our initial evaluation of the chamber, the back wall was tilted slightly, and there was an opening above it so energy bouncing off of the back wall went up and out of the chamber.

When we began to prepare for testing small-scale models, we needed procedures and equipment to evaluate the empty chamber reflectivity.

The principal method of testing the chamber involved a traveling metal sphere that was caused to traverse the length of the chamber, from the reflectometer antenna to the rear wall and, if desired, back again to the start.

I had a pulley system arranged using a thin Dacron line near the ceiling stretched parallel to the length of the test volume over pulleys at each end. A Dacron line suspended a lightweight, thin-walled, eight-inch diameter aluminum sphere so that it moved along the chamber centerline. The driving motor and a position pick-off device were coupled to the pulley at the open end of the chamber.

The reflectometer was in fact the microwave bridge in the Big Rumbling Cart. The output of the reflectometer was converted to decibels using a Scientific Atlanta Model 122B recorder and then plotted along the ordinate direction on an X-Y plotter. The sphere position was plotted along the abscissa direction.

An ideal response plotted in these coordinates, for a reflection-free environment, would have yielded a straight line with a negative slope of twelve decibels per octave of distance change. Octave means a ratio of two to one.

In practice, the equipment was adjusted for minimum signal coupled to the receiver while the horn antenna illuminated the empty anechoic chamber. Then the sphere was suspended in the center of the volume to be occupied by the test specimen and caused to swing slightly more than a quarter of a wavelength forth and back along the line-of-sight. The reflectometer was readjusted to yield the minimum variation of the receiver signal indication. This procedure assured the minimum coupling between the transmitter and the receiver and thereby greatly reduced possible errors caused by combinations of the transmitted waves with those reflected from a target. It also produced a calibrated reference level for comparison with polar backscatter patterns of the target. Typical adjustments using this procedure resulted in leakage of transmitter power into the receiver by thirty or more dB below the return from the calibration sphere.

In the chamber, waves reflected from various parts of the environment combined with the backscattered waves from the test sphere and formed interference patterns. The results were recordings showing deviations from the ideal sloping straight line. Sources of interfering reflections were located by interpreting those deviations, and the effectiveness of corrective measures was revealed by the next record.

This technique was a precursor of a more sophisticated location system that was implemented three years later at Groom Lake in Area 51 to test the A-12 and other mockups.

It quickly became evident that a better wall absorber was required.

The first attempts at improvement consisted of trying to rearrange the absorbing materials to prevent or redirect specular (mirror-like) reflections. Baffles and triangular ridges on floors, walls, and ceilings were tried and discarded.

The first absorber material that we purchased, Emerson and Cummings' "Echosorb," was thick foam blocks with hollow ogives whose surfaces were coated with a graphite-loaded paint. Each block was contained within fiberglass sheets. Their performance was unsatisfactory because there was too much of a dielectric constant difference between the material's surface and air and so too much energy was reflected and scattered.

We changed to B. F. Goodrich's "Hairflex" absorber that was a tangle of graphite coated animal hair resembling a black pot scrubber. We just put it over the Echosorb that was in place. That material worked well because its graphite loading was graduated and it did not have reflecting surfaces.

The original rectangular cavity, with a tilted back wall and all interior surfaces covered by "Hairflex" absorber, performed well and was still in use into the 1990s.

Our earliest measurements of isolation between antennas were performed in this chamber using backscattering techniques. This method was a direct outgrowth of the diagnostic techniques used to improve the anechoic chamber.

Quite early in 1958, during the effort to build a useful anechoic chamber, we recognized that side and back radiation scattered from the rims of the horn antennas was causing serious difficulties. I had the ends of the horn antennas surrounded by metal extensions of the horn sides lined with absorbing materials, some eighteen years before a NASA report of a similar invention![53] This expedient eliminated back radiation and most of the side radiation and had very little effect (less than one decibel) on the system sensitivity. Later we added absorbing hoods to the rims of large parabolic reflector antennas that were used for lower frequency tests.

Until the end of efforts to design low RCS stealthy aircraft and satellites, the Hooded Horn Antennas were standard equipment.

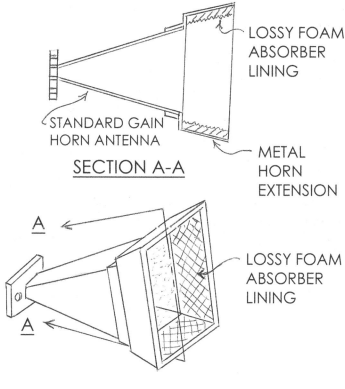

LOSSY FOAM
ABSORBER
LINING

STANDARD GAIN
HORN ANTENNA

SECTION A-A

METAL
HORN
EXTENSION

LOSSY FOAM
ABSORBER
LINING

A

A

"Hooded Horn" Antennas

At first changing models in this chamber was both time consuming and inconvenient. About a third of the floor had to be taken up and replaced each time a change was performed. Later a door was installed in one side wall to allow easier access to the models.

After we had suppressed the spurious reflections to useable levels, we installed a thin Styrofoam disk, about two feet in diameter and an inch thick, as a tray hanging by thin Dacron lines from the rotator in the ceiling. We thought we would just place the material or a model on the tray and perform measurements, but the returns from the disk were too great, so we abandoned the idea.

Styrofoam columns never were considered because reflections from their surfaces, joints, voids, and interfaces were known to be too strong. We needed to suspend test targets as nearly by themselves as we could.

The "Six String Hang"

The best suspension arrangement, invented by Jim Herron, utilized six thin Dacron lines arranged to avoid normal incidence. The triangular formations of the strings provided a measure of torsional stiffness that prevented oscillation of test specimens when rotation was started or stopped. The weight of the item being tested kept the strings taut. The "Six String Hang" was a major improvement in our technique, truly a key innovation.

Small, low dielectric constant plastic clamps were used to aid in adjustment of line lengths for positioning the various targets. The Dacron line suspension system was used for all subsequent backscattering tests in this and, later, our much larger anechoic chamber. It was used for more than thirty years, well into the 1990s. It was a strong system too—at one time we had a full-scale SA-2 missile mockup hanging up in our later large anechoic chamber.

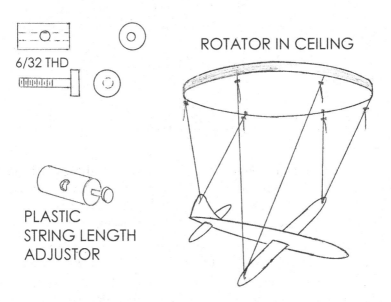

6/32 THD

ROTATOR IN CEILING

PLASTIC
STRING LENGTH
ADJUSTOR

Typical "Six String Hang" Support

To test our materials on scale model aircraft, we had to scale the materials themselves. To scale we had to change the electrical properties of the scale model and its materials so the ultimate effect would match the full-scale object. I suspect that if I had not had the antenna background that I did we might not have been able to understand the scaling laws.

Scale model technology had been developed to some extent long ago. Joseph Tykocinski Tykociner, at the University of Illinois, experimented with scaled models of antennas in the 1920s. Literature on scaling was not easily available until much later.[54] [55] [56] [57] [58].

One rule is that the higher the frequency, the greater must be the conductivity by the model scale factor. When we used conductive paint, we characterized it by "ohms per square." We assumed that its thickness was very much smaller than the dimensions of a square sample so it did not matter. Obviously a three-dimensional bulk absorber is different.

We also used Aquadag later when we were doing anechoic chamber work using very small scale models and had to do the best we could to model the absorber we would use on full-scale aircraft. "Aquadag" was a paint that contained graphite in a water soluble vehicle. It was the conducting paint that I had sprayed onto butcher paper for the screen room walls in 1953 to make the first anechoic chamber for the Lockheed antenna laboratory.

When we began measurements of backscattering from small scaled models in our first anechoic chamber, Kelly Johnson visited us frequently to watch our actions. He seemed fascinated by the polar backscatter patterns our recorder produced.

Since the models were small and our test equipment was very limited in power and receiver sensitivity, we were plagued by electronic noise in our receiver that obscured the level below which we could not measure backscatter.¶

We had reduced or eliminated disturbances or noise from other sources by using isolation transformers, voltage regulators, and direct current from six volt automobile batteries to power the cathode heaters in our receiver vacuum tubes.

One day as I was explaining this to Kelly, I happened to mention that one source of noise was "Johnson Noise"! Johnson noise[59] is caused by random fluctuations of current in a conductor due to thermal agitation of electrons from their equilibrium positions in conductors.

I immediately thought, *Oops! My career in the Skunk Works is over!* I told him that the term was in common use in electronic engineering,

---

¶   See Appendix F for an explanation of how we were able to circumvent that limitation in Salisbury Screen measurements.

and I showed him a reference in Terman's *Radio Engineers Handbook*[60] to assure him that it was true.

I once heard that some of the engineers who were designing the U-2 aircraft had pictures of women posing provocatively on the walls near their work areas. They knew Kelly would not approve of that, so they devised a system. If someone saw Kelly coming they would shout, "Present—Ducks!" All of the perpetrators would flip their girlie pictures over. On the backs were innocuous pictures of various birds. I suppose that at least some of them were ducks.

Working under the aegis of the CIA's consultants, we continued to attempt the development of relatively thin narrow-band absorbers of the Salisbury Screen type. Both the printed-circuit types and continuous film were tested.

The basic printed-circuit type consisted of squares of highly conducting silver-graphite paint sprayed onto a semi-conducting substrate. The parameters that were expected to control the frequency of maximum absorption were the dimensions of the squares, their separation from each other, and the effective separation of the outer layers from the highly conducting reflecting surface. The attenuation was expected to be caused by the resistive layer, TD, or a thin Mylar sheet coated by Mel's paint that we called "Tapered Paper" (TP) despite the fact that no paper was involved.

Double tuning was attempted by modifying the squares. It was done in an attempt to broaden the absorption bandwidth. Several different versions had holes of various sizes and shapes in the squares. Some tests using cruciform shapes were conducted.

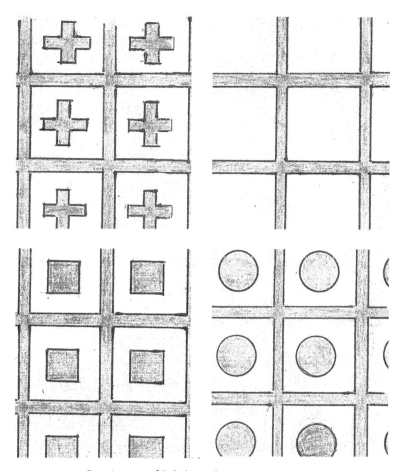

Specimens of Salisbury Screen Magic Layer

The results, in general, were disappointing; no significant increase in absorption or absorption bandwidth was attained.

Drum tests of the SEI materials continued in the Burbank chamber. In one set of tests, several different variations utilizing holes in the squares of the SEI material were tried, but no improvements in absorption or bandwidth for S-Band frequencies were attained.

We had begun designing the next generation multi-layer material at Edwards North Base using continuous film. After the anechoic chamber was built and we had moved to Burbank, we continued these efforts by scaling up material samples from S-Band waveguide size to large flat panels and cylindrical specimens. We were pleased to find that the data obtained earlier using the waveguide method at Edwards North Base correlated very well with the results of backscattering measurements of flat panel and cylindrical specimens performed in the chamber. The chamber measurements demonstrated that material performance measured under waveguide conditions could be translated to the equivalent free space conditions, the environment in which the absorber would be utilized.

We ran a series of tests that addressed the effects of different combinations of various ingredients in the resistive layer.[**] Based on the results, we were able to design a new buildup that replaced the TD paper with continuous film.

The next step was toward large-scale production. Careful control of all stages of fabrication was necessary for good results. The ADP group developed simple tools and fabrication techniques that allowed production of large amounts of very uniform continuous films.

The work on Salisbury Screens continued through 1958 and part of 1959. It was discontinued when work on a new aircraft began.

Security Breach

One afternoon in early 1958, Jack Hansen and I were standing outside the shop area of the north part of Building 82, discussing the day's events, when I heard what sounded like large trash cans or dumpsters rattling behind me. I saw a startled look on Jack's face, and then he said, "I think I just saw a car drive into the building!"

We went to the guard at the door and said, "We think a car just drove into the building," but the guard did not believe it.

Jack and I went into the building, and sure enough, there was a car with an unconscious male driver still in it, inside the building!

His car had crashed through a chain-link fence that terminated a little short street parallel to Hollywood Way, into the building wall, which, since it was corrugated metal, had given way but then returned to its original position, so there was no obvious hole in it.

Inside, the car had passed by a row of work benches at which people had been sitting only a few minutes before because it was, at most, fifteen minutes after a shift change began.

[**] Waveguide and coaxial resistivity measurements are discussed in Appendix H.

The shift change stampede had left no one in that area, so no one was hurt. The car went under a U-2 wing, missing the aircraft, and stopped just shy of a ping-pong table. Hitting that table would have been a real disaster!

We went back to the guard and said definitely there was a car in the building. He grumbled but he locked up his station and came inside. Once he saw the car, pandemonium ensued!

Apparently the man had had an epileptic seizure. He was removed while he was still unconscious.

U-2 Low Frequency Design and Testing

In early 1958, we worked on ways to reduce the vulnerability of the U-2 aircraft to detection by Soviet early warning radars. Our "Customer," the CIA, asked us to provide a means of reducing the backscatter from a U-2 aircraft in the 70 to 90 MHz frequency range. The corresponding wavelengths are fourteen to eleven feet. The United States had lent the 70 to 90 MHz radars to Russia as part of the World War II Lend-Lease Program to assist in their defense against Germany. Strangely, there was no discussion about reducing reflection in the vicinity of 170 MHz, the frequency of the more dangerous but less numerous "Tall King" early warning radars.

During a conference with the Customer's consultant, Dr. Franklin Rodgers, in a Washington hotel room design session involving Kelly Johnson, L. D. MacDonald, and me, it was decided that we might reduce the reflection by using a network of wires carrying lossy ferrite beads surrounding the aircraft. Spacing the wires one quarter wavelength from the metal fuselage, we would rely on the ferrite beads to absorb energy the wires intercepted. This scheme seemed reminiscent of previous attempts to implement a faux Salisbury Screen to attenuate backscatter of high frequency radar wave energy.

I had not been told about prior attempts to make similar arrangements work on U-2 and T-33 aircraft to reduce low frequency RCS.

Ferrites are ceramic compounds that contain iron as well as other metal atoms. Some are lossy—that is, they convert both electric and magnetic field energy to heat.

They were attractive because they seemed to offer an effective loss modality in small, lightweight beads. However, the ferrites available at that time, while effective for the low frequencies near 70 MHz, were inert for the higher frequencies required to test small-scaled models.

Scaled model measurements in our Burbank anechoic chamber using thin film resistors in lieu of ferrites showed promising results. Reduction of cross section of roughly 12 dB was obtained. That amount of attenuation could reduce the radars' detection distance by about half. The most promising arrangement was a network of resistors in a mesh of squares one quarter of a wavelength on a side disposed along the leading and trailing edges of the wings, the horizontal stabilizers, and on each side of the fuselage.

We decided to implement an analogous arrangement on a U-2 aircraft at Edwards North Base.

When I ordered several dozens of incomplete fiberglass fishing rods, our procurement supervisor John Ramsey objected rather strenuously until Kelly Johnson approved my order. The unfinished rods were tapered tubes that I selected to stiffen parts of the meshwork on the aircraft.

Meanwhile, Mel George had his people make several sets of fiberglass members that resembled an archer's bow. They were installed during the regular daytime shifts on the wing tips and the tips of the horizontal stabilizers.

Mac and I proceeded, after day shift hours in the hangar at Edwards North Base, to equip one aircraft with the low-frequency absorber network.

During the first evening, I used a Q meter to determine the number of ferrite beads to use to reduce resonance of a quarter wavelength long parallel wire transmission line that was short-circuited at one end where ferrite beads were positioned. Mac and I then spent the rest of the evening designing parts that we installed the next evening. A mechanic made all of the metal parts during the day.

Standard eighteen-gauge copper-clad steel antenna wire four one-hundredths of an inch in diameter was used for the principal parts. A wire was strung from the fuselage parallel to, and forty inches ahead of, the leading edge of each wing to the end of a strong fiberglass member at each wing tip.

Periodically, as nearly as feasible forty inches apart, wires were strung fore and aft inside tapered fiberglass tubes (unfinished fishing poles) to metal cuffs fastened to the leading edge of the wing by armament tape. Every forty inches along the wires parallel to the leading edge a group of lossy ferrite beads were strung on the wire. These commercially available FM, TV, and VHF receiver filters were the absorbing elements of this system. A group of beads was located on each fore and aft wire as near the cuff on the wing leading edge as possible. Similar but shorter systems of wires were installed along the leading edges of the horizontal stabilizers.

The trailing edges of the wings and stabilizers had a modified form of this treatment. In addition to a wire from the fuselage to a fiberglass member on the wing tip reaching forty-six inches aft of the trailing edges, a wire was strung from the fuselage to the wing tip fiberglass member parallel to, but separated from, the trailing edges of the wings and stabilizers. This allowed unencumbered movement of the flaps, ailerons, and elevators. These arrangements, which resembled wire ladders, were tethered to convenient places on the upper surfaces of the wings and tail by Dacron cords. Ferrite beads were disposed on the wires in similar fashion to that used on the leading edge treatment.

Additional wires were strung from a point on each side of the nose to appropriate attachments on the U-2's Slipper Tanks. They also carried ferrite beads.

A wire was strung parallel to and forty inches from the fuselage, on each side, between the trailing edge of each wing and the leading edge of the horizontal stabilizer on the same side. These wires, too, had several sets of ferrite beads disposed along their lengths.

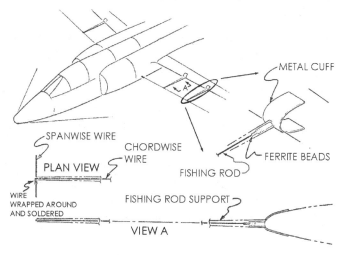

Details of the "Trapeze" Design

Perhaps that was the "Trapeze" that Sweetman attempted to describe.[††]

Testing U-2s at Daggett

Dynamic radar reflectivity measurements were performed in the vicinity of Daggett, California.

One day while on the Marine base at Daggett, California, during RCS testing of U-2 aircraft, I saw a coyote chasing a rabbit. It was so hot that both were walking. It took me a while to appreciate the seriousness of their situation.

A "Very High Frequency" (VHF) radar that could be tuned between 65 MHz and 90 MHz was made by a group probably directed by Dr. E. Rawson by modifying an RCA TT-10AL television transmitter. I do not remember the details of the low-frequency radar receiver.

An SCR-584 radar was modified to improve the receiver sensitivity and was used for S-Band tracking and testing. The radars were located in or near a building on the edge of an airstrip at the U.S. Marine base at Daggett. The VHF radar antenna was a modest-sized horizontally polarized Yaggi-Uda array pointed eastward.

A total of twenty-one flights for testing at 70 MHz, 80 MHz, and 2.8 GHz were flown using two U-2 Aircraft. One aircraft was treated with printed squares circuit material, and the other was coated by the continuous material.

Occasionally, severe interference at 70 MHz was encountered, which, at first, was thought to be signals from Television Channel 4 in Los Angeles received via antenna pattern side lobes. We were reminded of the effects of ionospheric refractions when especially strong signals that prevented radar measurements on an aircraft twenty or so miles away were identified as coming from Television Channel 4 in Kansas City, Missouri!

The interference was so strong that it caused the radar display to become blank. Dan Schwarzkopf was the person who had the presence of mind to listen to the radar receiver rather than to watch the display. Electronic engineer Dan Schwarzkopf was an important member of the MIT Lincoln Laboratory radar team.

Although we did not know it at the time, with a Wolf number of 180, sunspot activity was at the highest level recorded since the year 1372!

---

†† Appendix E discusses some historian accounts regarding U-2 RCS tests.

It was determined that the wires were moderately successful in reducing radar backscattering but were undesirable because of increased aerodynamic drag. Although the arrangement proved to be quite durable, we ended our efforts to reduce the low-frequency reflectivity of the U-2 aircraft.

In retrospect, I wonder why Kelly Johnson allowed us to install the Trapeze.

The S-Band testing at Daggett demonstrated that the reduction of reflectivity was less than had been expected. In fact, some flight tests were inconclusive, so one test was tried in which both a treated aircraft and an untreated aircraft were flown over the Daggett site. So little difference was measured that it was decided to test the treated aircraft statically on a pole in an effort to determine why the results were not better. The only available test range capable of holding a full-scale U-2 was at Indian Springs Air Force Base, near Las Vegas, Nevada.

Pole Testing at Indian Springs AFB

In 1958, the outdoor static test facility at Indian Springs Air Force Base near Las Vegas, Nevada, was made available to us. It consisted of a simple platform rotator remotely controlled from a building that served as a control and recording room, engineering offices, and an electronics laboratory. The rotator was about half a mile from the control room and only a few feet above the ground.

A corner reflector mounted on a wooden pole behind the rotator served as a standard for calibration for S-Band backscattering. Most of the backscattering measurements were performed using a frequency stepping S-Band radar probably designed by a group led by Dr. E. Rawson.

S-Band measurements made up the bulk of the diagnostic testing. Some attempts were made to perform low frequency measurements near 70 MHz, but technical difficulties prevented gathering useful data.

The S-Band frequency stepping radar employed thirty-one discrete frequencies within about a 20 percent bandwidth to illuminate the target. Range (distance) gating was used in an attempt to exclude extraneous reflections.

Frequency stepping provided a means for simulating the effect of target scintillation and removing the large excursions of signal level characteristics of reflections from large complex targets illuminated by monochromatic radiation. The thirty-one frequency steps were repeated 210 times a second and, because the target was rotated slowly (about one revolution in twenty minutes), 21,700 samples of reflections were obtained per degree of rotation.

These samples were processed by a special detector called a SQUOD, an acronym for Selected Quartile Output Device.

The input to the SQUOD was proportional to the power of the signal reflected from the target.

The output of the SQUOD was equivalent to the "root mean square" value[61] of all the signal samples in each frequency scan. It was calibrated to represent the equivalent echo area of the target in decibels referred to one square meter (dBsm).

All the backscatter polar patterns were displayed in terms of dBsm.

The wings and engine were removed from one of the U-2 test aircraft so it could be mounted, right side up, on the rotator. There was no provision for tilting the target; It was mounted as in level flight. Short mockup wings, each approximately ten feet long, were substituted for the real wings.

Most of the fuselage and all of the vertical fin and rudder of the aircraft were covered with SEI's Salisbury Screen absorbing materials. During the latter part of 1958 and the early part of 1959, printed circuit analogs and the continuous material absorbers were tested on the aircraft.

I heard that Dan Schwarzkopf reported that, during lunch in a restaurant next to a highway, he had overheard some people discussing puzzling sights they had seen recently. A mile or so away something seemed to rise up, go around and go down. It was our rotating aircraft's vertical tail!

Because the whole assembly could be seen from the highway several miles away, the aircraft was painted sand beige to make it less visible.

The test results generally were of the order of ten to twelve decibels (ratios of 1/10th to 1/16th) of reduction of backscatter, except for normal incidence, for which the attenuation at the design frequency usually was about twenty decibels (a ratio of 1/100th).

Inadequacy of the measuring system and reflections from the target rotator seriously hindered work on some details such as suppressing corner reflections from the intersection of the fuselage and horizontal tail members.

The use of frequency stepping may have obscured some beneficial results obtained by modifying the test object. A simple calculation indicated that twenty steps in a bandwidth of 20 percent will result in a net reduction of measured reflectivity by no more than about 12 dB.

A very interesting and important diagnostic tool was developed and tested at this site. It consisted of a corner reflector mounted on a trolley that was run forth and back along a pair of rails that were installed to one side of the rotator and were aligned nearly parallel to a line from the radars and the target rotator.

The waves reflected from a stationary target and the Doppler-shifted waves from the moving corner reflector combined in the receiver. Because they combined with all possible phase differences, their resultant varied with the changed frequency as the trolley progressed along its track.

A filter that could be tuned to the difference frequency (about 10 Hz if the radar frequency was 3 GHz) selected a narrow band of frequencies and extracted their energy that ultimately was used to deflect a recording pen thereby yielding a record showing a characteristic pattern of pulse-like deflections plotted as a function of the trolley's position along its track.

The filter was tuned by setting up a corner reflector at the center of the rotator and then adjusting the output to maximum as the trolley-borne reflector passed it. This procedure resulted in a maximum recorder deflection whenever two reflectors appeared to be at the same distance from the radar.

With a target set and left at a particular azimuth angle, the trolley we called "The Railroad" was caused to travel along its track at a constant one meter per second speed either toward or away from the radar. That is about as fast as an adult person can sustain while walking. The radar's range gate was moved in synchronism with the corner reflector's position.

Then, with the target positioned as desired, the Railroad was run to obtain a record. Next a line was drawn on a plan view drawing of the target at the appropriate azimuth angle and offset from the center of rotation by the amount indicated by the railroad record. After several such lines were constructed for several different angles of rotation of the model, a fix could be obtained on the phase center of a reflection from the target.

Generally the cause for each reflection could be located by inspection within about a wavelength. Then the efficacy of corrective measures could be estimated by inspecting subsequent polar backscatter patterns.

A relatively short time was available for testing the U-2 aircraft at Indian Springs before we were replaced by a Convair group testing the backscattering from mockups of proposed supersonic aircraft called the FISH and the KINGFISH.

They were Convair's last hope for winning the chance to build a stealthy supersonic replacement of the Lockheed U-2 aircraft.

The A-12—Competition
Stealth and Speed

"Mighty oaks from little acorns grow."
—A. B. Johnson, 1841

When it became known that Soviet low frequency early warning radars had detected the first U-2 aircraft in 1956 as it took off and flew along a Soviet border, and that the high-frequency missile guidance radars had tracked it, the CIA's reaction was to attempt to reduce the reflectivity of the aircraft as much as and as soon as possible. The original expectation was that the aircraft would be able to overfly missiles for about two years. U-2 flights were continued sporadically for nearly four years until Gary Powers was shot down in 1960.

Strong interest in supersonic vehicles arose with the realization that high altitude, high speed flight combined with the minimum radar backscatter was the best mode of operation for a reconnaissance aircraft.

A study begun in 1958 of the ability of such a craft to survive and carry out its mission in a violently hostile environment, such as might be expected by 1965 and later, pointed out, very clearly, the need for such performance. The report detailing the results of that study was published early in 1959. It was known informally in the Skunk Works as the "Cat and Mouse Report."[62]

It contained a strong recommendation for very high speed, very high altitude flight to hinder radar detection in addition to incorporation of materials and shaping in the original designs to reduce radar reflectivity.

Time was critical, so the CIA first evaluated using or modifying existing aircraft. I saw one of the candidates. It was the American made Martin RB-57B, a copy of the British World War II 'Canberra' bomber. I was very impressed by how clean the bomber was inside, which was a light cream color, so that I could see everything easily. But it could not fly high enough, fast enough, or far enough.

No existing aircraft could be modified for the mission. The CIA concluded that a new aircraft needed to be designed, and they initiated a design competition in 1958.

The aircraft design requirements incorporated recommendations from the "Cat and Mouse Report." Kelly Johnson's statements in that report that low radar cross section, high altitude, and high speed operation would be the most important factors in accomplishing surveillance missions were correct until the advent of orbiting reconnaissance satellites.

Some of the requirements were: effective broadband absorption, shaping, and other expedients to scatter energy away from the hostile radar; the highest possible speed (with its special high temperature problems); greatest possible range and payload; and a full set of reconnaissance, communication, electronic countermeasures, and navigation equipment.

The aircraft was to be designed to defeat Soviet low frequency early warning radars operating about 50–90 MHz, and high frequency, 3 GHz missile control and tracking radars. It needed to fly from Turkey to Norway across the Soviet Union. Its mission was to fly in, hopefully not be seen, gather critical information, and fly out.

Since none of us expected to make an invisible aircraft, the Archangel goals were estimated on the basis of minimizing an enemy's available reaction time. An aircraft flying 2,000 miles per hour will travel a hundred miles in three minutes.

Kelly's design team was formidable. It included aerodynamicist Richard Fuller, aerodynamicist Richard Cantrell, thermodynamicist Ben Rich, and chief structural engineer Henry Combs. L. D. MacDonald was in charge of all of the RCS reduction work and its coordination with the other disciplines. Mac, Mel George, Merlin Reedy, Mike Ash, Jim Herron, and I formed the original RCS reduction group.

The U-2 already was flying when I joined the Skunk Works to help reduce its radar signature. All radar backscattering reduction solutions for the U-2 were retrofits, which always have a weight penalty, and usually are not as effective as a technology that is incorporated into the aircraft design from the beginning.

I agreed with Dr. Bissell's opinion when he told Kelly that it was critically urgent to design radar signature reduction into the new supersonic aircraft to best achieve the program goals of low observability, superior speed, and high altitude operation. Kelly as an aerodynamicist had the opinion that aerodynamic considerations were to be the primary focus and RCS a secondary, even retrofitted, feature. Dr. Bissell insisted that RCS reduction was necessary.

Part of my job during the design competition was to convince Kelly to design low RCS into the shape and volume of the Arrow aircraft. I accomplished this by involving Kelly through a series of tests of fundamental shapes in the anechoic chamber, a parallel to his building of aerodynamic experience in wind tunnel testing.

We began with a series of tests late in 1958 that explored the properties of a triangular metal cylinder. These tests demonstrated the effect of shape in reducing backscattering. It was evident that when the size of the scatterer was large compared to the wavelength, the shape had a very large effect on the backscattering and attenuating materials had lesser importance. Whenever the size of the scatterer was not large compared to the wavelength shape had little effect and reliance had to be upon the use of attenuating materials.

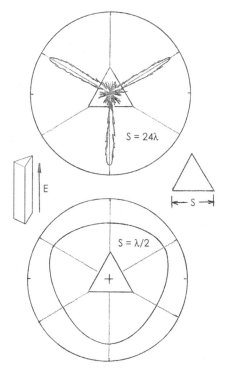

Triangular Cross-section Cylinder Backscatter

The total specular beamwidth of reflections from flat metal plates depends upon their size measured in wavelengths. An ordinary mirror reflects precisely back because even a small mirror is extremely large compared to the wavelengths of light. For a given size of a flat surface on an aircraft, the higher the radar wave frequency impacting it, the narrower the reflected beamwidth will be. The scattered energy can be directed away from the observer, resulting in a low radar signature if the surface is large enough.

As an indication of the ability to measure the properties of these triangular shapes, we graphically compared the measured backscattering data with a simplified theoretical relation. A more accurate calculation of the theoretical comparison would have shown a cyclical variation (caused by creeping waves) superimposed upon the straight line so it is possible that the measured data might have agreed even better. A special study of the relative reflections of rectangular flat plates performed about the same time (Dec. 1958) did, in fact, show such cyclical variations in the measured data.

We needed to confirm that the measurements were adequate. Relative echoes from other targets such as metal spheres, circular cylinders, corner reflectors, and flat plates, all correlated well with theory. We could both predict and measure radar backscatter reduction concepts to incorporate into the Arrow series designs.

These principles ultimately were incorporated into the design of the A-12 and its successors, the YF-12, the SR-71 aircraft, and the D-21 drone. Shaping the aircraft for aerodynamic performance and high frequency RCS reduction was ideal. Low-frequency radar wave reflections would have to be attenuated by lossy materials.

Much later this same information was utilized to guide the design of the Harvey proposal, the Have Blue, and F-117 aircraft. This phenomenon was the principle upon which the success of the F-117 aircraft's high-frequency stealth performance depended. Its low-frequency stealth depended upon resistive card technology, a form of surface attenuation treatment that would be developed for the design of the A-12 aircraft.

Kelly Johnson's All-plastic Plane

Our triangular cylinder tests demonstrated that shaping would greatly reduce high-frequency RCS. What could be done about low-frequency backscattering?

Kelly thought that an aircraft made of plastic materials might have sufficiently small low-frequency radar backscatter to defeat the 70 MHz Early Warning radars. I warned him that it would not. "You will see the internal structure and the square corners it forms. You will see the fuel."

Kelly wanted to test it anyway. Despite the fact that it was known that practical fiberglass structure would be dense enough to scatter four-inch S-Band radar waves, he still hoped that an all-plastic airframe might not backscatter fourteen-foot wavelengths significantly. Engine, landing gear parts, and any other metallic items were to be hidden by an, at that time, unspecified means.

One of the early scaled model plastic subsonic aircraft studied was a single place low-wing, tailless monoplane with long, high aspect ratio wings that were swept aft about thirty degrees. It and several variants were members of the G series designs.

Several all-fiberglass models that incorporated appropriate internal plastic structures were built and tested. One model was one-eighth scale and was too large for indoor testing, so it was tested at Indian Springs AFB.

An extensive series of tests performed of different kinds of absorbing structures explored the use of wedges of thin semi-conducting sheets, wedges of semi-conducting foams, and lossy foams combined with lossy sheets, all attempting to reduce corner reflections.

Thin sheets of absorbing material were disposed as vertical wedges around the periphery of the G-2 metallic center body. Later, similar treatment was applied around the periphery of a model whose metallic center body was joined to metallic box beams in its wings. This was the Model G-2A.

Backscattering measurements showed that the thick plastic sections required for strength and, especially corners, were very reflective. When kerosene fuel was added to the interior of the wings, the reflections increased and became characteristic of a solid piece of plastic. When the fuel in partially filled tanks was vibrated and standing waves occurred, the backscatter increased even more.

After attempts to hide the structure, fuel, and simulated engines yielded poor results, Kelly agreed to abandon that idea.

Arrow Design Series RCS Testing

During 1958 and early 1959 a new series of aircraft scaled models was investigated in the Burbank anechoic chamber. The Arrow series of supersonic designs eventually went through eleven versions and then was replaced by a design that became the A-12.

We thought that the anechoic chamber electronics might need to be improved to adequately evaluate models of aircraft designs.

Short pulse radars with range gating were studied. Extremely short pulses are needed to attain good resolution of details on small models. Such pulses require extremely wide bandwidths to carry all the required information. An electromagnetic wave travels about one foot per nanosecond in free space, the speed of light. One nanosecond is one billionth of a second.

However, the generation of short pulses of less than one nanosecond duration was beyond the capabilities of our equipment and our budget. The time required to develop such a system seemed too long. Fortunately, we would not need fine resolution to determine which design was the best, so we eliminated short pulse radar from consideration.

Other possible methods were considered, but none seemed to offer significant improvement over our original system. We continued to use the same type of reflectometer with which we had started for indoor measurements. This type of reflectometer was extremely sensitive to changes of frequency due to the use of the Magic Tee. Since the same antenna generally was used for both transmitting and receiving, it was a mono-static system that measured backscattered energy.

We did use separate antennas for transmitting and receiving when we used frequencies greater than 10 GHz because we could gain nearly six decibels in signal strength by eliminating the Magic Tee junction. Because the antennas for the high frequencies were small, their spacing was small and the systems essentially were also monostatic.

We replaced the commercial signal generators by Klystrons[63] to obtain more power. However, the Klystron microwave power generators were more sensitive to their environment. This type of equipment was extremely sensitive to changes of frequency.

Frequency stability adequate for an hour or so of testing time was attained by a combination of several measures. All the supply voltages for the Klystron transmitters were very carefully filtered and regulated. The Klystrons were immersed in large volume silicone oil baths whose temperatures were closely controlled. The Klystrons were mounted horizontally to minimize the variations of pressure caused by convection currents in the oil caused by bubbles formed under their hot parts. The Klystrons were surrounded by perforated metal low-pass pressure wave filters and the entire oil bath-Klystron assemblies were mounted on vibration isolators.

We utilized several sets of Klystrons and reflectometer assemblies to generate frequencies between 2 GHz and 10 GHz and several discrete higher frequencies. They were used for all backscatter measurements in the anechoic chamber.

Radar waves propagate spherically from their source. When they reach a distant target the sphere is so large that its surface is effectively planar. Ideally, to simulate real conditions in an anechoic chamber a plane wave could be created artificially.

The original anechoic chamber allowed only twenty feet of separation between the reflectometer and the targets. This was known to be inadequate to provide a sensibly plane wave at the target's location, especially for large models. We performed a series of measurements of flat sheet targets of many different heights and widths arranged in a plane normal to the direction of propagation and also in a curved surface to study the effects of phase error. The data was in the files under EDOBSAPE, an acronym for Experimental Determination of Beam Shape and Phase Error. These data served to indicate the magnitude of the errors that might result.

Some work was done using dielectric lenses to flatten the wave fronts but the results were unsatisfactory so they were abandoned. Also we tried Fresnel "zone plates"[64] made by painting highly conducting circular areas alternating with clear circular areas on thin sheets of clear plastic. These, too, were not worth the efforts to make and use them and so they were abandoned.

Some of the earlier work in 1958 on the effect of shape had demonstrated to Kelly Johnson that a wedge-shaped metal structure effectively can divert energy away from a cylindrical fuselage if the polarization* of the wave is perpendicular to its edge. However, it was

---

* Electromagnetic waves are composed of an electric field force component oscillating in a plane perpendicular to both the magnetic field force's oscillating plane and the direction the wave is going. The direction they move is called the Poynting vector. Polarization refers to the orientation of the electric field force plane.

necessary to make at least a part of the wedge an absorber in order to reduce backscattering of waves whose polarization is parallel to the leading edge of the wedge.

The A-12 fuselage shape was derived by curving the wedge's upper surfaces inward, rounding the top, folding the lower corners of the triangle upward, and rounding the bottom to improve aerodynamics. This was how the A-12 fuselage evolved.

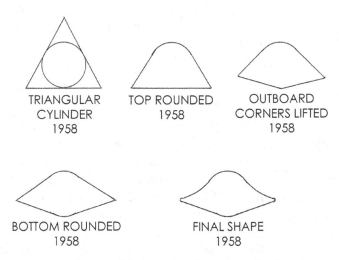

Evolution of the A-12 Fuselage Cross Section

Later modifications of the cross section developed into the final chine fuselage that is aerodynamically advantageous as well as a good anti-radar configuration.

The design we proposed to build was the A-12 incorporating radar backscattering reduction into the design. High-frequency reflectivity was reduced by careful shaping, tilting the rudders, and some application of ferro-magnetic materials. Ferrites never were applied to any of our stealthy aircraft.

Low-frequency reflectivity reduction largely was addressed by attenuation due to surface coatings in the form of tapered resistive paint over metal-supported plastic chine structures. The chines were as absorptive as possible at mid-band. We made the chine edges one quarter of a wavelength or about forty inches deep for most of their length.

During July of 1959, a series of tests using one-eighth scale models of the nacelles provided information about how to reduce the echoes from the front. As a result of the testing of various configurations, it was determined that the best balance between engine performance, aerodynamic considerations, and reduction of radar reflectivity would result from the use of nacelles mounted on the wings and nonmetallic radar energy absorbing inlet valves.

Considerable effort was devoted to the study of the reduction of backscattering from engine inlets and outlets. I knew that work had been done by others as long ago as the 1940s, attempting to reduce the returns by the use of shielding screens and attenuating bodies in the openings. Our early measurements gave us a baseline to start from and we rather quickly decided that we could use a lossy shape inside the inlet because our supersonic aircraft designs required a means for controlling the input air flow.

A lossy cone combined with a transition piece and streamlined supporting struts inside the nacelle were developed to suppress the return from an inlet. It became known as a "spike."

The forward eight inches of each spike assembly was made of metal and the remainder of the leading cone was composed of graphite-coated asbestos honeycomb surrounding the central metal structures. The outer covering was of silicone-asbestos coated with several layers of semi-conductive paint. The entire assembly was designed to present a mass of gradually increasing conductivity to an incoming radar wave.

Extensive testing of one-eighth scale nacelle models in the Burbank anechoic chamber and full-scale mockups out-of-doors at Groom Lake demonstrated the effectiveness of this method of reducing backscattering.

Special efforts were exerted on developing engine inlet screening methods in addition to the absorbing spikes. Modalities for reducing the reflections from the engine first stages by adding absorbing areas to the pylons that supported the inlet spikes and to certain areas on the spikes and the interior of the nacelles were investigated. Plastic nacelle rims were tested on a one-eighth scale nacelle and then discarded because they would not be strong enough. The leading edges of the nacelles had to be made of metal, and so both the inside and outside surfaces were strong scatterers. Radar wave energy could enter the nacelles and be attenuated or it could scatter from the rims outside.

Reduction of backscattering from the exhaust outlets would require a different approach.

That Fateful Meeting

"Chance favours the prepared mind"
—*Louis Pasteur*

In the late summer of 1959, I attended a meeting with several CIA, U.S. Air Force, and Lockheed people. The attendees included Dr. Richard Bissell, Kelly Johnson, L. D. MacDonald, and Melvin George.

The purpose of the meeting was to review our A-12 aircraft design proposal and to discuss the Customer's concerns.

There was considerable apprehension about the echoes from the nacelle exhaust outlets. The exhaust pipes were sixty inches in diameter, so they returned large amounts of energy at all frequencies of interest and over large angles to the rear.

A critical problem arose when the question of preventing echoes from the engine exhaust outlets was addressed. We knew that the only way to prevent such echoes was, in effect, to close the apertures. It was impractical to incorporate absorbing structures within the tail pipes.

We had done some scaled model tests using metallic screens of several different shapes that showed promise, but we were not enthusiastic about using screens of any shape or material.

After reviewing our scaled model backscatter reduction data during the meeting, there was a discussion about how to reduce the radar echo from the huge exhaust outlets.

Dr. Bissell seemed discouraged about the chances for success. He was so concerned about the problem that he considered abandoning the project.

Suddenly I thought of a solution. I suggested that we could put something in the fuel that would be ionized by the high exhaust gas temperatures and thereby absorb or scatter the radar energy.

My first proposal was to use cesium because, in vapor form, it has the lowest first ionization potential of all the chemical elements and therefore would be the best source of free electrons that would do the absorption and scattering required.

That suggestion was endorsed heartily by several of the Customer's consultants; one of the physicists actually stood up and exclaimed, "That's it!" There was a lot of excitement, and an enthusiastic discussion ensued.

Mel told me later that Kelly Johnson exclaimed that my suggestion may have saved the program.

Within about a week, in August of 1959, the CIA awarded a contract to design the A-12. Production of real prototype aircraft was contingent upon demonstrating a sufficiently low RCS signature by January 1960.

Subsequently, I received several generous bonuses.

A-12 RCS Full-scale Demonstration

We had five months to demonstrate that the RCS of our proposed A-12 aircraft was achievable under full-scale range testing conditions before we could receive a contract to design and build prototype aircraft. The first task was to build a full-scale mockup of the A-12 aircraft.

In the fall of 1959, we abandoned the idea of testing at the Indian Springs AFB facility. We needed a test facility that was much more secure, and where we could adequately measure a large, low radar cross section target.

Mac and I were asked to find a place to perform A-12 mockup radar backscatter tests. We visited Randsburg Wash at NAWS where the Navy had two very tall wooden towers spaced about one hundred feet apart so that radar targets could be suspended high above the rock strewn sandy earth. They reminded me of the similar arrangement that I had seen at China Lake during my work on rocket firing from aircraft at NOTS in 1943.

While we were there, they were testing a special gun mounted on a vehicle that ran on a railroad track and shot at real aircraft suspended between the towers. I saw the damage that one shot caused to a B-17 bomber. The shell entered the tail cone and went through the windshields after destroying much of the interior. I recognized the man in charge who had been an officer at NOTS when I was there. He did not seem to remember me.

We decided that we could not use their facility because it would be impossible to accurately measure radar backscatter from our mockup. The secrecy required could not be maintained. The towers were visible from Highway 395.

Ray Goudy flew Kelly Johnson, Richard Bissell, and Frank Rodgers to Watertown in Area 51 to select a site on which to build a new facility to do radar backscatter testing of the A-12 mockup.

Kelly did not like the area that Rodgers pointed out because of piles of rubble and uneven terrain. He looked West over to the dry lake, pointed, and said, "Locate the pole out there, a mile away." And lo, it came to pass!

A new, and much better, facility was established at Groom Lake in Area 51 of the Atomic Energy Commission (AEC) reservation north of Las Vegas, Nevada.

Visit to a German Laboratory

Sometime during 1959, I went to Germany with Doctor Edgar Kutcher, who had been a German infrared expert during World War II. I remember that the first morning as we left our Frankfurt hotel (before my coffee had done its work) being surprised to see so many Volkswagen automobiles!

We visited a secret laboratory in Heidelberg to observe some specimens of wideband microwave absorbers and their testing facility.

Their designs were intended for high frequencies whereas we were interested mostly in low-frequency absorbers to be incorporated into the A series aircraft. I decided that their excellent designs were too complicated and would be very difficult to produce in the quantities that we were expecting to require.

Their test facility, a single small room, seemed rather meager, although it was similar to others that I had seen.

During World War II, the Germans had attempted to reduce the radar signatures of the conning towers and periscopes of their submarine boats by using a coating containing magnetic materials. Their coatings may have been precursors to what we developed into our materials that were applied to some areas of the A-12 and SR-71 aircraft and covered most of the F-117 aircraft. We put approximately 1,500 pounds of it on each F-117 aircraft. Donald Bronsol was our expert who instructed the technicians who installed the material.

Building the Full-scale Mockup

Using the basic design of the A-12 aircraft configuration defined in the proposal, a full-scale mockup of the complete aircraft was designed and built in Burbank. The structure was basically an aluminum foil covered wooden shape supported by internal steel bracing. The mockup was designed to be mounted upside down upon a suitable support to emulate operational conditions. It would be illuminated by real radars.

The original absorber scheme required alternate metallic and absorbing wedges disposed along the length of the chines and around the periphery of the wings. It was built using triangular metallic structures that we called "teeth," interdigitated with lossy foam wedges for absorption.

A large amount of special low-temperature absorber materials whose characteristics were not yet completely specified would be required.

We set up our own absorber factory in Burbank. Special machines were designed and built to impregnate polyurethane foam slabs with semi-conducting paints.

The processing details quickly were worked out, and a large amount of mattress material disappeared into Building 82. Then it was delivered to Building 199. ADP aero engineer Harris Anderson told me that he had heard a rumor that management was preparing bedding so that people could live-in if a strike occurred! That seemed like a typical "cover story" promulgated by security people.

After the foam was impregnated and dried, it was tested in the laboratory to verify its absorbance, and then it was shaped and installed in the mockup.

The original machinery assembled to aid the impregnation process was known as "The Hucky-puk Machine" because shop supervisor David Darbyshire had referred to the absorber as "Hucky-puk." This equipment was able to accommodate foam slabs four inches thick, two feet wide, and four feet long.

The process consisted of immersing the foam in a pan of graphite paint, kneading it by gloved hand, and wringing the excess out. The wringer closely resembled an old-fashioned hand-operated clothes wringer. After wringing, it was dried in air in a low-temperature oven.

To increase the rate of production, a more sophisticated machine was designed and built by ADP that processed foam slabs four inches thick, four feet wide, and eight feet long. It was automated to the extent that it would impregnate the foam, wring out the excess, and deliver a foam slab ready for oven drying. It was adjustable to aid in controlling the density of the loading. Additional control was obtained by adjusting the contents of the impregnant solution. Mel was alleged to have a secret catalyst, his pipe ashes!

The new machine was dubbed "The Licorice Noodle Machine," probably by engineer Leroy English.

While it was being demonstrated to Kelly Johnson, a "terrible accident" occurred. Kelly got too close to the wringer and a large blob of black stuff flew onto the front of his shirt. Kelly may have exclaimed something like "My new white shirt is ruined!" Expecting to hear an explosive expletive, Mel George and Willard Bigelow were too shocked to notice that the shirt might have shown slight signs of wear. Kelly did have a sense of humor, and he knew how to use it!

The electrical properties of the foams were judged, as a basis for process control, by measuring the direct-current resistivity of each slab. The resistivity was correlated with attenuation, in decibels per meter, obtained by measurements in a standard rectangular waveguide using S-Band frequencies.

After some polyurethane foam had been processed and tested, the results were plotted and tracked very well along a reasonable empirically derived curve. When some data deviated greatly from the expected values, an investigation revealed that some polyether foam had been processed. Its impregnation characteristics were very different from those of polyurethane.

To produce the same amount of attenuation in a given thickness, the polyether foam had to have a bulk direct current resistivity much less than that of polyurethane. Since large quantities of polyether foam had been ordered for use in the full-scale mockup, the amount of commercially available graphite-containing paint had to be increased greatly. The extent of the loading of the foam was readjusted to compensate for the impregnation characteristics of the foam and production continued.

The lossy foam was cut into the shapes needed by two different methods. One was band sawing using a "bread-knife" blade that was sinusoidally serrated. The other used a "bucksaw" with an electrically heated wire instead of a saw blade.

After the initial large amount of cutting and shaping the material, the electric foam cutter was used very little and the shop air smelled much better!

The foam absorbers were installed in the mockup and covered by layers of TD paper to supply surface attenuation. To provide as gentle as possible an electrical transition from space to metal, we employed different numbers of layers of TD paper. In particular, one layer was employed from the leading edge back and additional layers were added at increments of distance from the leading edge. As many as eight layers were used. The equivalent conductivity of the chine surface treatment increased in steps as the radar waves approached the metal. This arrangement was known as "tapering" the resistivity or the attenuation. Optimum tapering was important to provide the greatest attenuation over the broadest frequency spectrum.

Sometimes the loading, and therefore the attenuation, of the foam sections was tapered by inserting pieces with differing bulk conductivities. In many cases it was necessary to taper both the bulk loading and the surface treatment to optimize the absorption over the greatest frequency range. Most of the tests and changes were done using the full-scale mockup.

While the full-scale model was being designed and built, a considerable amount of testing of absorbers and reduced-scale models was performed in Burbank. Both backscattering measurements in the anechoic chamber and attenuation measurements in waveguides were accomplished. Five different gradations of attenuating foam were established and used as standards.

Originally it was hoped that the full-scale mockup could be configured with treated chines on only one side, but that was not to be. Tests utilizing a short cylindrical section of the fuselage with only one chine showed that if the impinging radar waves were polarized with their electric fields perpendicular to a chine edge that "creeping waves" would encircle the cylinder and return to the radar. A second chine was required to allow the waves that followed the surface to be attenuated and escape to continue away from the radar.

After I had suggested that the outlets could be shielded by making the engine exhaust plumes electrically conductive, an effort was launched to determine the feasibility of the scheme.

The method I suggested consisted of injecting an easily ionizable substance such as potassium, sodium, or cesium into the fuel itself, into the fuel at the nozzles, or into the exhaust stream. Cesium seemed to be the material of choice because in the gaseous state it is the most easily ionized. However, at that time it seemed worthwhile to test the others. The expectation was that sufficient numbers of electrons would be liberated and remain free long enough to be effective.

Dr. Bissell's group went back home and discussed it. Pratt and Whitney and Lincoln Labs personnel reviewed the meeting notes, and the two groups met in Florida. I believe that Dr. George Valley of the MIT Lincoln Laboratory was an important member of the group. I attended that meeting.

A theoretical study of the thermal ionization of these materials by the exhaust gases revealed that it should be feasible so several substances were chosen to be tested. Until measurement results were available we would simulate the effect of the ionization by installing short plugs into the mockup's exhaust pipes.

Shortly after that meeting I went to the Pratt and Whitney research center near Jupiter, Florida, to initiate some ionization tests. There I met and conferred with George Armbruster, William Brown, William Cassady, Norman Cotter, Edward Esmeir, and Harley Nethken.

Mr. Nethken and I planned several tests and I returned to Burbank to gather some special test equipment and ship it to P&W.

Groom Lake Facility

While the mockup was being designed and built, the supporting structure for the Groom Lake outdoor testing was designed, fabricated, and put into place.

Leon Gavette, an ADP engineer, designed the rotator mechanism for use in supporting and rotating the mockup. It was an "azimuth-over-elevation" tiltable rotator device that was mounted upon the end of the elevator shaft. It was designed to lift 20,000 pounds and be usable in winds up to twenty-five knots, or twenty-nine miles per hour. Shear pins were incorporated that were designed to break under the forces caused by strong gusts or winds over thirty-five knots (forty mph), allowing the mockup to weather vane without serious damage. Kelly Johnson also wanted to be able to test exhaust ionization using an after-burning F-94-C aircraft on it! He said it had the loudest afterburner that he ever had heard.

That structure was capable of raising the mockup and positioning it as we desired for testing. The mockup would be mounted upside down on the tilting mechanism and the entire assembly was elevated fifty feet above a concrete pad and then rotated in azimuth. It could be rotated continuously in either direction for as long as desired.

The elevator shaft was installed in the center of a 102-foot diameter concrete pad provided for the backscatter measurement site. Its upper end could be made flush with the surface of the concrete pad so that the cart carrying a test item could be rolled directly over it to facilitate attachment to or removal from the rotator. I have no idea if or why the pad was 102 feet in diameter.

All the test specimens could be raised sixty feet above the pad on this pole.

Controls for the hydraulic system used to raise or lower the elevator pole were inside a sub-surface chamber off to one side of the shaft. Duplicate controls for tilting or rotating the model also were available in the chamber. Another set of rotation or tilt controls was in the control building a mile away. The chamber also could be used as a personnel shelter during cold, windy weather. An anemometer and a wind direction weather vane were located near the edge of the pad away from the Line of Sight (LOS).

Other contractors built or installed the buildings, the diagnostic radars and ancillary equipment, and the special facilities at each of two measurement sites on the dry bed of Groom Lake.

Specially designed diagnostic radars, located in a building a mile away on the dry lake bed, illuminated the targets and processed the reflectivity data. This facility was put into operation in November of 1959. Part of December 1959 was devoted to testing the equipment and performing field strength surveys near the pole. Initial operation in 1959 was on S-Band.

RCS Testing

The full-scale mockup was transported to Groom Lake in late 1959. The model had to be housed in a hangar on the base that was at least a mile away. It was carried out and back on a special cart.

Soviet spy satellites that we called "Ash Cans" were known to pass over at certain times, so we could not expose our tests. This caused many trips out and back.

The full-scale A-12 mockup was unavoidably slightly flexible and could stand only mild accelerations, so the control system was designed to prevent large starting and stopping accelerations. This and the limited pumping capacity were some of the reasons it took eighteen minutes to raise or lower the mockup to or from the maximum elevation. A complete rotation of the full-scale mockup required at least six minutes.

The minimum total time required to raise, rotate, and lower the mockup usually was greater than forty-five minutes. This would have reduced the testing time too much so changes to the elevated mockup sometimes were accomplished by using a "cherry picker" crane to lift men and materials to the required site.

Backscatter from the elevator shaft was reduced by means of a special shield that resembled a doubly tapered aircraft wing. It was a "clam shell" that was hinged at the leading edge so it could be opened to surround the shaft and then be pulled up into place and closed when the model was elevated. It closed around the pole when it went up and opened when it was lowered. Absorber pads were employed to reduce reflections from the rotator itself.

As far as I know, that was the first time that a streamlined shield was used to hide a model support pole. L. D. MacDonald and I did the rough sketch preliminary design, but I do not know who did the actual design and made it work.

When the real aircraft would be flying at its cruising altitude, the angle of the line of sight from the aircraft to the horizon was about four degrees downward. Therefore all backscattering patterns were measured using angles of tilt between four and fifteen degrees. By tilting the rotator, the equivalent of constant elevation angle backscatter patterns could be obtained.

Fifteen degrees of tilt was chosen as a limit because field strength surveys in the vicinity of the pole showed that the nose of the aircraft still would be well illuminated by the radars, so good measurements could be accomplished. Fifteen degrees of depression from the aircraft at cruising altitude would correspond to a ground distance of about fifty miles. At the A-12's speed, the aircraft would be over the observer in ninety seconds, hopefully too little time to react.

The "railroad" system tested at Indian Springs AFB was fully implemented at Groom Lake.

A second facility for testing smaller, typically one-eighth scale models and special shapes, was installed one-half of a mile from the radar control building in line with the facility at one mile. The model support was a conical air-inflated cloth bag about twenty-two feet long. The early version, "the old bag," had several straight seams. The improved design, just "the bag," employed spiraled seams to reduce backscatter from the seams.

A large conducting sphere used for radar calibration was located in a pit near the halfway site. It was mounted on a tiltable boom that was raised for calibration and lowered during measurements.

There were two different designs of calibration targets. One was a conducting sphere three feet in diameter, and the other was a similar sphere with an octant corner reflector built in.

Full scale and eighth-scale backscattering measurements continued at the Groom Lake facility for several years.

During September and October, while the full-scale mockup was being built, a one-eighth scale model of the A-12 had been built and sent to Indian Springs AFB for testing. Among the tests were the effects of tilting the rudders, effect of asymmetrical chines, engine inlet tests, exhaust outlet tests, effects of fillets between nacelles and inboard wing surfaces, and characteristics of the basic configuration without engine nacelles. Probably L. D. MacDonald and Ernest E. "Jack" Hanson should be credited with the idea of tilting the rudders fifteen degrees inboard. Tilting the rudders also improved the flying qualities of the real aircraft, particularly during turns.

Sometimes it was feasible to test smaller models on the Groom Lake short range while alterations were accomplished on the full-scale mockup or to substitute other test specimens if the full-scale rework was extensive.

In the first week of January 1960,[65] I discovered that, despite the inverted mounting of the complete mockup, there were paths by which energy could be scattered downward from the mockup, reflected upward by the concrete pad, and then re-scattered back to the radar. These reflections seriously interfered with the backscattering diagnostic measurements. They were identified when I noticed that some reflection phase centers (apparent points of origin) did not fall within the aircraft planform drawing when they were plotted from "railroad" data. Many of these interfering reflections, which became known as "spooks," were larger than those intrinsic to the mockup.

At first I suggested that tilted mirrors, aluminum sheets on wooden racks that we could make quickly, be used to scatter these spurious echoes away. When we obtained Hairflex absorbing material, it became standard procedure to cover the area of the concrete pad underneath the mockup with movable slabs of the absorbing material. Each time the mockup was lowered, it was necessary to remove them and then replace them before the next measurement.

An unintended benefit of the Hairflex absorbers was elimination of infrared shadows of the planform of the vehicle being tested that could have been detected by the Soviet satellites.

After the spurious returns were eliminated, backscattering measurements were resumed. A large amount of encouraging data was accumulated using this mockup.

In late January 1960, the approval to produce a quantity of these aircraft was received.

The A-12 OXCART

OXCART was the CIA code name for the aircraft that was to become the first able to cruise three times the speed of sound at nearly nineteen miles above the earth.

We had demonstrated with the full-scale mockup that the required A-12 RCS signature level could be attained using low temperature materials and substitutes for surface details that the real aircraft would have.

Before the contract to begin the design of prototype aircraft was received, several important design decisions already had been made. One of them was to use a titanium alloy because it could withstand high temperatures and weighed slightly more than half the weight of stainless steels. Kelly was adamant about reduction of weight because of its effect upon the altitude and the distance the aircraft could fly.

He sent a memo to engineers concerning weight reduction.[66] Although he was serious about weight reduction, his sense of humor shows in my copy.

10-11-60   C O P Y

WEIGHT PERFORMANCE CONTRACT

In accordance with our agreement made 2:35 P.M., Tuesday, Oct. 11, 1960,

I am asking each and every engineer to save at least ten (10) pounds of empty

weight by Tuesday, Oct. 26, 1960. Please fill out the data below and turn in to

Merv Heal by that date. It is acceptable for groups of up to five to make joint

returns (10# apiece or more, of course!).

Name:_____   Date:_____

Weight Reduction Means:

Weight Saved_____   Checked:_____
                                                  (Merv Heal)

Technical Approval:_____
                   (Boehme, Combs, Martin or me)

I'm sure glad you all agree that this is a splendid idea!

                              (signed)   Clarence L. Johnson

P.S. Resignation forms available to all non-conformists
      in my office!

Kelly's A-12 Weight Memo

From the beginning of the design of the aircraft, attention was given to the openings in the aircraft surface required for various reasons. Conductive coatings and screens were investigated for the cockpit windows, camera windows, air outlets, and antenna windows.

Waveguide beyond cut-off filters were designed to mitigate air outlet effects. One of the early solutions to the reduction of backscatter from openings (any sudden change in shape or electrical properties causes reflected waves) such as air outlets was my suggestion to use metal "egg-crate" assemblies of such size and depth that their openings acted as "waveguides beyond cut-off" and therefore, as though they were electrically closed. This idea was tested originally on partial models in the anechoic chamber and later retested and verified on the full-scale mockup. When the A-12 aircraft was built, several air outlets incorporated the egg-crate design.

The majority of our time was spent working on the chines, magnetic materials, antennas, engine inlets, and outlets. External RCS features were designed to withstand minus sixty to eight hundred degrees Fahrenheit and maintain strength for many hours of operation.

The low temperatures could be experienced during refueling. The high temperatures were typically encountered during high altitude, high speed flight.

Chines

Immediately after the contract was won, we continued to use the mockup and low-temperature materials to evolve the chine RCS design.

The interior absorber of the mockup chine had been loaded foam. Our initial investigation into high-temperature materials revealed that the bulk material would have to be a honeycomb, rather than foam. Ceramic foam was considered and rejected because it probably would not stand up to the A-12's flexing and vibration. Honeycomb was a better structural solution, and the CIA would make asbestos honeycomb available to us. Honeycomb would have a different effect on the RCS signature, so the chine design would need to be revisited using the low-temperature mockup.

Jim Herron and I designed a very large waveguide slotted line facility for testing large samples of materials using low frequencies. It was built in three sections, a coaxial cable to waveguide adaptor, a slotted waveguide measurement section, and a detachable sample holder. The entire assembly was mounted upon rails to allow easy separation.

The waveguide assembly was twenty-four inches high, forty-eight inches wide, and thirty feet long. It was designed to be used at any frequency between 125 MHz and 250 MHz.

Work was started on honeycomb using graphite-coated phenolic and graphite-coated polyester-fiberglass. Graduated loading of the honeycomb was achieved by dipping it into the colloidal graphite suspension multiple times to decreasing depths. The low-temperature loading technique was very successful and later was adapted to the manufacture of the high-temperature materials.

We had been in a rush to demonstrate the A-12 RCS performance. A large quantity of TD paper was left over from the U-2 work, and it was the only material available. We used it for our chine surface treatment despite its inconsistent resistive properties.

A much superior form of surface treatment was developed by Lockheed. Mel George's people sprayed semi-conducting paint of controlled, graduated conductivities, one layer over another, on a Mylar or fiberglass substrate. This tapered material again was referred to as TP. It was similar to Lockheed material that had been used during the U-2 RCS reduction efforts. Most of the scaled models and partial models were covered by variations of TP.

"Pre-preg" fiberglass cloth had to be cleaned before they coated it. The material would be left hanging in a paint booth over night to dry for the next day. One day I decided that it needed something attention-getting. I cut a sheet of butcher paper and sprayed it with red paint, cut it to shape and hung it alongside the fiberglass. The next day Mel was quite perturbed when he saw a pair of "long johns" on the line! He knew who did it, of course.

After much testing, it was determined that a logarithmic progression from 2,000 ohms per square to about 125 ohms per square in the direction of wave propagation represented a good transition between free space and the highly conducting surfaces of the metallic teeth and aircraft's skin.

After optimizing the chine design for low temperatures, we began to obtain or develop electrically equivalent high temperature materials that could be used in the A-12 aircraft.

Conducting paints, graphite-coated asbestos honeycomb, and graphite-coated asbestos sheets were developed along with materials and assemblies that could withstand large temperature fluctuations.

The high-temperature materials employed were basically asbestos, silicone elastomer, and graphite. ADP chemists developed all the paint formulations. There were several combinations of graphite, graphite and silver flakes, and inert carbon in a silicone elastomer. The highest conductivity paint, using mostly silver flakes, was used for antenna counterpoises (ground planes), lightning protection arc gaps, and for a few special bonding situations. Several other paints of different conductivities were used to provide surface attenuation.

A cosmetic, non-conducting black paint using black copper oxide was developed to cover the aircraft uniformly. It also significantly helped to cool the aircraft because of its high emissivity for the far infrared wavelengths.

The first two OXCART prototypes were built and flown with the teeth chine design. Some scaled model work by Hansen and MacDonald in June of 1961 indicated clearly that the low-frequency echoes could be reduced significantly by replacing the tooth-like structure with parallel chine frames. Also it was decided that the fuselage chines should be utilized to house aircraft systems, payload cabinets, and camera and antenna windows. The chines were redesigned as hollow structures and eventually became relatively thin slabs of absorbing materials, approximately one inch thick, supported by metallic structures. All subsequent A-12 and its derivatives utilized toothless chines.

A great deal of testing of the details of fabrication of the various absorber parts was performed so that, finally, almost the entire periphery of the aircraft was made of nonmetallic parts containing carefully disposed resistive materials whose radar wave absorptivity and excellent mechanical properties have contributed greatly to the success of the SR-71 type aircraft.

Anti-radar treatments compatible with manufacturing techniques were developed, especially methods of joining plastic to metal parts. As a result, most of the plastic parts survived the high-temperature environment for many times their original design lifetimes of twenty hours. In fact, the durability of the plastic parts has been superior to that of some of their associated metal parts.

Magnetic Materials

During the early part of 1960, the ADP group led by Mel George did considerable work on the use of ferrite materials as microwave absorbers. Dr. Dale Grimes of the University of Michigan served us briefly, and well, as a ferrite consultant.

Ferrites were of great interest to the Customer because of their hope that they could provide good low-frequency attenuation* with

---

* Ferrite materials exhibit a phenomenon called "dispersion," which means that their constitutive parameters (magnetic permeability and loss and reasonable weight and thickness and, also, could operate in the hot tail pipe to reduce S-Band reflections.

ADP made many samples of ferrites of different compositions, using different combinations of the leading metallic ions in combination with the ferrite radical. Some of the test specimens were smooth vitreous coatings on flat stainless steel sheets. Others were molded toroids of rectangular cross section for use in low frequency coaxial "slotted-line" measurements and some were pyramidal shapes that were mounted on flat metal plates.

A minor mishap occurred when someone set a curing oven temperature too high and melted a batch of pyramids. Their "bowed heads" surprised all of us.

Backscattering measurements of ferrite materials mounted on metal plates were performed in the anechoic chamber using mostly S-Band frequencies. Coaxial measurement equipment was designed and developed to allow reflection coefficient (in terms of VSWR) measurements over the temperature range from -60 degrees to 550 degrees Fahrenheit. Frequencies used in the coaxial measurements mostly were between 50 MHz and 1 GHz, although some measurements in co-ax were attempted using S-Band frequencies.

Lithium ferrites performed best over the greatest frequency range and temperature range. None of the ferrites tested had significant effects on backscattering above about 150 MHz.

The hoped-for absorption never was achieved with practical configurations. After a moderate amount of testing, we discarded ferrites and began work on a different kind of magnetic absorber. Ferrites never were applied to any of the A-12, R-12, YF-12, SR-71, D-21, Have Blue, or F-117 aircraft.

A magnetic field absorber using mostly powdered carbonyl iron in a dielectric resin binder was investigated. The result was an extremely thixotropic slurry that later congealed into a mass of iron particles held together and insulated from each other by the binder.

During the early low-temperature development, the binder was a lacquer. It was replaced by a silicone elastomer because it could be used over a large temperature range and particularly at sufficiently high

---

electric permittivity and loss) change with frequency. In practical terms, this means that their desirable properties were too narrow banded but tended to favor the lowest frequencies with which we were concerned.

temperatures. The result was a special magnetic absorbing material that was thin and aerodynamically smooth, could stand very wide temperature variations and large sound-induced vibration amplitudes, was easy to install, and was effective in absorbing a broad spectrum of radar waves.

A number of different shapes and sizes of iron and iron oxide particles were investigated. Some mixtures of iron and iron oxide, with and without graphite, were tried. It was determined that an overcoating of very small aluminum flakes could be used to tune the layer to attenuate more over a narrow bandwidth than would the uncoated material. However, the aluminum over-coating could not be made to adhere reliably to the silicone elastomer, so it never was used on real aircraft treatments.

Two different methods for application of this material were developed: spraying a thixotropic paint-like mixture and cementing preformed sheets in place. In sheet form it was known as C-138. The sheets typically were four one-hundredths of an inch thick. I always wanted to tell Mel that the "C" stood for "Concoction."

Mel tested a piece of this material by hanging a sample of it off the stern of his boat in Marina Del Mar. I have no idea how long it was there, but the test appears to have been very successful, because nothing happened to it.

The new material that became known as "Iron Paint" (or as "Iron Blankets" when used in sheet form) was almost literally that: it was about 80 percent, by weight, of magnetic particles, carbonyl iron, and ferric oxide in a dielectric binder.

The Iron Paint was mechanically thin but acted as though it was electrically much thicker. It operated by concentrating both the electric and magnetic field components of a wave that was passing parallel to the metallic aircraft's skin. This caused the wave to slow down and fall over into the magnetic surface. The magnetic material dissipated energy as the wave tried to propagate through it. Also, there was some slight absorption of energy directly from the electric field component because the dielectric loss extracted energy from the partially trapped guided waves.

The material's effectiveness near normal incidence decreased with decreasing material thickness. Because of the material's weight, we needed to use thin layers of the magnetic absorber. It was most effective for frequencies greater than about 2 GHz and for near grazing angles well away from normal.

Edward Lovick, Jr.

Extensive testing of this absorber was performed in the anechoic chamber using flat plates and on the outdoor range using the full-scale mockup.

The magnetic absorber was sprayed on a number of small critical areas on the A-12 aircraft. Because of weight, installation problems, and electrical properties (wave impedance, especially near grazing incidence), the iron/silicone mixtures were investigated and used only in relatively thin layers upon metal substrates. It exhibited remarkable service life under difficult conditions.

Iron blankets never were flown on the A-12. There was no known adhesive that could withstand the high temperatures encountered. Preformed sheets were glued onto the mockup and special test items.

Iron Paint became very useful later on when it was used to improve isolation among antennas aboard aircraft.

I liked to tease Mel George occasionally because he reacted like and reminded me of my brother. He sometimes was surprised when I occasionally said something about a chemical subject. An electronics physicist was not expected to know much about chemistry, so I tried to not reveal my limitations too often.

One time, after a discussion about "Zwitter ions," I remarked that the source of the skunk odor was butyl mercaptan. He was startled and skeptical.

Mercaptans are alcohols that have been modified by replacing carbon atoms by sulfur atoms. They are among the most malodorous substances known.

His reaction gave me the idea that we should have a sign over his chemistry laboratory doors proclaiming "THE BUTYL MERCAPTAN WORKS."

Greg Hill, who worked in the antenna laboratory, asked one of our experimental mechanics to make and install the sign, much to Mel's chagrin!

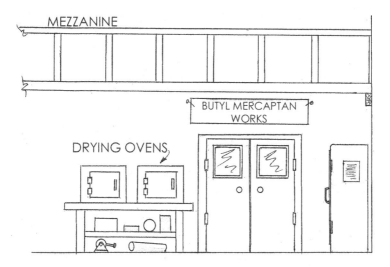

THE SIGN over the Chemistry Laboratory Doors

That sign was still there in Building 199 in 1983 when I toured the antenna and materials laboratories with a recently hired engineer, Sherre Love. Mel George was still chomping on his pipe stem about it, too.

Antennas

During this time, the early 1960s, antenna design and placement became a major endeavor and much radiation pattern as well as backscatter testing took place. Antennas were designed to be as effective as possible while, simultaneously, reflecting the minimum of radar energy.

A considerable part of the antenna design testing occurred in the Burbank anechoic chamber. In the beginning the various communications, navigation, instrument landing, and special purpose antennas were located on the basis of estimated performance and, later, that performance was tested by radiation pattern measurements in the chamber.

Backscattering measurements on the full-scale mockup and twelfth scale models were performed at Groom Lake to confirm the effects of the various antennas and some of the measures used to reduce their scattering. Fortunately, most of them required little modification or relocation.

The UHF Communication antenna was designed from the start by Jim Herron to be extended when needed and retracted during high

145

speed flight. It was the only antenna ever allowed to protrude outside the aerodynamic contours of the A-12 series aircraft.

Part of the fun of working in the antenna laboratory was the unusual odd jobs that would require us to improvise test setups and equipment to complete.

We wanted to measure the dielectric constants of gases. After some thought, I proposed that we line the interior of the small anechoic chamber with a thin plastic sheet, fill the chamber with gas, and then measure through the gas and sheet. Mike Ash, Jim Herron, and I did this, and it was very effective.

One of the most important aspects of the antenna design effort was finding or adapting materials, especially insulators, solders, sealants, and paints, which would withstand the high temperatures expected during high-speed flight.

Manufacturing methods for high-temperature absorbers, conducting surface paints, and highly conducting paints for special applications were continuing as subjects for development.

The electronic and the materials groups, together, developed quality and tolerance control methods for testing both mockup and flyable parts.

Engine Inlets

There were some areas, particularly inside the nacelle inlets as well as the titanium nacelle rims and outside surfaces, that required special treatment to reduce reflections. To cope with these problems, several different possibilities were investigated.

Ferrite materials were studied by Mel and his chemists. They made a number of different kinds and configurations. However, the results were not adequate, and there was considerable apprehension about engine damage if the material was dislodged, even from the outside of the nacelle rims. The inside of the inlet lip and the nacelle exteriors were left untreated by RCS reduction materials.

During the fall of 1961, other methods for shielding the engine inlets and the nacelle rims were investigated. Consideration was given to ablating materials on the tips of the spikes. My proposal that a stream of fuel with an ionizable additive could be sprayed from the spike tips was discussed privately among ADP personnel and discarded. High electric field electron emission from the spike tips was considered briefly.

During a conference about what could be done to reduce the backscatter from the engine inlets caused by the necessary titanium leading edges of the nacelles, I suggested that it could be possible to project streams of electrons into the air ahead of the inlet cones to ionize the air and absorb and scatter the radar energy. I envisioned something resembling a television electron gun, the part in a cathode ray tube that projects the electron stream.

I pointed out the fact that when electrons collide with molecules in the air, X-rays would occur[†] and that shielding might be needed to protect the pilot.

Someone asked how we could align the electron beams with the small holes in the aircraft's skin so I said, "Don't worry. The electrons will burn holes!" Sometimes I wondered if they really would!

The Customer approved the idea, and initiated a program codenamed Kempster.

Westinghouse X-ray engineers were consulted and preliminary tests were performed in their laboratory. The results were encouraging.

RCS testing of the possible effects of the idea was performed at Groom Lake. The eighth-scale A-12 model was equipped with assemblies of lossy foam nicknamed "puff balls" that simulated an estimated relative size, shape, and attenuation that might reasonably be attained. The basic data used to estimate the cloud parameters was obtained by measurements in the Westinghouse laboratory. Again, the test results were encouraging.

Westinghouse engineers built a moderately high-powered electron gun designed to operate, not in vacuum, but in air at the low pressures encountered at cruise altitude. The interior of the gun assembly was evacuated to a lower than ambient pressure, but still contained some air.

The original design used 100,000 volts for the electron acceleration and was to supply a beam current of 20 miliamperes. It required 25 KW to produce the 2 KW electron beam. The unit weighed about three hundred pounds. A flyable Kempster unit was completed in November of 1962.

Before extensive work was to be done to produce Kempster equipment, a simple in-flight test was performed by projecting the

---

[†]   "Bremsstrahlung" radiation (braking radiation, or in this case, X-rays).

electron gun's beam downward into the air ahead of an UHF radio antenna mounted on the bottom of an A-12 aircraft. The Kempster unit was installed in the "Q-Bay" (Equipment Bay). A tone-modulated signal was transmitted from the antenna. I do not remember the test frequency but it may have been about 225 MHz, the lowest frequency in the military communications band.

The electron gun was turned on and off periodically while the aircraft was flown toward a receiving station on the ground. The signal was reduced each time the gun was turned on, so the concept was considered verified and development of the production version was begun.

Kempster was the name of the prototype unit. The production design was called "La Croix," named for Westinghouse lead engineer Benjamin La Croix.

Because of the high power required to produce a sufficient number of high-energy electrons, and the limited amount of power available aboard the aircraft, it was decided that the electron beam would have to be turned on and off intermittently. Electron plasmas become transparent to waves whose frequency is greater than a "critical" frequency related to the electron density. During pulses RCS reduction probably could be accomplished only for the low radar frequencies up to about 175 MHz, high enough to defeat the Soviet "Tall King" early warning radars.

Lockheed engineer Donald Bunce was assigned the task of designing the installation of a Kempster unit in an A-12 aircraft. The most obvious result was the "Bunce Bump" on the upper surface of the port side chine. Sometimes it was called the "Bunce Lump" which became the "Blump."

Backscattering measurements showed that, for the test conditions, several decibels of improvement might be obtained. The tests were performed to estimate the reduction for 70 MHz and 170 MHz. There was no expectation that significant improvement would occur at high frequencies such as S-Band because the electron density required could not be attained.

In January of 1963, some additional tests of the estimated Kempster clouds were performed on the eighth-scale model A-12 because new information from Westinghouse seemed to describe them better. Unfortunately, the cloud shapes and sizes were scaled up from model tests in static air so the real shapes may never be known.

There was some anxiety about the generation of X-rays when electrons were stopped by neutral molecules. Since it was reported that a blob approximately twenty-five feet in diameter with a much more intense central core of roughly ten feet diameter which could produce X-radiation capable of penetrating the aircraft's skin would be expected, some X-ray shielding tests were planned. However, they were not performed until early August.

One Kempster gun was mounted in the Q-bay of Aircraft SN125, projecting its beam straight down. X-ray tests were conducted in a Groom Lake hangar by moving a portable inspection unit, pointed at the cockpit, on a twelve foot radius and sixty-four inches below the Kempster opening. The Westinghouse engineers used an Andrex unit to simulate the 150 KV design of the La Croix source.

The pilot's normal equipment was in place and did contribute a small amount of X-ray shielding but a need for more was indicated.

On the basis of these tests, sheet lead shielding about 1 millimeter thick was applied to the pilot's seat and some other areas in 1963. This thickness was capable of attenuating 150KV X-radiation by about a factor of ten.

A Kempster unit was installed in an aircraft and two flight tests were performed during 1964. Although the test configuration was not realistic and the frequency was too high, encouraging results were obtained.

It never was expected that the pilot would be completely shielded so, later on, in 1964, Westinghouse people recommended presumably safe flying schedules based on dose rates, percentage of whole body exposure, and integrated total dose. Our medical officer, C. I. Barron, MD, apparently did not contest their recommendations. He may not have been informed about the tests. Since only very limited flight-testing of this device occurred, there probably was no cause for concern.

It was decided that the shielding required for the more powerful LaCroix unit would be too heavy. I believe that was what ended the program.

The Kempster/La Croix testing was finished, and discontinued, in mid-1965 when one flight test was run.

While the Kempster development work was going on in the Westinghouse laboratory, a plan to test other possible methods for shielding the engine inlets was conceived by Dr. Joel Lawson at SEI, and codenamed Emerald.

Emerald was a cooperative effort involving three groups. In March of 1963, ADP people Mike Ash, Jim Herron, Robert Taron, and me, led by Joel Lawson, performed a series of tests in the supersonic wind tunnel at the Lockheed Rye Canyon Research and Development Center.[‡]

This facility was a blow-down tunnel capable of operating supersonically at high Mach numbers. The blow-down tunnel consisted of a large room that served as a plenum in which air was pumped until a desired pressure was attained, a set of "doors" (valves) that could be opened quickly to allow air to rush through a large tube to a rectangular chamber in which a test specimen would be subjected to the moving air. Special thick glass "Schlieren" windows on opposite sides of the rectangular section were provided for photographing the actions of test specimens.[67]

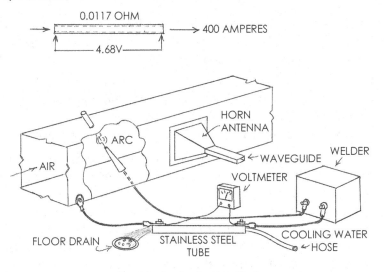

Electric Arc Ionization Test

When we removed the inch-thick glass windows and replaced them with six thin Mylar sheets, three on each side, the wind tunnel operating crew was almost terrified. They feared that objects or we would be sucked into the thin-film covered openings. We noticed that they all hid in the well-protected control room!

---

‡ Renamed in 1983 to Kelly Johnson Research and Development Center, Lockheed-California Company.

Bob Taron seemed skeptical of the entire operation. As things transpired, the only damage that occurred was to some of the Mylar sheets that we had to replace after each test run.

For these tests the tunnel was operated in the supersonic mode, typically three times the speed of sound at altitude (Mach 3). Three different series of tests were conducted.

During the test runs tremendous roaring noise occurred. The whole building seemed to shake and then suddenly there was silence. Each test may have happened in less than a minute, but we were so busy that it seemed much longer.

For one series an arc between carbon electrodes inside a windshield mounted on a "sting" (a typical wind tunnel support) was used as a possible source of electrons. Some of the carbon electrodes contained different additives (i.e., aluminum or copper powder).

An arc-welding machine, operated well over its 400-ampere rating, was used to supply power to the positive carbon electrode via a stainless steel tube one inch in diameter and four feet long. The current was measured by taking advantage of the tube's resistance and measuring the voltage between its ends. Water was run through the tube to cool it, from a water hose into a drain in the floor.

The same machine also was used to supply current for an arc between an aluminum wire and a block of aluminum, and the carbon electrode arc with aluminum powder injected into it. Special injectors were used to introduce the wire and the powder.

Attempts were made to use an S-Band interferometer to determine the properties of the air downstream from the arc.

Special mounts carrying the horn antennas were installed on opposite sides of the tunnel throat. The waveguide circuits were run under the tunnel throat.

Before blow-down the interferometer was nulled by adjusting a phase shifter and an attenuator and the settings were recorded. During the test the operators tried to readjust the interferometer to regain the null. This required fast work under trying conditions, but it was done by Mike Ash and Jim Herron. The changes in attenuation and phase shift were to be used to determine the scattering particle or electron density.

The last test run was the most exciting of all. After the usual noisy event there occurred a series of loud thumps that shook the whole building and almost caused panic! We thought it was an earthquake.

The large valve doors were opening and closing violently. It was determined later that the cause was failure of a vacuum tube in the valve door control system. At least we were not to blame.

The Emerald tests were inconclusive. It was true that the S-Band test frequency was much too high for even a most optimistic estimate of free electron density, but at least some evidence of their presence was expected. Probably the only effect seen was caused by the mere presence of material particles. In any event, the tests were discontinued, and the idea was abandoned.

Engine Exhaust Outlets

Our first tests were performed in April of 1960 by sending microwave energy through the exhaust stream of a J-57 engine running on afterburner on a test stand at P&W in Florida.

The engine test pad was a concrete slab located in a shallow lake. Its surface was about a foot above the water level. I was told that an alligator was accustomed to eating food set out on the pad. Be careful where you leave your lunch or where your feet are! I never saw the alligator, I never lost my lunch, and I have both of my feet!

Measurement of the ionization in the plume required an arrangement of equipment that resembled a simple Wheatstone bridge.

Energy was divided into two waveguide branches. One branch contained two directional couplers, a variable attenuator, and a variable phase shifter. The other branch employed two antennas between which the exhaust stream was located.

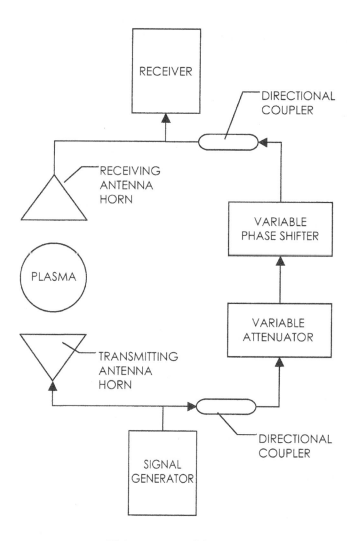

Dielectrometer Schematic

The bridge initially was balanced to result in a null indication in the receiver.

After the ionized exhaust stream was interposed between the antennas, the bridge was rebalanced. The plasma properties then were determined from the changes in attenuation and phase shift.

In order to place our horn antennas as close to the exhaust stream as we could without damage, I held a wooden stick out until it began to smolder and used that as our limit.

We measured the attenuation (loss) and the delay (phase change) caused by the ionization for two very different frequencies, 3 GHz and 10 GHz.

Several measurements were performed at a number of locations along the exhaust stream starting near the outlet. These tests were run almost at sea level, the air was relatively wet and the measurement frequencies were much too high. Even so, we measured appreciable ionization for several diameters downstream. Our first test series utilized a sodium salt as the fuel additive because it was readily available. Potassium salts were used in some subsequent tests.

We were surprised that we observed so much more ionization than we had expected.

The explanation for the more copious free electron production lies in the fact that very much less energy is required to remove an electron from a surface or a cluster of atoms than from a single atom in the gaseous state.

The "work function," a measure of the energy required to release electrons from alkali metals sodium and potassium in the solid state, is approximately half that required to do so from cesium in the gaseous state. The result is a great reduction of the energy required to accomplish ionization.

Also, it is important to notice that the "surface work functions" for sodium, potassium, and cesium essentially are equal so that, in the solid state they are equally effective.

At first I and others involved assumed that the electron donor would be in the gaseous state whereas the experimental results indicated otherwise. A happy result was that a significant reduction of the weight of additive material was attained, and that the exhaust gas temperatures would be adequate.

More controlled physical testing was necessary to determine the relative amounts of particles in the gaseous state or the solid state and the effects of the exhaust gas temperature.

Testing was terminated in Florida and arrangements were made to continue testing in the P&W Willgoos Turbine Laboratory in East Hartford, Connecticut, where much better facilities were available.

The tests in East Hartford were performed in a ten-inch diameter quartz tube to contain the plasma of free electrons and excited atoms, and to allow much better control of the measurement conditions.

Several frequencies, 3 GHz, 6 GHz, 9 GHz, and possibly 21 GHz, were used to aid in determining electron density and the electron-atom collision frequency, the parameters required to calculate the radar-scattering effects.

Again, the results were encouraging, so several special cesium-containing fuel additives were produced and made available for testing in a real A-12 aircraft.

There was a short period in early 1960 during which SEI, Pratt and Whitney, and I tried to calculate the levels of ionization to be expected as a result of injecting special additives into the engine exhaust streams and the effects of that ionization upon radar backscattering. Since there was general independent concurrence that the probability of success was quite high for frequencies below about 175 MHz plans for RCS testing scaled models of the engine and its exhaust were formulated.

The Willgoos test data were used to calculate the electron density and the collision frequency distribution in the exhaust and, from this, to define the shape and length of the equivalent absorber/scatterer to be modeled on the A-12 mockup used for backscatter testing at the Groom Lake facility.

The full-scale RCS mockup was equipped with "plumes" of absorbing materials to simulate the real exhaust plumes. The plumes were simulated by mounting thick Hairflex absorber on wooden structures attached to the exhaust nozzles of the mockup.

RCS tests showed that an additional benefit of the plumes was a slight reduction of the backscatter when the nose of the aircraft was pointed toward the radar. This effect was caused by the simulated ionized exhaust reducing the abruptness of the change in conductivity of the exhaust openings in their transition to space, thereby allowing the radar waves to leave the aft end of the aircraft more easily.

The SEI group in Cambridge continued to work on scaling rules to allow extrapolation of the Willgoos test data to flight conditions.

The results of calculations and laboratory tests all indicated that good shielding of the exhaust outlets would require at least 80 percent afterburner operation under cruising conditions.

At the P&W Florida Research and Development Center, a group designed and tested several fuel control valves to accommodate the required fuel and additive flow rates required.

Willgoos plasma studies had used solutions in fuel of 25 percent to 50 percent sodium, potassium, and/or cesium. One effective cesium additive was 50 percent cesium valerate, but it was not fuel soluble, so it would have had to be injected into the exhaust stream just aft of the nozzles.

In order to simplify the injection problem the Customer had some work done on a cesium compound, cesium stearate, that was soluble in the fuel. A fuel soluble compound that finally was used in flight tests was 30 percent cesium metal in dialkyl phosphite.

The last test of the effects of fuel additives occurred in mid-1965.

Static RCS Tests

Anti-radar testing on the A-12 mockup and scaled models continued for more than two years until the advent of the R-12, the prototype of the SR-71.

In 1962, a comparison of a U-2 and an A-12 was performed by mounting one each of the real aircraft right side up, without fuel and engines, on the large levitator-rotator at "The Area" (Groom Lake).

After the U-2 tests, an A-12 aircraft was mounted on the pole. It had the chines covered with aluminum foil, and it had attenuating engine inlet spikes, plastic attenuating rudders, and simulated absorbing exhaust plumes. The backscatter was generally 1/10th as much than that from the U-2, except in the rear quarter where it was about 1/30th as much.

A comparison between the static backscattering from the full-scale mockup and that from the real A-12 aircraft showed very good agreement.

The A-12 Aircraft in Flight

April 26, 1962, was an important date. It was officially the day the first A-12 aircraft was scheduled to fly. I was not at the field, in area 51, but I heard about it. At that time the airport there was called Watertown. There is a Watertown, a city in New York where Director of Central Intelligence (DCI) Allen Dulles was born. At Groom Lake, except in the rainy season, there was very little water around.

I read or heard that the official day was to be April 26 when the Customer was scheduled to be present. However, the day before, one of the pilots, Louis Schalk, according to the story I heard, was doing some taxi runs and, without realizing it, "accidentally" lifted off the ground because the aircraft was carrying a very light load of fuel. Well, "accidents" do happen.

The official first flight, observed by both Lockheed and Customer personnel, occurred early on April 26, 1962.

Anti-Radar Flight Tests

In April of 1960, a flight test facility for measuring radar echoes dynamically was started at Groom Lake in Area 51 in Nevada. Several radars and large steerable antennas were set up near the Command Post (CP) buildings. The test data was recorded on magnetic tape and then was sent to a processing facility in Las Vegas. Results were available a short time later, usually the next day.

Wayne Pendelton was an important member of the group who established the facility.

During the latter part of 1963 and January 1964, several flights of an A-12 were performed over the dynamic flight test range using the ground radars at Groom Lake. The radar echoing characteristics were measured while the aircraft flew under cruising conditions.

One flight of an A-12 to test the effects of fuel additives on the conductivity of the exhaust plume occurred in December of 1964. Additional tests occurred in 1965 and in 1967.

The last test of exhaust plume ionization effects was done in the fall of 1967, using an A-12 aircraft flying over the Groom Lake flight test range. That was the last of the anti-radar effort.

At about the same time another short series of A-12 flights under cruising conditions was accomplished to test the efficacy of the basic anti-radar treatment.

Three flight tests to assess the effectiveness of the anti-radar treatments on the A-12 aircraft were performed. Two were in December 1963, and one was in January of 1964. Each flight consisted of four passes, two each for horizontally and vertically polarized S-Band waves. The aircraft had all the skin joints taped with aluminum tape. It was flown in the lower sub-sonic speed range so it had the inlet spikes extended.

Data were recorded for UHF (173 MHz) and "squoded" S-Band (2.71 to 2.99 GHz) but the UHF data was not considered to be trustworthy because of lack of reliable calibration. It is interesting that, on one pass, the UHF communication antenna was not retracted and it did seem to have an influence upon the S-Band return.

Several A-12 flights over the Groom Lake dynamic range in June of 1965 provided data for a comparison with data obtained on the A-12 full-scale mockup. Although the flight test data were sparse, good correlation was observed.

Sometimes we would test at night at the Groom Lake facility. There were times when testing was going well and waiting for data was somewhat boring. I and a few others would go out and howl and try to make contact with coyotes. It never worked, but you could have heard a lot of howling!

Flight tests of an untreated U-2C and a U-2R aircraft were performed over the Groom Lake range in the summer of 1968 to try to determine their backscattering characteristics for S-Band and C-Band.

The end of the effort to reduce the aircraft backscattering came in the summer of 1968. The A-12 aircraft were stored and the static mockups were destroyed by burning and burying the ashes. Luther Duncan MacDonald watched as the full-scale mockup was consumed by fire.

A-12 Antennas Refinement

Some of the Electronic Counter Measures (ECM) antennas had difficulties that seemed odd at first. After some flights it was noticed that the jammer helical antennas had shrunk in size, and that a ball had formed at the end of the antenna tips.

The A-12 environment, nearly 100,000 feet, was practically a vacuum and the dielectric strength of the air was very much decreased from that at sea level. The antenna tips had melted because a corona had formed and then a large amount of transmitter power had drained off into the corona and that had melted the metal.

My Navy experience with high-power radar transmitters helped me to identify the problem and the cure. We put a small metal ball on the tips of the replacement antennas, and they proved to be stable. The ball termination was not susceptible to corona like the original sharply cut off tip design had been.

Then we started having trouble with the jammer antennas' coaxial feed cables connectors burning. The air was so thin and the temperature so high that the air in the connectors directly adjacent to the metal was ionizing. Pulling the air molecules apart by electrical forces was violent. Pitting, and ultimately burning, resulted.

Again my experience helped. In the past I had coated high-voltage power supply wiring for television receivers to prevent this very type of problem. Typical picture tube accelerator voltages in television receivers ranged from 15,000 to 25,000 volts. My 1964 Zenith Model 29JC20 color television used 25,000 volts.

The solution was to coat the metal with a non-conducting dielectric material. In this case the temperatures were so high that conventional paint would not work. Our solution was a silicone resin, the same material used as the resin in the chine lay-ups. We filled the air gaps in the connectors with high temperature silicone grease.

Jim Herron and I performed several tests to determine why the High Frequency (HF) communication equipment in an A-12 aircraft did not work reliably over the long distances needed for callback.

We were well aware of the modes of propagation available at that time: ground wave; sky wave; ionospheric refraction; the effects of wave polarization rotation; and sun spot eruptions.

Each morning, for three days, we were airlifted by helicopter to a flat area atop a small mountain near Groom Lake. We set up our battery powered HF transmitter-receiver the first day and left it in place each night while we were airlifted down to the base. Our call sign was "Murgatroid" as in "Watertown, this is Murgatroid. Send lunch, please."

From Watertown, you could look across the airstrip to the flat-topped hill. The backside of it that you could not see was a steep drop almost like a cliff. When they took us up they would go around to the back side, rise up and perch on the flat top. Ordinarily when they took us down they would lift up, fly high, and go down gently. The last time they picked us up they tipped the helicopter and went down parallel to that hill, sliding down the terrain. If they were trying to scare us, it didn't work.

Our tests did, indeed, reveal that the HF communications were quite limited. I concluded that the cause was the excessive resistance to high frequency current flow by the titanium skin of the aircraft.

The A-12's titanium alloy had fifty or more times direct current resistance than the aluminum alloys typically used for aircraft. The high frequency "skin effect"[68] resulted in the titanium alloys exhibiting many more times as much resistance. The skin effect was a function of the frequency. The resistance increases as the frequency increases. In addition to the skin effect, the increase of the temperature of the aircraft due to air friction under cruising conditions increased the resistance even more. The result was much more energy loss during two-way communication. Ergo, much reduced communication distances. The effective line-of-sight communication distance could be only a small fraction of that available if the aircraft was made of aluminum.

An unintended benefit was that a hot all-titanium aircraft should have lower RCS than should an all-aluminum aircraft.

We experienced similar degradation of radio direction finder performance due to poor sensitivity of its sense antenna caused by the skin effect and the thermal increase of resistance of the titanium.

Another factor that limited the utility of the HF equipment in the aircraft was a serious impedance-matching problem that caused very high radio frequency voltages due to the inability of the available antenna "tuner" to cope with them.

This condition came about because one terminal, of two required, was at the aft end of a six-foot section of the nose that was electrically isolated by a plastic ring from the rest of the 107-foot long airframe. I used to explain that the airframe actually was the antenna while the short section was only an exciter. I sometimes referred to that section as "the tail that wags the dog."

The other terminal was on the remainder of the aircraft. In effect, the terminals were near the end of a very long radiator and so the impedance was very unsatisfactory for low frequencies.

Mike Ash and Bob Taron measured the impedance at the HF antenna terminals as a function of frequency using the 1/8th scale aircraft model atop the large pole used for radar backscatter measurements at Groom Lake. The model was isolated several feet above the top of the metal pole by a box-like structure made of plywood.

The instrumentation in the model consisted of a simple radio frequency oscillator, modulated by an audio frequency oscillator, a radio frequency impedance bridge, and a simple radio frequency receiver, all powered by automobile batteries. The two dials of the bridge were augmented by pulleys that were driven by Dacron strings from hand-cranked pulleys mounted on a wooden desk at the base of the pole. The pulleys were turned until the output of the receiver was minimized.

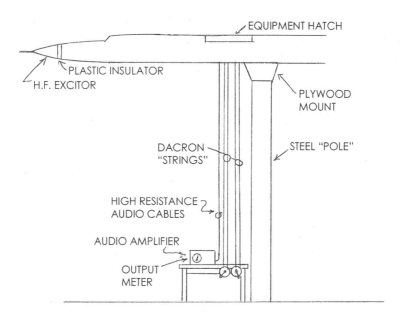

A-12 HF Antenna Impedance Test Set-Up

The receiver output was indicated by an analog meter connected to an audio frequency amplifier on the desk at the base of the pole. The receiver output was connected to an impedance step-up transformer in the model. The output of the transformer then was connected to two fifty-feet long automotive ignition conductors that, in turn, were connected to the high impedance winding of a similar transformer on the measurement desk. The low-impedance winding of that transformer was connected to an audio amplifier that operated the analog meter. I had utilized this method to minimize scattered energy during antenna radiation pattern recording during the early 1950s.

Mike Ash or Bob Taron manipulated the cranks to obtain a minimum deflection of the output meter and then one of them would be lifted up to the model by a "cherry picker" crane, open the top of the instrument compartment, read the bridge dials, and record the data. Then he would change the radio frequency, re-tune the receiver, close the instrument compartment, and return to the ground. This operation was repeated many times until an adequate set of data was acquired.

Finally the data was plotted on specially enlarged, three-feet-in-diameter Smith charts.

Mike mentioned that the cold nighttime wind made the measurements somewhat less interesting than they should have been!

Ernest E. "Jack" Hansen and I were engaged in the daytime testing the HF transmitter in an A-12 aircraft while it was in a hangar at Groom Lake. The purpose of the test was to determine the suitability of an inductor to be used to isolate the six-foot portion of the aircraft's nose that was to be one terminal of the antenna. The inductor was a bi-filar coil (two parallel wires) that carried electric current to heat the Pitot tube.

I tuned the transmitter to various frequencies and keyed it. When I tuned to the lowest frequency, 2 MHz, the high voltage across the gap caused corona to develop on the inductor's forward terminal and then cause the insulation to burn. Quickly we suppressed the small flame and discontinued the tests.

After the very minor damage was repaired, further testing was not needed.

While I was sitting in the cockpit I suddenly realized that there was an enormous fuel tank behind me!

The impedance data and the high probability of fire caused us to prohibit operation of the HF transmitter below 4 MHz.

Lightning Tests

Early in 1964 there was some trouble with the plastic rudders of one A-12 aircraft delaminating so they were removed from the aircraft at the Groom Lake base. It was decided that the failure had occurred because sea level air entrapped inside the fins during their manufacture expanded under the high temperature flight conditions. One-eighth inch diameter holes were drilled in the silicone-asbestos rudders to allow the pressure to equalize.

I was in the hangar standing beside Kelly Johnson while he was conferring with several engineers. I happened to look up and see the two steel pivot posts for the rudders silhouetted against the western sky through the open hangar door. I asked him if they looked like lightning rods.

His reaction was swift and direct! He immediately directed me and engineer Peter Gurin to perform lightning tests and devise protection from lightning strikes.

Pete arranged to have one rudder transported by air to the General Electric lightning laboratory in Pittsfield, Massachusetts, where we worked with Albert Rohlfs and E.R. Uhlig and their most powerful equipment. The laboratory was in a large metal shed.

We used their 7.5 million volts generator to simulate the initial strike and their 200,000 volt high current generator to provide the remainder of a typical discharge.

During the actual discharges we were inside an enclosure whose ceiling and walls were wooden frames covered by metallic "chicken wire" fencing and whose floor was copper sheets. All were connected together and formed a Faraday Cage for our protection. The controls and recording equipment also were inside.

For the first few tests I had a large number of short segments of copper wire arranged around the leading edge, along the top, and down the trailing edge of the rudder close to its metal base. Each one-inch long wire was separated from its neighbor by about one half of an inch, leaving an air gap between each conductor. This arrangement allowed the ionized air that spread from each gap to carry the very large currents, that otherwise would damage or destroy the rudder, to the metal structure where much less damage would occur.

The wires deliberately were made short to avoid resonance for any of the radar frequencies that we were concerned about. They were used to initiate spectacular arcs of ionized air around the perimeter of the fin.

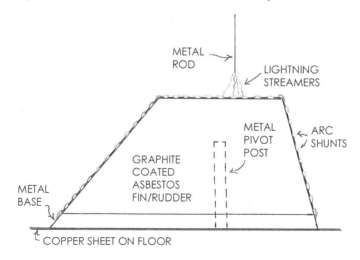

A-12 Plastic Fin Lightning Protection

The first tests were very satisfactory, so I had the wires replaced by patches of paint containing silver and graphite on armament tape[§] disposed similarly around the periphery of the fin.

Again, the tests were very satisfactory. The silver paint patches initiated the arcs very well and suffered very little damage to themselves. They performed as well when they were covered by black copper oxide paint. This scheme was recommended for use on the aircraft.

Radar backscattering measurements at Groom Lake showed that the lightning protection patches did not increase the radar echoes.

During late July and early August of 1964, I supervised another series of lightning protection tests at the G. E. lightning laboratory. This time the efforts were directed toward protection of the HF communications equipment installed in the nose of the A-12 aircraft. Mr. Robert Plott of the CIA accompanied me during these tests.

I had a crude mockup of about six feet of the nose section made of a copper screen-covered wooden frame the size and shape of that part of the aircraft, including real aircraft parts needed for lightning protection.

The new lightning protection hardware consisted of metal anti-corona rings, a circular spark gap to protect the antenna connection, the pitot heater wires, and the plastic gap cover. The pitot heater current was conveyed across the gap by a bi-filar coil whose inductive reactance was sufficient to minimize its effect upon the antenna impedance while, simultaneously, holding down the high frequency components of the lightning current until the ionized air could shunt them and the low frequency components to safe levels.

For these tests I had silver paint squares about three quarters of an inch on a side separated by about a quarter inch on armament tape put across the gap. Some tests used one tape while others used two diametrically opposite tapes.

---

§   Similar to "duct tape."

A-12 Nose Antenna Lightning Test, Edward Lovick (Left) and Robert Plott, CIA

Arc Shunts in Action

Edward Lovick, Jr.

All the results were very satisfactory. Tapes that were used several times showed very little erosion of the paint so that became the lightning protection modality, silver paint squares spaced across the gap. This series of tests was conducted using only 4.4 millions of volts!

While we were there we also tested some leading edge parts of the chines to verify the protection scheme. After a few successful "shots," we eliminated the protection and literally blew the parts to bits, thereby confirming the value of the protection.

I know of only one lightning strike to an A-12 aircraft. The only evidence, aside from the pilot's comments, was some discolored spots on the right-hand side of the fuselage just aft of the cockpit.

I was told about a hair-raising incident that happened before Pete and I arrived. It was early in the morning of a gray and rainy day when one of the men who worked there parked his car and got out, put up an umbrella, and began walking toward the entrance to the large metal laboratory building.

Some of his co-workers who were in or near the entrance happened to see him coming—with lightning streamers emanating from the metal tip of his umbrella!

Finally, as they literally held their breaths, he gained entrance and put down his umbrella. He remarked that he had felt "a prickly sensation" while walking in! He was within seconds of a lightning strike that could have ruined his resume!

LMSC Missile and Satellite Testing

Since the early 1950s, Kelly Johnson had been working with the Lockheed Missiles and Space Company (LMSC) to develop reconnaissance satellites.

At various times during the development of aircraft with reduced radar echoing properties we performed backscattering measurements of satellites and missiles for Lockheed Missiles and Space Company.

The first of these was a series of tests in September and October of 1961. It was codenamed PANATELLA.

A one-fifteenth-scale model of a double ogive shape made of wood and covered by aluminum foil was tested in the anechoic chamber in Burbank. Only nineteen tests were performed using the scaled equivalent of 190 MHz to simulate a low-frequency search radar. Several configurations including all metal except for camera windows, flat ends corresponding to bulkheads, absorbing ends utilizing lossy foam, and even some iron paint were tested. The results showed that the ten layers of different conductivity lossy foam in ogive configuration on each end, was best for hindering long-range detection by a hostile radar.

Another set of satellite tests was codenamed EGG. It was basically an oblate spheroid with a metal skin. Since its mission was photographic it was to contain two cameras that would produce panoramic pictures. This resulted in the need for two large windows in the bottom.

We constructed an eighth-scale model, including simulated cameras and the estimated gross interior structural features that might have been visible through the camera openings. The shell was of fiberglass covered by aluminum foil. Nine layers of conductive foam surrounded most of the bottom except for openings for the cameras. The top was left untreated because of the need for a radiating surface for temperature control of the real satellite in orbit. The foam material was terminated on the top side by contouring it to prevent too sudden a change in electrical properties.

Seventy-two different tests to simulate the backscatter of four frequencies were performed and all the test data was given to LMSC.

During the first week in February 1962, a set of backscattering measurements was performed using a slender, all-metal missile as a target. Two different models of ROCMIZ, a full scale and a one-sixth scale, were mounted on the pneumatic tower on the half-mile range at Groom Lake and tested under twenty different conditions of nose on, nose off, three frequencies and two linear polarizations.

During October of 1962, we mounted an Agena D rocket on the levitator-rotator at Groom Lake and measured its backscattering characteristics using several frequencies in S-Band and C-Band.

A series of tests on the Agena D with a reconnaissance payload was performed in November of 1962. A real Agena was mounted vertically on the levitator-rotator, and backscattering measurements were done with and without the antenna rods and with camera windows open and closed using L-Band and S-Band frequencies.

While the full-scale Agena D measurements were being performed in Nevada, similar measurements corresponding to lower frequencies were performed in Burbank using scaled models and frequencies in the anechoic chamber.

Eight different eighth-scale model variations were tested using 1370 ± 150 MHz to simulate 171 MHz and 650 ± 150 MHz to simulate 85 MHz. All the test data was given to LMSC representatives. Kelly Johnson was very involved with rocket and satellite design and development with LMSC.

Approximately a year later, in 1963, a series of scaled model measurements was performed of radar echoing from satellites designated as Case IX.

These efforts were directed toward measuring the backscattering and then reducing it. Some of the techniques that were applied to satellites were: lossy "egg-crate" structures shielding cameras; thin wire mesh over camera openings to approximate a metal cover; changing of shape to promote scattering in other than the retro-direction. Both commercially available lossy foam and ADP lossy foam were wrapped around the model.

In October of 1963 another LMSC satellite model was tested. This one was codenamed "GAZER" because it, too, was a photo-reconnaissance machine.

We constructed an eighth-scale model for anechoic chamber tests. It was essentially a metal cylinder with flat ends. A typical low frequency anti-radar treatment employed several layers of conductive foam wrapped around the cylinder. A total of ninety tests using five frequencies were performed. All these data were given to LMSC.

Anechoic Chamber Evolution

In late 1958 or early 1959, the first anechoic chamber was moved to Building 175, a miserable sort of place where P-38 aircraft had been assembled during World War II. It was partially open to the outside. We had to build a bird guano shield. My Navy background helped here—I never looked up with my mouth open!

We had been flooded out of Building 82, and the new Building 197 facility was not yet available. Building 82's wiring was from the 1930s, when paper was used as wire insulation. The wiring ran in conduits under the floor and a storm flooded the conduits, disrupting electrical power. We were working on both the U-2 and Archangel efforts and could not afford down time during repairs.

The first anechoic chamber ultimately was moved to Building 197, an add-on to Building 199, the location of the ADP group in Burbank who were engaged in materials research, fabrication of absorbers, antenna design, development and manufacture and backscattering measurements. It was still there in 1990, behind the old A-12 honeycomb edge core dipping equipment, and within sight of Mel George's office.

In December of 1963, we started the design of a new and much larger anechoic chamber. Actual construction was accomplished in the first half of 1964 and the facility was put into intensive use immediately for antenna and backscattering measurements.

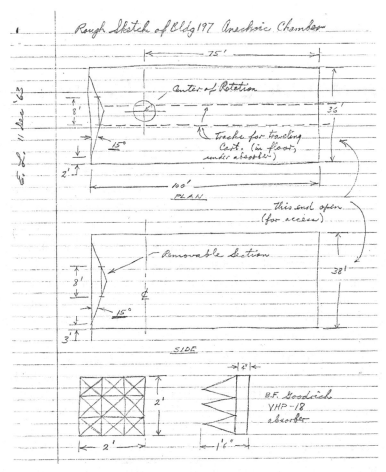

Design Sketch of Bldg. 197 Anechoic Chamber

The large anechoic chamber, of which I did some of the preliminary design, used pyramidal shaped wedge absorber made of polyurethane foam with graphite impregnating the material. The design called for the lossy plastic foam absorber to be mounted on a plywood liner in the building. The walls, ceiling, floor and one end were to be covered. More than four thousand absorber blocks were required. Nearly six hundred sheets of half-inch plywood and a large amount of two-by-four lumber were required for the liner.

The largest interior volume that could be accommodated was 120 feet long, 36 feet wide, and 38 feet high. However, it was decided to use only one hundred feet of the length to allow working space behind the closed end for special purposes such as radome tests that were anticipated.

A pair of metal tracks to support and guide a special trolley was to be set into trenches in the concrete floor of the building.

It was planned that a special cart that could be used to transport models and workmen to the rotator or to support an antenna testing tower could be run out and back on the tracks. The entire floor, except for very narrow gaps to clear the trolley supports, was to be covered by absorbing blocks. The trolley was to be controlled locally by men on the trolley or remotely from the open end of the chamber.

The traveling cart, or trolley, was designed to roll to any position along the center of the chamber and to lift up to four men and a large 250-pound target twenty-two feet from the floor. The floor of the work platform was intended to rise nineteen feet and the safety railing surrounding it was planned to support the test item.

In addition to being usable as an elevated work platform, the cart was designed so that, when the platform was at its lowest height and the safety rails were removed, an antenna positioner could be installed and the chamber then could be used for antenna radiation pattern measurements.

Because the walls, ceiling, and floor were covered with light gray absorber materials, people could experience vertigo when hanging up or removing the scaled models. We painted black stripes around the walls above and below the height of the model to provide a peripheral vision horizontal reference.

Backscattering measurements were to be accomplished using targets suspended from a rotating section of the chamber ceiling by Dacron lines in the six string hang formation. The rotator was to be six feet in diameter and was to be controlled remotely.

At the open end of the chamber we placed the transmitting/receiving equipment on a horizontal beam that could be raised and lowered to work on it, or position it differently relative to the model. The massive support for the reflectometer and other equipment consisted of two large steel "I" beams set vertically and braced to the building, supporting the horizontal beam. In the beginning no arrangements for a control booth were provided—it was added several years later.

The design for the anechoic chamber was implemented and used, with relatively minor changes, for approximately thirty years. At the time it was built, it was the best and largest anechoic chamber, in terms of operating convenience and lowest background levels, in the country. I learned later there were larger ones, but they were not as good.

As time passed, a large part of the work at the Groom Lake site and in the Burbank anechoic chambers was concerned with antenna development and performance in situ. The relative amount of backscattering measurements declined rapidly and essentially ceased early in 1967.

Derivatives and Developments

There were several derivatives of the A-12*: the D-21, the YF-12, and the SR-71. Two prototypes of the YF-12 interceptor were built. The D-21 reconnaissance drone and the SR-71 successfully went into production.

The D-21 "Little Whizzer"

During 1962, a small pilot-less reconnaissance vehicle was designed to be launched from an A-12 in flight. The design incorporated many of the anti-radar principles as well as aerodynamic configurations that were developed for the A-12. It was designated Case II and then, later, the D-21 and often was referred to as the "Little Whizzer." It got that name because some air traffic controllers had reported noticing something traveling very high and very fast. The CIA took care of that problem.

This vehicle was much smaller than the A-12 aircraft and was designed to be air-launched from an A-12 cruising at Mach 3 and then fly by itself along a pre-programmed track. It had to be launched at high speed to start its ram-jet engine.

A drone would not put a pilot at risk. If it landed in enemy territory, it would crash to destroy itself. With its smaller size, it would be less detectable. Preprogrammed before a mission to fly a certain course, it would end each mission by going out to sea so that the sensor package could be dropped for retrieval. An aircraft would try to catch it in the air. If it fell into the water, it would float until a boat recovered it, finding it by its beacon.

The recovery beacon system used two antennas so that it would be heard regardless of the orientation of the sensor package in the water. The antennas were connected by coaxial cables so that when one was in the water, it was short circuited and would not transmit while the

---

* For a more systematic discussion of the A-12 derivatives than my personal recollections, you may want to visit Wikipedia's Lockheed A-12 Variants entries.

antenna that was in the air could transmit. If both antennas were in air, both would transmit. Mike Ash and I designed that arrangement.

Small-scale models of the D-21 were built and tested for anti-radar properties in the original anechoic chamber in Burbank. Some scaled model tests were performed with a D-21 mounted on top of a modified A-12.

While these models were being fabricated, a ten-foot long typical section of the D-21's full-scale fuselage was built in Burbank and tested at Groom Lake to examine the effects of changing chine configurations.

A full-scale D-21 mockup was built and delivered to Groom Lake in the spring of 1963. The D-21 "Little Whizzer" incorporated most of the anti-radar techniques developed previously.

Backscattering measurements were performed using eighth-scale models and partial and complete full-scale mockups. By mid-1963, backscattering data was available corresponding to 70 MHz and 170 MHz from tests of the eighth-scale D-21 model and for S-Bands and C-Bands from the full-scale D-21 mockup.

At this time, the engine inlet rim was metal and was coated with the iron paint absorber. The chines were covered by sixteen steps (one to sixteen layers) of TD paper to simulate the intended treatment.

The results showed that the D-21 was about equivalent to the A-12 for 70 MHz, and approximately 10 db less reflective for 170 MHz, S-Band and C-Band. The chines then were modified by changing the resistivity taper ratios which improved the 170 MHz attenuation. Tests showed little change for S-Band and higher frequencies.

Several of these machines were built in preparation for flight testing. In 1965 RCS tests of scaled models of the improved D-21 atop the A-12 were performed in the new, large, anechoic chamber in Burbank.

Some flight testing of the combination of the D-21 launched from an A-12 occurred in late summer of 1965. The modified A-12 was designated M-12 for Mother (later changed to M-21) and the D-21 was referred to as the Daughter. Notice that twenty-one is twelve reversed. The M-21 had been modified to add a second crewmember, a flight engineer.

After a fatal accident and loss of both an aircraft and a drone, this effort was discontinued in favor of launching the D-21 from B-52 aircraft.

YF-12

The YF-12 probably was the most lethal attack interceptor aircraft ever built. It had a nose radome and radar to support attack duties. It carried eight missiles internally that could be launched at Mach three or faster. When cruising at nearly 100,000 feet its radar could search ahead 350 miles. Its operating ceiling was almost 100,000 feet, and it had about the speed of the SR-71. After two were built, Air Force funding for additional YF-12s was not acquired.

R-12 Aircraft

The reconnaissance version of the A-12 needed a second seat for an RSO, to navigate and operate the cameras and other sensors. The design of the R-12 aircraft was well advanced by the beginning of 1964.

The A-12 full-scale anti-radar mockup at Groom Lake was modified to represent the R-12. Since the main differences between the A-12 and the R-12 were in the forward part, the fuselage section aft of fuselage station 715, the wings, the engine nacelles, and the rudders were modified but essentially retained. A new forward fuselage section was installed on the old aft portion and the new configuration was used for radar backscatter measurements.

Full-scale anti-radar testing at Groom Lake in 1965 was mostly concerned with the R-12 or SR-71 configurations.

SR-71 Aircraft

The R-12 was a preliminary design that evolved into the SR-71 aircraft.

A new side-looking radar was added to the SR-71. It used windows instead of a conventional radome.

The windows for the side-looking radar had some impressive advanced frequency gating features. The radar antenna was a collection of slotted waveguides laid parallel and joined to each other that probably could be seen by enemy radar at a long distance if it was not hidden.

The windows were designed to be reflective at all frequencies except very near the one used by the aircraft's radar. The radome designers had to design the windows' pass-band taking into account that the antenna moved and looked through the complex shape at a variety of different angles, so they tended heavily to use the limited computer resources available at Lockheed.

I believe that Bill Moule was the lead designer of the radar windows. If it was a collaborative effort, then it is possible that Denys Overholser and William "Bill" Schroeder were involved. I remember seeing Denys Overholser later than this time, usually surrounded by piles of computer paper as he worked. They used ray tracing in those days to design radomes, which is similar to the physical optics method of RCS modeling. Bill Schroeder wrote Lockheed's groundbreaking physical optics RCS prediction computer programs code after becoming a radome designer.

SR-71 Flight Suits

The aircraft derived from the A-12 were partially pressurized, and they could go almost up to 100,000 feet, where the air density is about one percent of its sea level value.

The crewmen wore pressurized suits that, according to Paul Crickmore,[69] were developed from Gemini space suit designs.

The highest I heard about was a little over 90,000 feet. The reason they didn't go higher was because the Customer wanted quite a lot of equipment installed that significantly increased the aircraft's weight. And flying at 90,000 feet was quite an accomplishment too, at a little over 2,200 mph ground speed.

Eglin AFB Over-water Tests

One SR-71 aircraft was deployed to Eglin AFB, Florida, for flight-testing of radar backscattering. During the summer and early fall of 1966, measurements were performed for S-Band, C-Band, and X-Band frequencies. The data gleaned from these tests were sent to a group at General Dynamics, Fort Worth, Texas, who were doing vulnerability studies for the Air Force.

L. D. MacDonald and I were present as observers.

The flight tests were flown out over the Gulf of Mexico.

The usual practice was to send an aircraft out early to drop a highly conducting sphere to calibrate the test radars, but one day the supply of spheres was depleted so that no testing could be done.

I thought that there must be something else that we could substitute, so I enlisted the aid of engineer Russell Walrose to help me. We went to the Sears store in Fort Walton Beach, Florida, and selected several basketballs that we rolled in an aisle of the sporting goods department.

The manager was more than a little interested until I told him that we would buy all that rolled straight—which we did. We also bought some aluminum wrapping foil and some rubber cement and went back to our motel where we spent most of the evening covering the balls with foil.

I do not know whether or not the balls were used to calibrate radars. Sometimes I wondered what people who found foil-covered basketballs floating in the Gulf of Mexico may have thought.

One day there was some excitement because the 6 GHz tracking beacon seemed to have failed and the measurement radars lost the aircraft. However, the aircraft returned to base safely. There was some speculation about the possibility that ionization of residual fuel additive may have contributed to the loss of radar echo. I doubt it.

More likely there was sufficient warm air over a layer of cool moist air to cause "ducting" that caused the radar energy to be refracted downward so that most of it never reached the aircraft.

Ducting is a phenomenon that occurs frequently off coastlines. During World War II, I heard reports of radar echoes being received from very distant objects, much farther than the normal detection distances, across part of the Indian Ocean, probably caused by ducting.

Active Cancellation

A group of people visited us in Burbank and presented a description of an electronic scheme for reducing radar backscatter from aircraft. Their proposal involved several transponders placed on the periphery of an aircraft to receive radar signals. Then, a computer was to be used to calculate the angle-of-arrival, its reciprocal, and the appropriate amount of power to send back out of phase with the incident waves to cancel or reduce the signal to the radar.

Later we observed demonstrations in their laboratory, using an impressive amount of equipment that showed very good results.

This arrangement seemed too complicated and potentially unreliable, so I designed small autonomous plug-in repeaters, each dependent only upon a small amount of direct current power, to be placed around the periphery of an aircraft to do the same thing.

I do not know whether or not either scheme has been implemented on any vehicle.

An SR-71 aircraft moving at 2,000 miles per hour over the ground moves 2,933 feet per second. A radar wave will travel from nose to tail and back in 2 ten millionths of a second during which time the aircraft will have moved about 7/1000 of an inch! For all practical purposes, it would be standing still, because the speed of light is nearly 335,000 times the speed of the aircraft.

Gary Powers

I met Francis Gary Powers[70] and worked with him for a short time after he came to Lockheed after his misadventure with the Soviet Union.[71]

He and Mel George were given an assignment to try to determine the best color of paint to use on highflying aircraft to reduce their visibility to other aircrews.

We arranged two large mirrors as a periscope in our large anechoic chamber so we could see and photograph a 1/12th scale model of a U-2 suspended in the chamber.

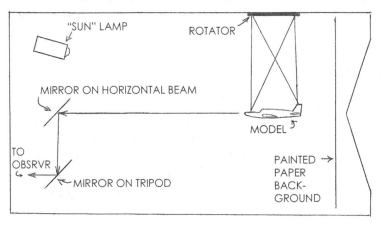

Periscopic Mirrors in the Large Anechoic Chamber

The back and portions of the sides of the chamber were covered by large sheets of paper painted light blue to simulate a sky background. High-powered sunlight lamps were used to illuminate the model.

The model was painted several times with different colors and color schemes and observed and photographed.

One or more flight tests using a U-2 had shown a puzzling discrepancy between airborne observations and photographs of patches of color on the aircraft. While the photographs showed the colors quite well, visual impression was that they all appeared nearly the same—light beige. Orange seemed about as good as any of the light paint colors that were tried to camouflage the U-2.

I never saw a report about the results, but I wondered if ultraviolet radiation at altitude was strong enough to affect the pilot's ability to see the colors even though they wore sunglasses or their helmet face plates were tinted.

Photographers knew that, even at much lower altitudes, UV filters often were needed to allow good color rendition so, perhaps, a filter on the camera was used but was not remembered. Kelly Johnson once said that the SR-71 "Blackbird" looked blue at high altitudes.

From a great distance the moon shines brightly—but up close it looks like dirt!

Gaseous Radar Wave Attenuators

An article in the *Los Angeles Times* newspaper dated October 24, 1969, alluded to a happening similar to the Bornholm incident reported in the 1950s. Again, it appears that nothing was done about it.

Later, in the fall of 1969, perhaps stimulated by the article published in the *Los Angeles Times* newspaper, Mike Ash, Jim Herron, and I tested nine candidate gaseous materials in a microwave resonant cavity designed more than ten years earlier by Mike.

While he was working in the Lockheed antenna laboratory before he joined us in ADP he designed a cylindrical multi-mode resonant cavity[72] for use in testing dielectric materials at very high frequencies and very high temperatures, often more than 500 degrees Fahrenheit. Its basic material was Inconel X, an alloy of nickel that was plated inside by gold to ensure maximum conductivity. Gold was chosen instead of silver because it is very much more resistant to oxidation by air.

To electronics engineers Q is a number[73] that can be interpreted as a "quality factor" that indicates efficiency. It is useful in many engineering calculations. It also represents the "sharpness" of a resonance.[74] It is in some respects analogous to Reynold's number, familiar to aerodynamicists. The very high Q that was attained by Mike's design allowed us to measure a wide range of dielectric materials properties, including dielectric constants and loss factors.

When we in the Skunk Works began to use Mike's cavity heated to relatively high temperatures, we experienced severe degradation of its Q. The cause was determined to be migration of the gold plating inside the cavity wall into the Inconel. It actually dissolved into the Inconel.

Mike was able to find a plating company that had developed a combination of palladium and rhodium that worked very well as a barrier layer to hold the thin layer of gold firmly in place and retard its diffusion. After the interior of the cavity was re-plated by gold the very high Q values were regained. Mike worked with chemist Eugene Giachino to accomplish the refurbishment. Mike forgot to tell us that the removable end had a left-hand thread!

The most interesting gas we tested was deuterated ammonia because it exhibited significant absorption near 3 GHz.

Also, we tested thirteen gaseous materials in a hermetically sealed anechoic chamber.

I wrote a report, dated December 5, 1969, detailing our results, but it was not released.

U-2s and the Jungle Environment

U-2R aircraft were used during the Vietnam War flying over the jungles in attempts to locate the Viet Cong.

During the Vietnam War, there was a suggestion that a well-known effect that a time varying sinusoidal function (voltage) as it forces a current through a non-linear circuit element generates harmonic functions (currents).

It was expected that the third harmonic of a radar wave frequency would be generated by current flowing through rusted or corroded metallic junctions in vehicles and or weapons concealed by foliage and that it could be detected by suitable receivers in U-2 aircraft.

In 1969, Ed Martin and I briefly discussed antennas that could be designed to be installed on or in U-2 aircraft. However, I do not know if there was any attempt to do so.

There has been a program called METRRA[75] (an acronym for Metal Re-Radiating Radar) to develop practical metal detecting equipment.

Early RCS Prediction Code Development

In the spring of 1962, a group led by Dr. Herbert W. Lorber at Edgerton, Germeshausen, and Grier (EG & G) in Las Vegas started a program to calculate the scattering from objects of complicated shapes. The ADP group cooperated with them to measure the backscattered energy from scaled models. The results were excellent in terms of agreement between calculated and measured data derived from highly conducting (all metal) targets, but quite disappointing when attempts were made to apply the theories to the enormously more complicated case of targets made of composites of conductors, semi-conductors, and insulators. Efforts to derive useful information continued until the end of 1964.

By the 1970s, computers had improved to run programs by means of punched cards. With the shaping principles we had identified in the 1950s and refined and flown in the 1960s, and our inlet, exhaust, materials, and antenna RCS reduction capabilities, we were well situated to take on the next aircraft design challenge—crashing the party we were not invited to—the XST program.

The F-117—Doing It with Mirrors

"If you would from radars hide
Try tilted mirrors side by side."
—Edward Lovick, Jr.

Serendipity: The gift of finding valuable or agreeable things not sought. The concept upon which the development of the F-117 stealthy aircraft was founded was a classic example of serendipity.

I heard that J. Russell "Russ" Daniels discovered an Air Force "Fighter Mafia" interest in obtaining a large number of small, stealthy, undetectable-by-radar piloted aircraft for air-to-ground attack. He asked Ed Martin,[*] the Director of Science and Engineering, to talk to DARPA and Air Force people to let them know (after obtaining CIA permission) that, for several years, Lockheed had been producing stealthy aircraft for the CIA and the Air Force.

Edward Martin had been in charge of manufacturing some of the U-2 aircraft.

---

[*] The following material is paraphrased from "Pioneers of Stealth 2004 Nominees."

"Ed Martin—Lockheed Martin. As Director of Science and Engineering for Lockheed (Advanced Development Projects) he discovered DARPA's interest in low observable aircraft and enhanced survivability methods. (He) Made the initiative to convince DARPA of Lockheed's experience with Low Observable aircraft and expertise for a new generation of aircraft. (He) Recruited the original design team for Lockheed's XST (later Have Blue). (He) Convinced Lockheed Corporate to devote company funds to test the "Hopeless Diamond" that proved the faceted design concept worked. (Validated the computed radar backscatter data). (He) Directed the prototype design and development of the Lockheed XST project during its initial feasibility engineering phases. (He was) Responsible for the initial aircraft configuration concepts and the winning program entry in the first competitive low observables program."

Ed was told that the money for the XST[†] program already had been allocated to other companies. If Lockheed wished to participate, they would have to fund their own proof of concept work.

Dick Scherrer was a design engineer in Leo Celniker's ADP Preliminary Design Group. He was assigned the task to develop a conceptual stealthy design.

The Fighter Mafia group wanted a stealthy attack aircraft that could disable or destroy a very dangerous Soviet Union field artillery vehicle codenamed "Gun Dish." It consisted of an armored vehicle carrying a rotary gun (like a Gatling gun) that could fire several thousands of "rounds" per minute with devastating effect. Its fire control system used a radar operating near 15 GHz whose wavelength was about eight tenths of an inch.

The gun could be aimed at a target very quickly, as I observed while sitting inside a reconstructed vehicle at Fort Huachuka, Arizona, while a technician operated it.

Sunlight coming through bullet holes in its sides emphasized the fact that it had been used in the 1967 Israeli-Egyptian war!

A crucial bit of information that I gave to Dick Scherrer was that, if a flat reflecting surface was large enough compared to the wavelength of impinging radiation, its reflection would be specular, or mirror-like. By tilting it sufficiently, most of the energy could be directed away from returning to its source.

In December of 1958, Mike Ash, Jim Herron, and I had measured the backscattering from triangular cylinders and had demonstrated to Kelly Johnson that very nearly specular reflection would occur if the sides of the triangular cross section were more than about 25 wavelengths wide. At 15 GHz, that would correspond to about twenty inches. As the reflecting surface measured in wavelength[‡] decreases, the primary reflection lobe centered on the specular vector widens.

---

†   XST stood for Experimental Survivable Testbed.
‡ λ is the conventional mathematical symbol denoting wavelength.

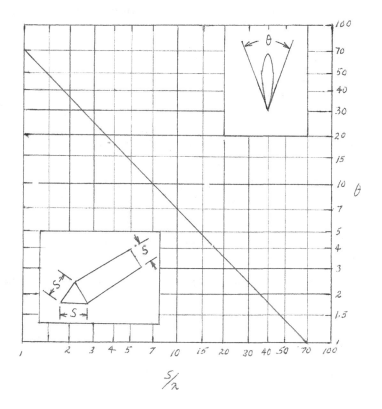

Reflecting Surface Size and Specular Beam Width

In the early 1970s, the computers and or computer programs available to us at Lockheed could not calculate adequate representations of complicated curved surfaces characteristic of aircraft technology, so curved or warped surfaces were approximated by collections of flat areas.

Basically the Lockheed computer program could not correctly calculate the backscatter from curved or warped surfaces or edges. Also, it could not predict the different responses to radar wave polarization. It was a very simplistic program and in fact, it was basically an optical ray tracing program.

Working with Denys Overholser, Dick Scherrer realized that, despite inadequacies in Lockheed's ECHO code, it might be possible to design an aircraft that would take advantage of some of the results of the calculations.

Bill Schroeder, who was a mechanical engineer and a good mathematician, wrote the original ECHO computer code. His protégé was Denys Overholser. Denys was able to run the simple code and generate huge piles of paper! Denys, please do not take umbrage at that remark.

I do not know whether Denys Overholser had any significant practical experience in the art and science of electronic measurements. I do not know what his educational background was (because I never asked him) but I think it may have been electrical engineering. It made little difference because he was more than up to the challenge.

The results of the radar backscatter calculations were so favorable as to be almost not believable. They promised a real breakthrough in the technology.

Ed Martin directed a proposal to the Air Force to build an aircraft based upon Scherrer's design and the predictions of the "ECHO" computer code, which was a good marketing tool.

Ed invited me to participate. We had been in the Navy radar group in Chicago and we had worked at Lockheed both before and after World War II Navy service.

Our original in-house name for the proposed aircraft was Harvey, named for an invisible rabbit from a 1950s movie, *Harvey*, starring Jimmy Stewart.

Harvey's faceted design was a significant departure from prior ADP aircraft, and management was unwilling to fund a proof of concept RCS model and tests. After failing to get ADP management interested, Ed approached Dr. Andrew Baker in Lockheed Corporate. Dr. Baker played a major role in helping Ed obtain company funding for the RCS demonstrator[§].

The "Hopeless Diamond" was a simple RCS test body that was used successfully to validate its computed backscatter by measurements at an outdoor test facility. It was named by aircraft preliminary design engineer Ed Baldwin. Aerodynamicist Dick Cantrell was responsible for stability and control design factors. He was skeptical of the possibility of controlling a flying faceted aircraft.

---

§   Ben Rich had published a very different account of the initial contact with the Defense Advanced Research Projects Agency (DARPA).

Later he declared that he would teach it to fly—and he did, with considerable help from Robert C. "Bob" Loschke.

There were aerodynamicists who were aghast at the whole thing until wind tunnel tests were performed. Possibly some people didn't know about or remember the Coanda Effect (discovered in 1932 by Henri Coanda) in which a fluid—air in this case—tends to follow a surface until it is forced to leave for some reason, such as an abrupt discontinuity.

My contribution at that time was to propose a special treatment for the engine inlets. It consisted of an "egg crate"[¶] designed to operate as a collection of cut-off waveguides intended to prevent entry of radar waves into the front parts of the engines while allowing adequate air flow.

The smallest grid openings I was allowed by the propulsion engineers were too large to cause cut-off at the Gun Dish frequency. Their cut-off frequency was less than half the Gun Dish frequency.

At higher frequencies the grid would act like waveguides and let the energy go through, so we made the tubular parts of the inlet grids out of lossy materials. There was no metal in those grids. They were fiberglass with resistive coatings, and the resistive coatings were step tapered, not very conductive on the outside, and more conductive as waves progressed in, and finally fairly conductive. In this case the desire was to make the inlets blend into the surrounding absorber coated metal surfaces.

Ed Martin, whose experience included Navy radar training, immediately recognized the merits of this modality.

The engine performance was degraded somewhat, but the egg crates solved the radar backscattering problem. They also straightened the airflow to the engines somewhat and that was beneficial.

We successfully tested the prototype grids in the large anechoic chamber in Building 197.

Ed was looking for a way to aid the marketing of the XST proposal, which led to Have Blue and the F-117.

¶ The egg crate inlet was derived from the metallic A-12 vent openings I had designed in the early 1960s. The original reason for this kind of grid was to make certain surfaces on the bottom of the A-12 aircraft appear to radar waves to be metallic like the surrounding airframe surfaces. The holes in the grids were waveguides beyond cut-off, so that they did have a reflection coefficient very nearly like a metal sheet.

Shortly before he and several others went to present our proposal, I suggested to him that calculation implied that the aircraft seen nose-on would seem like a 7/16th inch diameter metal sphere to a 15 GHz radar. He liked the idea, so I obtained ball bearings from our shop for him. Ed took a bag of the bearings to his meeting with the Customer.

He told me later that after that information was disclosed a lot of bearings were rolled on the conference table![**] I never recovered my tool check.

A contract to build a full-scale Have Blue mockup to validate the radar reflection capabilities of our design was received and implemented. Simultaneously another company, Northrop, was building their entry for the competition.

Have Blue RCS Test Competition

RATSCAT (RAdar Target SCATter) was an Air Force research facility located on Holloman Air Force Base, New Mexico.

Before we were awarded a contract to build aircraft there was a contest between Lockheed and Northrop to decide who would build stealth aircraft. Northrop had a design that was somewhat similar to ours. I did not know the details because I saw it briefly only a few times.[76]

Northrop and we shared the same hanger at RATSCAT, separated only by a large dingy gray curtain suspended from the hangar ceiling. The curtain did not extend all of the way up. Neither company was supposed to look at the other company's model.

For the A-12 to SR-71 testing at Groom Lake we had used a large cylindrical steel vertical post to elevate a full-scale mockup of the A-12 and other mockups fifty feet above the ground for backscatter testing. We had seen evidence of it interacting with the model, so we had put B.F. Goodrich Hairflex absorber on the ground at the first bounce location, and had put metal clamshell wrappers around the pole to shield it, specifically to eliminate the cylinder's direct reflection.

But that was a different frequency and RCS level. With an aircraft whose radar reflectivity was nearly as small as that of a 7/16-inch diameter steel ball bearing, the Groom Lake pole interaction easily would overwhelm the Have Blue signature.

[**] Ben Rich or his ghost writer had a different version of this incident. Ben was not directly involved in its origin.

At RATSCAT, before we began testing, they were having problems with full-scale model support. Since it began operating in 1964 and for several years thereafter, the RATSCAT facility had used crude, by mid-1970s standards, supports for its radar targets.[77]

They had problems with the model supports at RATSCAT because huge foamed plastic "elephant legs,"[78] sometimes as many as nine, were utilized. They were inconvenient and unsatisfactory for safety as well as radar backscatter measurements. There was an incident during a time they were trying to test a real airplane when it fell off of the Styrofoam posts and may have killed a man.

We had to design a much better support pole.

I believe that the impetus for its design was difficulties in measurement of our Hopeless Diamond at the McDonnell-Douglas Grey Butte facility near Palmdale. The backscatter from their model support was too great to allow our model to be discerned!

I heard that Lockheed ADP engineer Dick Scherrer provided a key suggestion. He proposed that an all-metal pole be built. I was not involved in his discussion with Denys Overholser but it was to be a metal pole, shaped like a tapered knife blade, leaning toward the radar.

A rotator mechanism could be attached to the metal pole. Unlike the A-12 support design in which the rotator was external to the mockup, our rotator was contained within the model to allow concealment. Lockheed and Northrop would provide their own rotators.

A pole prototype was built and tested at Grey Butte. It successfully was used to test The Hopeless Diamond.

The RATSCAT pole was designed to support test items forty feet above the ground. It was tested for strength in Building 82. It was heavy, requiring a crane to move it around. Ultimately it was used for all of our Have Blue and F-117 backscattering tests at RATSCAT. It proved to be very sturdy.

Its backscatter was so small that it could not be detected by all but their most powerful measurement radar. It was, in fact, a major improvement in support towers.

Engineers who designed aircraft wings probably designed the new pole. Unlike the pole used at Groom Lake, it was hollow and utilized stressed metal skin for strength and stiffness. Wiring to conduct power to tilt and rotate the models was contained inside the tower. I believe the pole was coated by our C-138 or BX-210 ferro-magnetic absorber materials.

A very important feature of it was the ease and speed with which a model could be attached to the top. Previously several hours were required to mount or dismount a model. The new design reduced the times to less than an hour for each task.

One dark evening I sat in my rented automobile in the University of New Mexico parking lot up on a mountain side near Alamogordo during a severe thunderstorm watching the RATSCAT area and wondering what might happen to the new pole if it was hit by a lighting bolt. Although there seemed to be several air-to-ground strikes near it, no damage occurred.

Before we began testing the Have Blue model at RATSCAT, Northrop was having trouble with their rotator motors.

The cause of the motor failures was the large alternating currents from the power supply that caused the direct current motors to overheat and burn out. The power supply was designed to increase its output in discrete steps by increasing the amplitude of a series of short pulses. The intent was to allow an operator to start and stop target rotation gradually in order to prevent damage due to inertia.

Apparently the designers did not realize the magnitudes of the alternating current (Fourier) components of the pulses compared to the direct current as a result of the discontinuous (pulsed) power supply output. The alternating current components caused heating but did not contribute to the operation of the motors.

I saw a rather large pile of burned-out half-horsepower motors in the lower level of the radar control building.

Jim Herron designed an entirely new and very efficient rotator that was installed into our model. It was only about eighteen inches in diameter and not much more than that in height. A very small direct current motor that ran, unloaded, at a maximum speed of about 9,000 r.p.m, worked through a very efficient gear train to rotate our mockup about one revolution in fifteen minutes. He also had installed a filter that reduced the alternating currents to safe levels. We used that rotator on our new tower design for all our tests at RATSCAT.

Testing at RATSCAT was very difficult many times. For example, often there was great difficulty with calibration of the test radars. Usually a reflecting sphere was used because backscatter from spheres has been amenable to calculation. Occasionally some other shape, such as a triangular corner reflector or circular cylinder, was used.

Richard Scherrer recorded the reflection from a radar target over and over for an entire day and discovered that the resulting patterns varied by twelve decibels, a power ratio of sixteen to one. The cause finally was related to the rise and fall of the underground water table in synchronism with the Earth's tides!

The RATSCAT facility is located on "white sand"—powdered gypsum[††] that nearly fills a huge bowl almost surrounded by mountains. Rainwater drains into the bowl and sometimes even rises above the gypsum.

One such event was referred to as "Lake Oshiro," probably "in honor of" Frederick Oshiro, a Northrop electro-magnetics engineer.

While driving to the RATSCAT site, and driving back, on a moonlit night the white "sand" dunes were absolutely beautiful. There were times when the wind would blow briskly, and it looked like water was flowing across the road, but it was just the gypsum drifting across, and that was interesting too. The first time I saw it I thought it was water.

One time a strong, steady wind was blowing as I drove out to the site, and when I got there the car stopped. There was so much gypsum dust in the air it looked like fog. So I decided to check the air filter on the carburetor and found it clogged. I just took it out, thumped it on the ground, put it back and the engine ran well. It was not all just scientific fun.

Energy radiated by any antenna spreads away from the intended direction of projection.

Because both the radar antennas and the targets (calibration bodies or models) must be relatively close to the ground and as far apart as feasible to minimize wave front curvature in the vicinity of the target, a large amount of the energy may be reflected from the ground plane, or the water below, to the vicinity of the test object and there combine with the energy that travels directly through space to the targets.[79]

If the reflected waves arrive at a time to be in phase with the direct waves they reinforce and, if they arrive some odd multiple of a half period too late, they will interfere and tend to cancel each other.

---

†† Calcium sulfate 2-hydrate, $CaSO_4 \times 2\,H_2O$.

If the reflecting plane moves up or down, the total distance the reflected waves travel will change, causing the energy on the target to fluctuate and hence the calibrations will vary.

When it was recognized that the major cause of the calibration difficulties was water table movement in the ground, the first efforts to correct the situation involved having helicopters from nearby Holloman Air Force Base hover over the space between the radar antennas and the target support in an attempt to dry out the water. No improvement was obtained.

The next remedy tried was more successful. I suggested that a "diffraction fence" be installed about halfway between the radar antennas and the target support.

We had a diffraction fence installed to block the first Fresnel zone where the reflection was occurring and that worked out quite well. The first fence was basically a frame made of wooden two-by-fours that supported aluminum sheets tilted away from the radars and well away from the vertical.

Improvement was attained when the fence was covered by radar absorbing material (RAM). Satisfactory calibrations were obtained. Theoretically, blocking the first Fresnel zone should have been sufficient, and it appeared to be so.

Later, B. F. Goodrich "Hairflex" absorbing material was laid on the ground under the model where another bounce could occur.

Perhaps a better arrangement would have been to cover the reflection area with fine mesh metal screen in concrete. Target illumination could have been increased by utilizing the power otherwise lost by blocking the reflected waves.

Early in the testing, our Customer was concerned about Soviet satellites discovering the XST model configurations. Someone devised a large conical covering to conceal the models from view. About thirty feet in diameter, the lightweight cloth cone was suspended over the test model by a cable from a crane. We called it the "Coolie Hat." The Coolie Hat, cable, and crane could not be in place while we were testing. If there were no satellites scheduled to pass over and we were ready to begin measurements, the Coolie Hat would be removed.

The Lockheed computer program predicted remarkable results. Some of the results were quite sensational because the aircraft, theoretically at least, would return very much less reflection than an equivalent all-metal one when viewed head-on. Those of us who knew what had been going on were quite certain that we could come close to the computed results that had been shown to the Customer.

The first series of tests at RATSCAT showed that our results for very high frequencies were excellent. The backscatter measurements using our full-scale model were remarkably similar to the computer calculated predictions.

For the original tests Northrop had designed and built a full-scale mockup to be used for backscattering tests that covered very low frequencies as well as very high frequencies.

The Lockheed model had been built specifically to counteract only the high-frequency Gun Dish radar. No attention had been paid to the low frequencies because we were not required to. The first tests showed the Northrop design to be superior.

We returned to our side of the hangar shop and rebuilt parts of our model, using low frequency technology similar to that which we had developed for use on the A-12, YF-12, and SR-71 aircraft.

We needed some special foam absorber material to put into the peripheral edges of the mockup.

Program manager Alan Brown asked Mel George to send some from Burbank. There was none available so he asked Merlin Reedy to "start from scratch."

Unfortunately the foam processing machine that had been used years before had been dismantled. Merlin quickly enlisted Mike Ash's aid to produce the foam.

Mike was able to find some of the old parts and, with the assistance of Casey Woldanski and Bill Jost, reconstructed a crude but adequate substitute.

Before the machine was constructed some foam was impregnated by rather primitive means. Merlin Reedy and Mike Ash donned rubber boots and became "grape stompers," literally kneading the foam with their feet in a tub containing the impregnant, a colloidal suspension of graphite in a water-based vehicle.

Mike remembers that the recipes for the impregnant solutions required ammonia. When he asked Merlin about how much to add he was told to "pour in ammonia until you cannot stand the aroma and that will be enough!"

While we were testing the Have Blue model at RATSCAT several test frequencies were used and one of them happened to be a harmonic of another.

It turned out that one of the exhaust outlet grid cells on each side of the centerline, looking at the back of the airplane, was resonant at that harmonic. Its reflectivity was 30 db (1,000 times) greater than that of the surrounding structures! We treated that cell with a simple absorber and eliminated the reflection. Peter Gurin diagnosed that one.

If we had not used those particular frequencies we might never have known about that resonance. I have wondered since then that if during actual flying of that aircraft other frequencies would be resonant, perhaps just because of a different part of the exhaust grid.

At RATSCAT, occasionally I saw coyotes at night. Sometimes they would come up right under the radar antennas. Perhaps someone was leaving food out for them. They were not afraid of the bright lights.

Occasionally I would go onto the roof of the radar building, or just into the parking area, and watch the lights from Alamogordo appear to rise up over the hilly areas and go back down again, depending upon the temperature gradient in the air. I was surprised at how much change I would see.

Sometimes several Air Force officers were on site observing our progress with our testing and development work.

One evening while the model was in the hangar, I decided to measure the resistivity of some of the tubes in the inlet grids. What we had done for the model was make, in effect, thin plastic shells that were coated with the resistive materials, and the shells would slide into a fiberglass replica of the inlet grid, so that we could take out those resistive card tubes if we wanted to—and I did.

I went into the hangar and took a large number of them out. I was very happily checking them and then putting them back. Someone discovered that I had taken them out.

My opinion when I designed them was that, since there was a large number of them, there would be random or nearly random variations in the coatings, and if the variations were not very great it should not make any difference overall whether or not they were returned to the same cells from which they had been removed. It turned out, of course, that it did not, but I was almost sent back to the factory for that action. They did not know that I had designed them.

Murray Slone, who was a materials engineer, invented and developed a very clever and effective device and procedure for testing the grid cells. It utilized a relatively long solenoid (a coil of wire on a plastic tube) that could be inserted into each grid cell. When in place its impedance was measured by using a vector voltmeter and the result was compared to its impedance in a standard grid cell. It was most useful in comparing cells to find those that were not sufficiently similar to cells known to be satisfactory.

There were several times when we had interesting experiences with the edges on the aircraft. They were made of fiberglass with coatings of graded resistance, and I enjoyed testing them by measuring their resistivities.

There was a problem that arose early in the testing of the edges at low frequencies. There were discontinuities along the edges where pieces were joined together and, at a certain frequency that we happened to be using, there were some rather peculiar perturbations in the backscattering patterns. Horizontal polarization caused them but vertical polarization did not.

I recognized a pattern characteristic of an array of two antennas superimposed on the scattering pattern. All we had to do was eliminate the discontinuities and the problem went away. That was fun.

RCS testing showed that our design was superior and, in fact, very nearly performed as the calculated data indicated. The results clearly demonstrated a major improvement in designing for very low radar reflectivity.

In 1976, Lockheed was declared the winner of the full-scale RCS demonstration competition. We were awarded the next phase contract, to build two prototype aircraft.

Alan Brown

Our friend Alan Brown, who for a time was my supervisor, is an interesting person. He is an expert engineer who also has a very well-developed sense of humor. Very likely he has talents that even he has not realized.

Earlier in life he performed on stage in England as a singing actor! He is a musician (piano player) who has made at least one musical instrument. In particular, I remember a beautiful harp that he made and played.

Alan told me about an episode that happened at the RATSCAT radar backscatter measurement facility in New Mexico.

Sometime previously before he became a member of the Skunk Works, during a trip through the Middle East, his English-style clothing was lost and he had only Arabic clothing to wear. Later he was able to obtain suitable clothing, but he kept the Arabic raiment.

One day at RATSCAT while we could not test, or were between tests, he was seen out in the desert walking toward the radar control building wearing his Arabic headdress. Although, to him, it may have seemed perfectly logical to wear it in the hot desert daylight, it caused consternation among the security people. Fortunately, he was not shot!

Alan told of a time when he had just returned from that trip and had not yet recovered his normal clothes. He was asked to make a sales presentation about the Lockheed L-1011 aircraft to some Japanese potential customers. He walked into the meeting room dressed as an Arab. His boss was shocked and the Japanese were greatly perturbed. I do not know whether or not they bought any aircraft.

Sometime before he was inducted into the Lockheed Skunk Works, he had served as an instructor for several technical courses at the University of Southern California.

Now, in "retirement," he still lectures or teaches technical courses, often in foreign countries. I never have attended one of his university lectures, but if I did I would expect a very informative and entertaining experience.

Denys Overholser

I did not know Denys Overholser very well, although he and I did share several experiences. One of these was a trip up from Alamogordo, New Mexico, to a restaurant in a hotel we hoped to reach at Cloudcroft. It was 9,000 feet above sea level at the top of a mountain. We did not make it because there was too much snow covering the narrow unpaved road.

I was driving and Denys was sitting in the right-hand seat where he had a clear view through some trees of a very steep hillside next to the road. Partway up the road to Cloudcroft we started slipping and could go no farther. Then, to make matters more exciting, we began sliding backward down the road. Denys had a great view of the trees going by!

We went to visit a solar observatory at Sunspot. Denys was driving. Snow covered the roadway so that we had difficulty going over rises in the undulating road. There was one particular hump that we failed to go over so Denys volunteered to push the car while I drove it.

Now I do not want to go anywhere with him if there is snow on the road because it is my turn to push!

James Reichert

James Reichert was a very important member of the Skunk Works. He was one of our most important experts on paints and painting, especially of the critical paints used to attenuate radar reflections from the edge treatments.

Jim also was an expert on applications of plastic materials such as epoxys, polyesters, polyethers, silicones, and others. He supervised much of the fabrication of plastic parts of the F-117 aircraft that utilized those materials.

In his "spare time," of which he had very little, he did independent research flight-testing of propellers. Jim was a former Marine fighter pilot who had considerable experience in flying several different aircraft and helicopters.

I believe that William "Bill" Stullick was an important member of Jim Reichert's group. He was an expert radio controlled model builder and that was an important factor in helping Bill Jost and me during some tests of mechanically tunable RCS reduction modalities.

Lightning Tests

During the development of the Have Blue aircraft I took some typical leading edge parts to be tested at J. Anderson Plumer's lightning laboratory near Pittsfield, Massachusetts.

My experience with "Andy" was very pleasant. He and I tested several samples in his facility after hours when his employees were not present. The results were as expected; that is, very good protection.

However, I am not aware that this protection modality ever was incorporated into the design of the Have Blue or the F-117 aircraft.

Windshield Optical Tests

I had an interesting experience that may have been a result of a conversation with Alan Brown.

I took a Have Blue or an F-117 windshield into an optics laboratory supervised by Jac Schmidt and set it up on an optical bench so that I could project a collimated beam of light from a slit onto one surface at a near grazing angle and measure the reflections from the various interfaces within it.

A photo-electric cell detector connected to a microammeter allowed me to compare the relative strength of reflected light and determine layer thickness, layer absorptivity, and layer uniformity. I wrote an informal report of the results and then forgot about it. Perhaps the technique could have been used as a quality control modality.

Have Blue Prototype Flights

The original wind tunnel tests of the Have Blue design were quite encouraging, so they continued working on it, and finally two of the original design were built and flown quite well.

The lack of flaps made them difficult to land.

One was lost because of a damaged landing gear, which eventually caused the loss of the airplane because the pilot Bill Park could not land it. One wheel support was bent slightly under the fuselage during an aborted hard landing attempt and would not move up or down. Kelly Johnson ordered him to abandon the airplane. Bill ejected but sustained injuries that ended his flying career.

The other was lost as a result of a hydraulic fluid fire that caused a loss of control so that the pilot had to abandon it.

Doctor Allen Atkins and I were at the Groom Lake base working on some backscattering data when the second mishap occurred. We went to the control room and saw a video recording of the aircraft falling and crashing. The pilot, Ken Dyson, ejected as the aircraft pitched upward violently just before it fell nose down to earth. He survived with serious injuries incurred when he landed on some very rough, rocky soil. Fortunately, he recovered.

Cancellation Tests at Grey Butte

During our times at Grey Butte, I learned more about rattle snakes than I wanted to. Much of our testing was done after dark so we had to be very careful about encountering snakes. There were "Mojave Green" snakes that are the most deadly of the fifty-seven varieties of rattlesnakes.

An article in a Palmdale newspaper warned its readers to be very careful about picking up green garden water hoses and urged them to obtain yellow or orange hoses. I saw several snakes killed. After they died they changed color from grass green to tan.

While I was investigating active cancellation technology I tried what might be termed "semi-active" cancellation. I had our shop equip a generic shape target that may have been The Hopeless Diamond with a system of movable scatterers that could compete with the scatter of the target body. William "Bill" Jost was the engineer who supervised the implementation of the systems in the test model.

The expectation was that combinations of scatter from conducting rods or flat fiberglass strips with resistive coatings and spacing from the edges of the target body could be found that would minimize the total backscatter from the target for given frequencies.

Bill Stullick was our radio-controlled model expert who helped us design battery-powered servo systems that could be operated remotely from the backscatter test control room at Grey Butte to adjust the spacing of the secondary scatterers to minimize the target's backscatter.

Our first evening, during a test, we were startled when someone called out, "Your model is on fire!" It almost was.

Bill Jost and I and several others discovered that a resistor in the power supply circuitry could not carry the current and had, indeed, "burned up" and created a large amount of smoke—and excitement. After replacing the defective resistor with a much sturdier one, we resumed testing.

The systems performed very well and we were able to find combinations that would cancel the total reflections well below the electronic noise levels of the measurement equipment. That was fun, sitting in the control room while adjusting the spacing by radio control.

As far as I know, nothing was done to utilize our results.

Medical Classes

While I was involved with the A-12 and SR-71, I became interested in the possible beneficial effects of controlling the negative ion level in the air the pilots breathe.

During 1977 I began taking evening courses in medical subjects at UCLA thinking that I would leave Lockheed and become a physician. Although I enjoyed the learning, I decided that such a change would not be cost effective, particularly because of the great increase in the cost of malpractice insurance.

The fact that I would have to spend several years in school and in low-paying, entry-level work convinced me that I should stay with Lockheed and read medical literature as a hobby. I still have most of my class notes and my medical books, that I sometimes consult.

I Declined Management—Again

Ben Rich offered me the senior management position in charge of observables in 1978.

I declined because I realized it was just too much fun doing the technical work and associating with the people who did it. I did not like the routine planning and reporting. Also, I realized that there had been great attrition among management ranks.

In 1981 I received Lockheed's Robert E. Gross Award for Technical Excellence. Kelly Johnson was my sponsor. The wording on the plaque states that I received this Scientist of the Year designation "For his extensive contributions to the new technology incorporated in advanced avionic and microwave systems." During the event a photo was taken of me, my wife Lucille, and Kelly.

1981 Robert E. Gross Award

Edward and Lucille Lovick and Kelly Johnson

ADP Preliminary Design Group Activities

I became involved with the ADP Preliminary Design Group when Ed Martin invited me to participate in writing the XST Phase I proposal. In the following years, I participated in several other design activities.

The Stealth Bomber

After the Have Blue program was well underway, and in fact almost finished, I began working with Leo Celniker on a bomber program.

Leo is a highly intelligent person. His forte was aircraft design, and he was very good at it. He was very knowledgeable about high speed aerodynamics. Leo was Chief Preliminary Design Engineer in the Advanced Development Projects. Dick Scherrer reported to him.

I had been involved with measuring backscattering from 1/20th scale models that involved curved surfaces. The measured data agreed moderately well with the calculated data in many respects. The calculated data always was for a single frequency whereas all of the scale model measurements involved pulsed signals, so that they simulated to some extent the spread spectrums of real radars, and therefore the representation of the maxima and the minima in the scattering patterns were more accurate.

Later it was demonstrated with large scale and full-scale models at RATSCAT that the small scale models were quite accurate in their representation of the backscatter. Of course, 1/20th scale models were not as detailed, lacking such things as windshields, aileron openings and all the warts that go on the real aircraft.

I suggested to Leo that we did not need to have sharp edges and faceting like Have Blue. He really did not need convincing. Rounded surfaces promoted much better aerodynamic performance.

He had a full-scale model of the bomber built with rounded wing and empennage leading edges. The fuselage also was rounded instead of having all those difficult-to-manufacture facets that were characteristic of the Have Blue and F-117 aircraft. A huge number of man-hours were devoted to making those F-117 facet edges meet at straight lines and at points.

The backscattering results from RATSCAT tests were excellent. Leo was satisfied that we had demonstrated that we did not need to have facets. The Lockheed F-22 Raptor does not have facets!

We tested the bomber model at RATSCAT during 1979 and were very successful in reducing its radar reflections. Despite having demonstrated what we believed was a superior design, Northrop was awarded the stealth bomber contract. The B-2 Flying Wing was the result.

Sometimes while we were at RATSCAT there would be hours or days during which we could not test. During one of these periods Leo and I decided to drive ninety miles to El Paso, Texas, and attend a *Lawrence Welk Show*. (Saturday, March 10, 1979.)

We also went to Juarez, Mexico, to find some real Mexican food. We parked our rented car in a municipal parking lot and walked into the business district.

After inspecting several places, we decided to eat in an Italian restaurant! Then we went window-shopping and Leo purchased some things for his wife. We then decided to take a taxi back to our car. The driver asked us to wait while he plugged in a headlamp, which he did after retrieving one from inside the car and then had some difficulty starting the engine. The ride back to the parking lot was like some I had seen in old movies!

The Stealthy Submarine Boat

One day in the early 1980s, a young Skunk Works engineer, Phillip Rogers, came into my office with some very interesting questions and comments. He had been attempting to photograph flow patterns indicated by wicks on a scaled model of the Have Blue aircraft in a water flow basin at the California Institute of Technology. He had not been able to, although he could see the model and the wicks.

We determined that the reason was that the supersonic energy used for automatically focusing the camera was bouncing off the surface of the water and preventing useful pictures. The reflection loss at a plane interface between air at sea level density and fresh water, for normal incidence, is about 29.5 decibels, or more than 99 percent, and even greater for angles off normal.

Rogers then asked if it would be feasible to use that information to design a stealthy submarine boat using the analogy of the faceted aircraft but, in effect, turning the problem inside out! A submarine boat is analogous to a bubble in some respects.

After some discussion, relying upon my Navy sonar teaching and some graduate study of oceanography, I said that it seemed worthy of some testing.

He arranged to have some models made and we tested them locally in a small supersonic cleaning facility with encouraging results.

Soon afterward he and I went to a test facility in Cambridge, Massachusetts, that was working for the Navy on reducing torpedo propeller cavitation noise.

They had a large rectangular water pool that was supported upon a number of inflated automotive truck tire inner tubes for vibration isolation. The walls and bottom appeared to be made of concrete. The water surface was mirror smooth.

The bottom of one end of the pool was several feet lower than that of the other end, and the two were connected by a smoothly curved ramp, as in a typical swimming pool.

For security, we and several of their engineers worked at night, after the regular crew had left the building. Since we had limited time available, we usually worked almost the entire night.

They arranged a bridge across the pool at the centers of the long sides and installed a rotator in the center of the bridge. Our models were suspended in the water by a rod driven by the rotator. Several supersonic sonar transducers were immersed, one at a time, halfway down from the surface at the deeper end of the pool and were used to measure the backscatter from the models.

Frequencies between 2.5 MHz and 5 MHz were used because it was necessary to scale the wavelengths to correspond to the scale factors used for the models. A very much simplified estimate of the wavelength of a 5 MHz sound wave in fresh water is about twelve one-thousandths of an inch. The speed of propagation of longitudinal (sound) waves in sea water depends upon temperature, pressure, and salinity and varies wildly. We made no attempt to simulate such conditions.

We used a sphere to calibrate the backscatter data.

PLAN VIEW

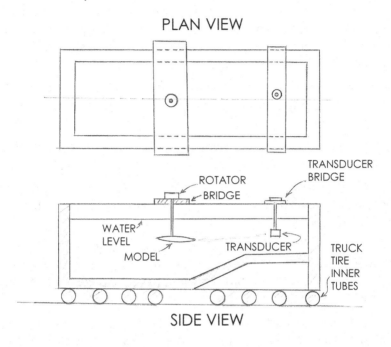

SIDE VIEW

Water-filled Test Basin

The test facility supervisor occasionally provided some entertainment during our lunch break around three in the morning. While we ate, he would play his guitar and sing!

During our time at the Cambridge facility, there were snowstorms. When we emerged after our last testing night the snow was so deep that we had difficulty finding our car in the parking lot!

Our results seemed quite satisfactory, so Rogers arranged for some tests at the U.S. Navy's Leesburg sonar transducer calibration facility in Bugg Spring near Okahumpka, Florida. There similar test facilities were available in a small, deep pond. This time we went by floating walkway out to the test rotator.

We were told that there was an alligator "nest" at one end of the pond. Fortunately, although we saw the nest, we never saw an alligator.

Again, the test results were promising so further tests were planned using larger, more realistic models.

The Navy had a large sonar test facility in Lake Pont Orielle in Idaho. I do not know whether or not Rogers was able to continue his investigations. All I remember is that I saw drawings describing the installations and they resembled typical outdoor radar backscatter test facilities, except that they were upside down and underwater.

Helicopters

Sometime during the mid-1980s, I became involved in a short study of the possibilities for reducing the radar detectability of helicopters.

I had talked to engineer Bill Gardner who told me that he had mounted a four-cup anemometer on the roof of a barn near a home he had for retirement. He had intended to use a surplus military K Band (25 GHz) radar to measure wind speed, but it had failed to work.

I thought that was a hint that helicopter blades might be made to reflect little radar energy.

Phillip Rogers and I went to visit the state of Georgia's police radar expert at the Georgia Institute of Technology. After a short discussion, we set up an experiment in a small yard next to one of the school buildings.

We mounted a four-cup anemometer on a wooden tripod and he clamped a police radar onto the window glass of the driver's side of his automobile parked about fifty feet away. Then he directed the radar toward the anemometer by swinging the door.

I stood well to one side of the tripod and directed a stream of air from a leaf blower to rotate the anemometer.

The first results were terrible! The radar indications showed extremely erratic speeds, varying from very low to unreasonably high. I stopped the blower.

At that time an automobile passed nearby and the radar showed a reasonable speed so it appeared that the radar was working well.

It seemed obvious that the blower was causing the interference, so I placed a metal sheet that just happened to be leaning against the nearby building to shield the blower from the radar.

The next test was conclusive—the radar did not detect the rotating anemometer cups. Just to be certain, we repeated the experiment several times with the same results.

We returned to Burbank thinking that we could greatly reduce radar reflections from helicopters.

My interpretation of the results was that equal but opposite Doppler shifted returns from two rotating elements, be they spheres, cups, or helicopter blades, corresponded to sidebands of an amplitude modulated carrier frequency. The "advancing" element would increase the returned frequency while the "retreating" element would decrease the returned frequency by an equal amount. In addition, they would be 180 degrees out of phase—just the conditions required for amplitude modulation of a carrier wave. If there was no steady carrier (the radar frequency return from a helicopter body, for example), a receiver would not demodulate the radar returns and so the rotating elements would not be detected.

There were several caveats.

Each revolution, if one element hid another, a carrier frequency return (not Doppler shifted) would occur. The ability of radar to detect it would depend upon its magnitude and repetition rate.

Another was that the return from an odd number of rotating targets could be reduced but not cancelled.

Unless the advancing and retreating elements backscattered the same amount, cancellation could not occur although some reduction might occur.

As far as I know, nothing was done with this information.

The Sea Shadow

In 1975, Lt. Commander Wes Jordan, USN, asked the question "Could a stealthy ship be designed using the faceting principles incorporated into the F-117?" Leo Celniker, as head of the ADP Preliminary Design Group, thought it would be possible. With a combination of Lockheed and Customer funding, a design approach was developed. Early in the preliminary process, Ugo Coty* was designated the Project Engineer.

It would be a challenge to design and demonstrate low RCS performance on the sea. Unlike an aircraft seen against the sky, a too stealthy ship could stand out as a smooth spot in the sea clutter. A ship's wake can remain for quite some time, pointing to the location of the vessel. Assessing design performance under simulated or real conditions in secret would be difficult.

The Sea Shadow configuration was designed to reflect radar waves away from threats positioned near the horizon. That meant that the sides of the ship would need to lean inboard, away from the ocean.

The solution was a Small Waterplane Area Twin Hull, or SWATH configuration, rather than a conventional single hull. It resembled a catamaran with underwater "wings." The submerged hulls were shaped to counter the strut waves to minimize ship wake. All of the ship's above-water surfaces were angled relative to each other in such a fashion that no corner reflectors would exist.

A tremendous amount of work and innovation went into developing secret test facilities. Tests of fifteen-foot and thirty-foot demonstrators convinced the Customer to go ahead with the full-scale Sea Shadow.

---

*   Ugo Coty compiled an unpublished history in 2006 of the Sea Shadow program, which was e-mailed to me by Yilmaz Deniz. We used his early history contents to verify the timeline. Ugo included contributions from some of the people who had worked with him. Hopefully, this account will be published for the public in the near future.

Dr. Nicholas Damaskos

Dr. Nicholas Damaskos was an important consultant to the Lockheed Advanced Development Projects. He was sponsored by the CIA during the OXCART program. He visited us frequently to discuss materials and measurement techniques. He and I became friends and colleagues.

Nick was a consultant to the Sea Shadow project from the beginning. He analyzed test data during the scale models phase, finding the signature data in the sea clutter. Nick provided critical absorber materials for the full-scale Sea Shadow.

Sherre Love and Windows

Sherre Love was a young engineer on the Sea Shadow program. A recent engineering graduate from the University of California, San Diego's Revelle College, she was assigned to design the windshields and windows to prevent radar echoes from the bridge's interior. She also designed the engines' air inlet to capture incoming radar energy.

Sherre made important contributions to the design of the Sea Shadow. The windows were particularly difficult to design because they had to allow excellent visibility for crew members inside the craft while simultaneously preventing radar wave energy from penetrating them and then backscattering to hostile radars. She was eminently successful in both design goals.

Sometime in 1983, Richard R. Heppe was appointed Vice President of the Advanced Development Projects. He decided that the area in which the radar backscatter engineering group worked needed some drastic changes. In particular, he decided that we occupied too much space and so he dictated reduction of office space and elimination of many desks.

I happened to be sitting in an office with several other people when a young lady came in and sat in a chair next to me. She seemed to be cold and somewhat confused, so I offered her my sweater. She accepted it and seemed relieved.

After I was moved into a different office that I shared with another engineer, Dale Cooper, I invited her to work with us in our office because of Heppe's dictum. There was no reasonable place for her to work. She had to share a desk!

We became friends and quite often worked together.

Norman Nelson replaced Heppe as Vice President of ADP on May 16, 1984, when Heppe replaced Graham Whipple, who retired from the presidency of CALAC. Then things seemed to proceed much more calmly.

I had the good fortune to attend one of the frequent progress report sessions in which she was required to present her results to our Customer's representatives.

Sherre was the only woman in the room. When her turn came, she stood at the podium and said, "My name is Sherre Love, and I do windows!" After that she owned the audience.

The day she came to work with us was one of several very important days in my life but I did not know it then.

In 2001, two years after I lost Lucille, Sherre and I were married.

I asked Sherre to describe her experiences in her own words.

> My job interview in 1983 at the Skunk Works was pretty typical, I believe. I was aware of the job because a fellow engineering major and former roommate from UC San Diego, Lisa Brey, had suggested me as a candidate to her program management.
>
> She told me that I couldn't know what I would be doing but to trust her, I would love it. What more could you ask for? It was much more intriguing than my other main job choice at the time, writing software for satellites.
>
> So I drove to Burbank, interviewed, and got the job as a design engineer. Sam Smyth, my design manager, immediately introduced himself and walked me through a P-3 hangar, pointing out some of the parts that he had designed on the aircraft. He said that seeing what you had created on a flying aircraft was one of the most satisfying aspects of design work. I didn't have to wait long in a holding area, because I was granted an interim security clearance.
>
> The first surprise I had was weather related. The interview and first few days of work had occurred during hazy days when the haze appeared blue so that I didn't realize how little visibility there was.

I was staying with friends in Santa Monica until I could save enough money for the first and last rent payments for an apartment, and so I drove over the Sepulveda pass into the Valley each day.

One morning I was surprised to discover that there were large mountains close to the plant that I hadn't even known existed! That was a greater surprise than watching the parking lot pavement ripple during an aftershock of the 1988 earthquake, although not by much.

On my first day inside Building 311, I was introduced to my coworkers. It was suggested that I immediately learn how to use CADAM, the computer-aided design software, and skip drafting with paper and pencil. I was relieved, because I am left-handed and had no experience drafting, but was aware that lefties tended to make pretty smudgy drawings. Sam Smyth had taken me to one of the old lofting rooms so that I could see the surface, the plastic guides and heavy lead "ducks" they used to physically set an edge to scribe the loft lines against. That really made me appreciate the advances that had been made!

I was introduced to Mike Gilbert, a CADAM expert, who promptly made all sorts of stuff zoom furiously around the screen. I'm sure I said, "Wow!" in admiration at his creative skill. In fact, Mike had confused me by just moving the drawing around on the screen.

After weeks of CADAM training, I reported for my first assignment to the room where the designers worked. Although there were only about thirty people on the program full-time, we were separated into several small rooms.

I was told that one of the World War II-era desks was mine (my own desk! And very substantial metal), then I was walked to a terminal, and was given a job to design a part of an RCS test fixture. I had arrived!

Hours later so did Dick Heppe with my program manager, Ugo Coty. Ugo was apparently trying to get more space for his group, and Heppe was fighting it. Heppe stormed in and began opening and slamming drawers on the desks while we all watched from the computers. He got to mine, and went through it, shouting, "You don't need more space! Look at this, this desk is empty!"

I was nervous and didn't know whether to say timidly, "Excuse me, sir, that's my desk. This is my first day and so there's nothing in there." Well, I didn't say a word. It didn't matter—I think someone else said it for me. Heppe looked a little nonplussed as he looked at my scared face, and then he and Ugo left. And we did get that larger room later.

Space in that building was a big deal. Some days I would walk in and someone's door I used to pass on the way to ours would simply be gone. When they changed things, it happened overnight.

I was lucky to have an old fashioned Skunk Works experience in the 1980s at Lockheed. Ugo had a small group, and he did all the dueling with the managers above him, leaving us to get the work done quickly and well. And we pitched in to get the jobs done, with a great variety of tasks that I really enjoyed.

Sam Smyth was a great supervisor. Besides being the best designer in the company, as evidenced by how frequently he was called to other programs in and out of ADP to lend his design skills, Sam was very wise about people.

One time he had farmed a generic, detail design job out to a designer outside our group, but the man wasn't finishing the job. We went and stood over his drawing board, looking at the lack of result. Then Sam got a piece of paper and, drawing what he wanted in three views, he asked the designer for his opinion about one aspect of it. When we left, Sam told me that some designers had trouble visualizing in 3-D, and would not admit it out of fear for losing their job.

I learned that if I ever noticed something not getting done, dignified, indirect guidance might get the best results for all. I practiced that philosophy throughout my aerospace career. Sometimes it even works on Ed!

It was a marvelous experience to design the windows for the Sea Shadow. I got to learn so much about materials, structure and fasteners, corrosion, window manufacturing and quality screening, RCS design, and testing. There was a ship specialist, Yilmaz Deniz, to help us airplane designers make sure things would be seaworthy.

I had no idea that there was a stealth fighter in the building, as I had been given one of, if not the first, blue N on my badge. All that I knew that meant was that I couldn't go where almost everyone else in the group could, except for using one portion of a hallway. But I honestly never even thought about that. No problem!

I helped to design a test fixture to measure the RCS performance of one of my windows, and then got to attend a night of testing, which included a nighttime lift in a cherry picker. That experience confirmed that I had a difficult time staying awake during third shift.

I was taken out to China Lake to see where the scale models had been tested. I remember Ugo wanting to show me the model, which was stored in a large shed secured by a padlock. When he found out that no one present had a key, he declared he owned the lock and could do whatever he pleased with it, got some bolt cutters, and cut the lock off of the door, right in front of the China Lake security escort. In fact, I wouldn't be surprised if Ugo borrowed those cutters from the security guy. Ugo was terrific—he had the goods, and he got things done!

I attended the installation of the windows into the Sea Shadow up in Northern California. As I recall, we were picked up in an unmarked white van without side windows, at the airport, then we were asked to duck down and hide our faces for a time. We drove through some curtains, and ultimately ended up in the floating dry-dock that contained the ship.

It was my first visit to a shipyard; I still remember the smell of the welding, and the sounds of grinders. They used a crane to bring the windows into place, and then used the fasteners and fillers I had selected to seal them up. I still have the hard hat they gave me.

I was back up again to help install the inlet. My job had been to devise a three dimensional design inside a boxlike opening that would cause radar waves to bounce around so many times before exiting that they would be sufficiently absorbed. Nick Damaskos had the job of designing the absorber.

We had no ray-tracing programs at that time, so I did two-dimensional ray-tracing by mirroring an incoming line off of each surface. If it worked in cross section, I would then do the same in three dimensions. I remember that I fairly quickly found a geometric solution that seemed to work. When I showed it to Sam, he said fine, now find another. After I protested, he said he wanted me to develop a dozen or more designs. It was a fun exercise, starting over with a different approach that many times.

The design that was chosen was built as a unit that was dropped in the boxlike hole on the top of the ship. I "assisted" Tim Gray, a very capable materials guy working for Jim Reichert, to spray an electrical transition coating around the edge of the inlet to complete its installation. The really neat thing was that the Sea Shadow was floating inside the building at the time!

No railings, a top deck that wasn't much wider than the inlet, and at the waterline between the sheer sides of the ship and the dry-dock walls there looked to be ten feet or less clearance. Whew! I wouldn't want to fall down there and get shmushed.

I remember Ugo's incredulity when in spite of all the security precautions, a Russian trawler showed up when the Sea Shadow was RCS tested at sea the very first time!

With my design tasks over, I was assigned to assist in processing the RCS test data. Bill Lorber explained to me, using a missile as an example, how to recognize scattering sources in RCS charts, and even how to do predictions by hand in anticipation of what might be seen in the data.

I also got my first helicopter ride when I was taken out to the island where the RCS data was being collected. Ed Lovick had warned me that a helicopter had the glide ratio of a rock; fortunately, it wasn't demonstrated!

Having a basic or parametric expectation of what you'll see in data prior to reviewing it was a practice that I used as I progressed from Sea Shadow designer, to RCS analyst at Northrop, to Infrared designer and analyst at Lockheed and in the Phantom Works at McDonnell-Douglas, to IRAD and CRAD[†] manager, and ultimately to becoming the Customer representative reviewing programs for the Navy while at the Naval Research Laboratory in Washington, DC.

I was working in DC when I called Ed Lovick for his eightieth birthday after many years. In 2001, I returned to California, and we were married. Nine wonderful years, a pilot's license, and soon a book later, here we are!

In 2006, the Sea Shadow had its twentieth anniversary and was declassified. In September it was made available by the Navy for donation, along with the Hughes Mining Barge that had served as its floating dry-dock.[80] Sam took some photos[‡] showing the windows, and the inlet, which is the dark angular aperture on the top deck visible in the lower photograph of the stern.

---

† IRAD is Independent Research and Development, funded in large part by a corporation. CRAD is Contract Research and Development, funding completely by a Customer; this is the ultimate goal in technology development research funding.

‡ Sam Smyth is offering his significant collection of aircraft photos to museums or universities. E-mail ed@edtheradarman.com if you can help.

BOW

STERN

The Sea Shadow, Photos Courtesy Sam Smyth

Sherre mentioned an earthquake that occurred in 1988. I was sitting at my desk in my office that morning when the shaking began. I tried to get out of my chair but could not, so I sat and watched a concrete wall crack and crumble, and then the lights went out. I retrieved a flashlight that I kept in my desk. My office was on the bottom floor so I eagerly left the building. It seemed that most of the building's residents already were out in the parking lot. During several aftershocks we saw the parking lot ripple. Ben Rich said, "You all can go home."

Stellar Engineers Incognito and Influential People

I worked with several men during my career who did not have college engineering or physics degrees, but who seemed to me to be more brilliant and frankly useful to Lockheed than most of the "PhDs" I encountered. In the PhDs' defense, they usually were too specialized from their curricula, and lacking in hands-on general experience. However, these stellar non-degreed engineers suffered in their career advancement because they did not have that paper. They were major contributors to the programs, and these are some of the problems they solved.

Two men who made significant technical contributions to the U-2, the Arrow series, YF-12, SR-71, D-21, Have Blue, and F-117 programs, as well as several other programs, were Mike Ash and Jim Herron. Their work in the antenna laboratory and the backscattering anechoic chambers as well as "in the field" at Groom Lake, Nevada, the McDonald-Douglas Grey Butte site near Palmdale, California, RATSCAT at Holloman AFB, New Mexico, and Edwards North Base near Lancaster, California, was outstanding. Together, they probably made more antenna and backscatter measurements and calculations than anyone else.

Mike Ash

Before he joined us in the Advanced Development Projects, Mike Ash had been employed in the Lockheed Burbank Antenna Laboratory where he had done remarkable work.

He and engineer Robert "Bob" Taron tested a thirty-foot diameter "Rotodome" antenna enclosure designed to be carried by a Navy WV-2E patrol aircraft* at a special installation at Windy Gap near Newhall, California. That was a very difficult task under bad weather conditions and a very short allowed time. As was characteristic of them, the tests were timely and very successful.

---

* A Lockheed 1049 Constellation-type aircraft.

Mike designed and tested a strip-line feed connections system for a scaled sixteen-element antenna array. Only by hands-on experience can one appreciate how much fun that was!

He became involved in radome boresight testing and correction for several projects. Among them were height finder radomes for the Navy WV-2E, the first filament-wound radome for the F-104 USAF fighter, and the first production radomes for the Navy P-3 patrol aircraft.

Some time during this work he designed a multimode resonant cavity to be used to test dielectric insulator materials used in antenna and radome fabrication. Luckily we later discovered that his design could be used at temperatures up to 1,200 degrees Fahrenheit!

Mike Ash was involved in the design and development of a localizer-glide slope antenna for the A-12 aircraft. It was a slot parallel to the fuselage centerline located in front of the windshield that was multiplexed to operate as two antennas. It served the localizer and the glide slope receivers. As part of that job, he wrote an adjustment (tuning) document and then instructed some Air Force technicians how to accomplish needed maintenance adjustments.

He also participated in the design and development of the YF-12's instrument landing system localizer and glide slope antennas that were located under the radar antenna in the nose radome. Later he wrote a maintenance document and instructed Air Force technicians about adjustments of them that might be needed.

Bob Taron designed and Mike Ash developed some special X-Band circularly polarized Electronic Counter-Measures (ECM) antennas for the SR-71 aircraft that were especially difficult. They were small, tapered helices made of very fine (No. 23 AWG) wire recommended by Raymond Burton inside a conical copper horn.

Designing and building those antennas meant not only the electro-magnetic and mechanical design, but also heat treating the wire to precipitation harden it to prepare it for the up to 700 degrees Fahrenheit thermal environment. Mike was able to find a company who made springs who made the helices. The final and probably the most difficult part of that design was making the small helix radiate a rather large amount of power while they were immersed in very rare air.

The very fine wire of the helix was coated by a dielectric material to prevent corona formation but that seriously degraded the antenna's performance.

Then, using an uncoated helix, Mike designed a very thin polyimide cover, shaped like a sailor's hat, that was installed in the aperture of the horn, effectively trapping relatively dense air that inhibited formation of corona. Additional corona prevention was attained when Mike filled part of the horn with very low density polyimide foam to support the helix when it was subjected to severe vibration during flight.

A major part of that ECM system was a thirty-five-foot long waveguide transmission line that connected the antenna to its receiver. That was a very difficult job, but Mike was well suited for it.

I was not involved with its design or development, so I have asked Mike to elucidate. With his permission, I am taking the liberty of quoting some of his remarks contained in an e-mail he sent to me.

> Quoting Mike:
>
> I had a time one day with some crude bending mandrels, several ten-foot sections of X-Band waveguide,[†] and a hacksaw up at Palmdale to design that waveguide with only E plane bends[‡][81] through that maze in the chine of the SR-71.
>
> And we kind of got our nose rubbed in some new concepts trying to come up with a transmission line for the thirty-five feet of waveguide that was required for the receiver part of that system. I think that ultimately the waveguide dimensions came out of the Microwave Research Corporation back near Boston—but the material and the extrusion with the extreme finish came from local vendors—and even the measurement of the internal surface finish introduced some exotic optical

† X-Band waveguide is tubing a half-inch high by one inch wide outside dimensions.

‡ "E" is the conventional mathematical symbol used to represent the electric field vector component of an electro-magnetic wave while "H" represents its free space magnetic field vector component. E plane bends are much more forgiving than H plane bends.

concepts that became a learning process. If memory serves, I think we delivered a system with less than 2.0 dB loss for the thirty-five-foot length.

That loss is very near the theoretical best that can be attained with straight sections of that size aluminum alloy waveguide.

Mike Ash was a hero—he saved a severely injured Lockheed electrician's life by pulling him off a high power circuit. For most people that would have been a very dangerous act, but Mike knew how to do it safely, and he did not hesitate.

I was not present, but I was told about his action. Mike did not talk about the event. He is genuinely modest.

Those remarkable accomplishments were by no means the end of Mike's story. He was very important in the efforts to produce the first "stealth" radome for the SR-71.

Leo Celniker was the project engineer who directed Mike to provide the radome. William "Bill" Moule designed the radome as a three-stage filter that was bi-refringent, responding differently to orthogonally polarized waves.

Mike, at Leo's urging, asked engineer Ed Patino to "encourage" Bill to cease refining his design and release it so that the shop could make one for testing.

The design required 22,000 accurately sized and spaced holes drilled in three brass plates whose thickness and flatness were critical. Mike credits Jerry Ephraim and his crew for superb cooperation and workmanship in producing the radome.

The plates were soldered together in an autoclave operated at more than 200 pounds per square inch (psi). It was safety valved to 200 psi but had not been operated over 150 psi until Mike required it. The temperature needed to solder the plates was about 400 degrees Fahrenheit. Mike had to convince the plastics shop supervisor that it could be done.

Jim Herron

Jim Herron was another remarkable person with whom I was fortunate to work and to know. He, Mike Ash, and I collaborated in developing the fundamental scaled model backscatter testing facilities and practices used by the Skunk Works.

Jim became an expert in measurements of backscatter from small scale models and probably measured more such data than anyone else. He produced hundreds of meticulously recorded and cataloged records. He also was an expert in interpreting their meaning.

Before he joined us in the Skunk Works, Jim had served in the Navy and, later, in the Air Force. I do not know his early technical background, but he was very versatile in mechanical designing and fabrication.

Both Mike Ash and Jim Herron continuously improved their technical skills. They learned mathematics and computer programming quickly and well. I was very impressed by their accomplishments. I like to believe that I could have done as well as they did without formal engineering schooling.

Jim Herron designed the UHF communications antenna and redesigned some of the Customer-supplied counter-measures antennas for the A-12 aircraft. He and I worked together designing the sense antenna for the Automatic Direction Finder (ADF) system, and he and I field tested the High Frequency communication system.

Russ Daniels, who was ADP vice president at that time, arranged for me to "fly" a crude early version of the A-12 simulator for a short time, and that was a nice experience. I hope that I thanked him adequately.

Once again I might have gone up the management ladder because I knew Russ Daniels and Kelly Johnson, and I had met several other influential people. But actually I was doing well, having fun enjoying what I did being an engineering physicist, so I did not pursue it.

There were several people who were not members of Kelly Johnson's Skunk Works who indirectly influenced some of the work I did.

Dr. Allen Atkins

Dr. Allen Atkins was a USAF representative working with us on the Have Blue aircraft testing at RATSCAT on Holloman AFB, New Mexico.

He and I became friends. When we returned to Burbank, Allen, Natalie, Lucille, and I enjoyed going out to dinner several times. Then he left to become the head of DARPA for a while.

Dr. Robert Elliott

I knew Dr. Robert Elliott very well from my time at the University of Illinois.

He was one of the very few to refuse Kelly. A superb mathematician, well known for his writings about electromagnetic theory, he did not want anything to do with the often senseless hassles with "security."

While I was attending classes at the University of Illinois, I had taken his course on writing technical reports. Later, after he had become an instructor at UCLA, I enjoyed attending his class on crystallography. He was an excellent teacher. I especially enjoyed his beautiful English writing. His first university degree was Bachelor of Arts in English.

Dr. Thomas T. Taylor

Another teacher I was privileged to know was Dr. Thomas T. Taylor. In 1952, I took his course on advanced antenna theory at UCLA. He was an excellent teacher. I kept very detailed notes for reference. Many times they were very useful.

Sometime during the late 1980s, I lent some of them to an engineer who worked in the Skunk Works. He wrote a report that incorporated almost a reproduction of parts of those notes. He received a high grade from our Customer for it. I still have those notes.[82]

Afterword

I retired from Lockheed in November 1990. Free from the daily hassles of government security, I expected a pleasant retirement.

Lucille and I produced five children during our fifty-two years together: Carol (married to Dennis Sybrowsky), Ronald (wife, Ann), David (wife, Jeanne), Patricia, and Richard. I have five grandchildren: Courtney, Katie, Dallas, Jennifer, and Nolan.

Sherre telephoned me during the morning of my birthday from her home in Annapolis, Maryland, to wish me a happy eightieth birthday. I was surprised and delighted! We had not talked to each other for almost thirteen years!

In 1999, Lucille organized a family gathering to celebrate my eightieth birthday. She had not been feeling well for several weeks. We thought it was the flu. That evening after we came home from the party, Lucille suffered a massive heart attack. She died in the hospital. I was devastated and felt lost.

Several weeks later, I decided that I needed to do something to take my thoughts away from my loss.

I began preparations to reactivate my pilot's license. I completed a ground school review but was not very motivated to continue. I was depressed and lethargic.

Sherre Love had left Lockheed a year before I retired, in anticipation of the Burbank plant closing. She worked for the McDonnell Douglas "Phantom Works" in St. Louis, Missouri, and then for the Naval Research Laboratories in Washington, DC. I did not expect to see her again.

In the spring, Sherre traveled to Los Angeles on her way to a conference at the Naval Air Weapons Station, China Lake, California. I met her and accompanied her on the long drive to and back from the base for the conference. I did not attend any of the meetings. Then she returned to Annapolis.

Soon thereafter I telephoned her and we began cross-country telephone calls. I realized that she also was unhappy and seemed depressed. Finally, after professional counseling, she decided to obtain a divorce.

I immediately asked her to marry me. That was the best suggestion that I ever made!

Sherre and I were married May 16, 2001, at 4:00 PM in the Wedding Chapel at Disney World in Orlando, Florida, eighteen years after we met! We have settled into a nice lifestyle.

She and I have studied advanced music theory at a local community college. Sherre played violin while I played trombone in its jazz big band. Sherre surprised herself by beginning to play the drums in that college big band. Now we have a drum set in our living room!

Frequently we attend several music events, Sunday afternoon jazz club meetings, jazz festivals, and regularly visit major professional big band rehearsals.

Another important activity for us has been completing pilot's ground school and several instructional flights. Sherre worked toward qualifying for her pilot's license while I prepared for my bi-annual re-qualification "check ride."

We attended the 2006 AOPA event in Palm Springs, California, and were given awards for being the oldest pilot there and for being the newest pilot there. Sherre had received her license only a few days before! We look forward to pursuing our bi-annual re-qualifications after the book project is complete.

We are members of the Aircraft Owners and Pilots Association (AOPA), the Experimental Aircraft Association (EAA), the (Lockheed) P-38 International Association, the Pioneers of Stealth, the Blackbird Association, and Roadrunners International. The latter two are organizations of people who were involved in the design, development, or operation of highly classified stealthy reconnaissance aircraft during the Cold War era.

Sherre is a member of Women in Aviation and the Ninety-Nines, Inc., an association of female pilots that was formed by Amelia Earheart and ninety-eight women pilots. (I am her "49 ½ er"). She is also treasurer of the Valley Jazz Club, a non-profit organization in the San Fernando Valley keeping classic jazz alive and well.

I am a member of the American Legion, the Association of Old Crows, and Eta Kappa Nu, an honorary electrical engineering society.

We are living happily ever after.

> *This is the book we sought to write*
> *Of both our lives and love so right*
> *We have enjoyed it, every bit,*
> *My love and I have finished it.*
> *We have finished what we've begun*
> *We hope no damage has been done*
> *No parts or pieces gone astray*
> *And that the smoke will clear away!*

In summary, science and engineering can be fun. Analogies are an important and powerful way to create new things and get things done. Changing the nature of equations' coefficients in one discipline can be used to derive new things in another discipline. The starting point for creating new ideas on one project or in one field begins with drawing upon what is read, seen, and experienced throughout a lifetime, analogies, and cross-pollination of other fields and colleagues.

"Education is what remains after one has forgotten what one has learned in school."

—*Albert Einstein*

THE END*

---

*   For now.

Appendix A: Smith Charts
and Z-Theta Charts

Devised by Phillip H. Smith, the Smith Chart first appeared in 1936.[83] A revised and more easily used version appeared in 1944[84] and still is useful today,[85] even if modern computer software is available.

The Smith Chart[86] represents a remarkable achievement. All possible complex numbers[87] with positive "real" parts are mapped mathematically into the interior of a circle. It was designed to solve problems involving hyperbolic functions of complex arguments, especially electromagnetic[88] transmission lines and impedance matching.[89]

I blame British university mathematics professors for bollixing up complex numbers. They apparently could not rationalize the idea of the square root of negative one, so they called it "imaginary"! They should be forgiven, however, for the usefulness of the concept, particularly in applications to electrical and mechanical engineering.

Complex numbers are combinations of "real" and "imaginary" parts. They are extremely useful in solving many different kinds of practical problems. Perhaps the best way to learn about them would be to study a mathematics textbook,[90] a physics textbook, an electrical engineering textbook, or an Internet source such as The Math Forum @ Drexel, http://mathforum.org/library/drmath/view/55566.html.

There are three basic types of electrical components: resistors, capacitors, and inductors. Reactance is the measure of the effect of capacitance or inductance on current, and it varies with frequency. The upper half of the Smith chart represents equivalent series connected resistance and inductive reactance elements. The lower half represents equivalent series connected resistance and capacitive reactance elements.

The entire perimeter represents one half wavelength of standing wave minimum shift. Halfway around is equivalent to one quarter of a wavelength minimum shift.

ZERO on the left-hand side represents a short circuit (zero resistance). Progression clockwise halfway around the outer circle (toward the generator or away from the short circuit) leads to a point where the impedance is infinite. The line from ZERO to INFINITE represents all normalized values of resistivity. The upper part of the chart represents impedances composed of series connection of resistance and inductive reactance. The lower part represents impedances composed of series connection of resistance and capacitive reactance. The horizontal line represents all possible values of "pure" resistance.

Any circle centered on point C represents all possible impedances corresponding to a given value of VSWR. The VSWR is defined as the intersection of the circle and the right-hand side of the horizontal axis running through point C.

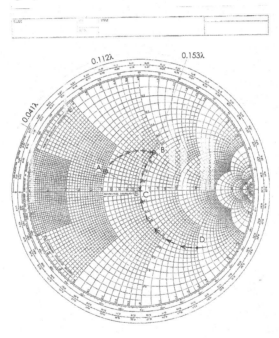

Simple Operations Using Smith Charts

In the figure, the point "A" represents a normalized impedance that does not represent a "matched" impedance. Normalization is a mathematical procedure that changes the scale to some more convenient value. For most problems involving transmission lines, every value on the chart has been divided by the absolute value of the transmission line's characteristic impedance, which always is assumed to be a "pure" resistance because the transmission line is assumed to be lossless. There are procedures available to account for losses in real transmission lines.

The point at the center of a Smith Chart represents a perfect impedance match. Point B represents point A transformed (moved along a segment of a circle) by a loss-less transmission line 0.112 wavelength long to the circle that passes through the center of the chart at point C. Addition of the proper circuit element to convert point B to point C represents completion of the matching problem. Point D represents a different type of problem in which a simple addition of a circuit component can accomplish an impedance match.

Generally it was not feasible for us to secure nearly perfect impedance matches for antennas that were designed to operate over moderately wide frequency ranges without "tuning."

The military specifications required transmitting antennas to cause no more than a VSWR of two-to-one. That causes rejection of 11 percent of the incident power at the antenna terminals and also increases the loss in any transmission line connecting the antenna and a transmitter. Receiving antennas were allowed to cause no more than five-to-one VSWR. That causes loss of 44 percent of the incident power if the receiver is matched to the transmission line and additional loss in any transmission line connecting the antenna and a receiver if the receiver is not impedance matched to the transmission line.

High power transmitters required automatic narrow band impedance matching devices or "tuners." High-powered transmitters require excellent impedance match because reflected waves can result in dangerously high voltages and reflected power can overheat and damage or destroy the transmitter.

In practice, the first step in using a slotted line and a transmission line (or waveguide for higher frequencies) for measurements required the transmission line to be short-circuited, and the locations of minima to be read from a calibrated scale attached to the slotted line structure. Standing wave minima occur every half wavelength back from the short circuit component. All slotted lines were equipped with metric scales.

The short circuit component was replaced by a "load" (antenna) that usually shifted the minima locations and reduced the VSWR from extremely large to a much smaller, easily measurable value.

The VSWR measured with an antenna in place was read from a specially calibrated voltmeter.

A circle was drawn about the center of the chart using the VSWR value, read from the portion of the pure resistance line from one to infinite, as its radius (the right-hand side in this illustration).

A line was drawn from the center of the chart to a point on its rim that corresponded to a minimum shift as a fraction of a wavelength toward the generator that crossed the VSWR circle at a point representing the normalized impedance of the load.

These are only very simple examples of operations that can be accomplished graphically using Smith charts.

Solutions of actual problems can be very much more complicated and may best be solved by a computer.

The Smith Chart is only one of several versions of charts that can be used to solve the same classes of problems. The Smith Chart is based upon transformation of rectangular coordinates whereas the Z-Theta chart[91] is based upon equivalent polar coordinates. Sometimes a "Z-Theta chart" is called a Carter chart.

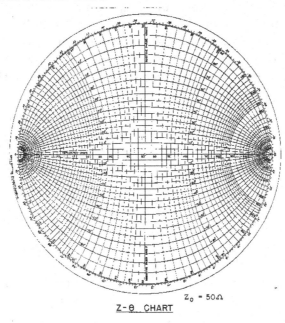

$Z_0 = 50\,\Omega$

Z-θ CHART

"Z-Theta" Charts

Z represents impedance magnitude and Theta represents an associated phase angle.

Appendix B: Analogies and Graphical Aids

A simple straightedge can be used to explore quickly a large range of solutions to a class of problems. In this example, a line can be drawn between any two known values of the three variables A, C, and D. The solution for the third variable is the value on its scale which is crossed by the line connecting the two known parameters.

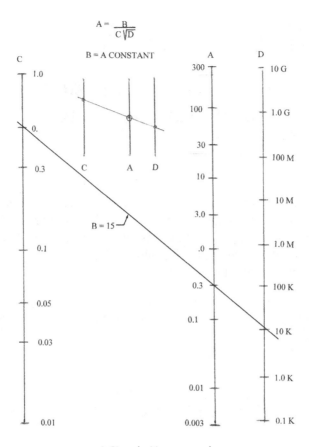

A Simple Nomograph

Before the advent of sophisticated calculators and computers, when the slide rule was king, nomography[92] was an important methodology for quick and convenient approximate solutions of engineering problems. Nomographs still are published in the "Pilot's Operating Handbook" for small aircraft.

While I was a student at the University of Illinois, I acquired an excellent textbook on the subject of creating nomographs.[93]

After learning to recognize certain properties of equations[*94] [†95] and how to select appropriate graph paper, the effort required to obtain useful results may become much less. A very simple example is illustrated by the next figure.

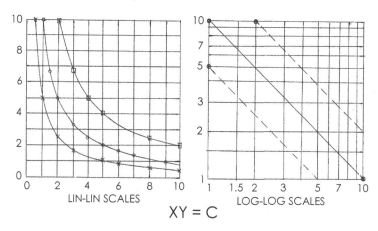

LIN-LIN SCALES   LOG-LOG SCALES

$$XY = C$$

Graphs Using Linear or Logarithmic Coordinates

The equation $X \cdot Y = C$ represents a family of hyperbolas. When the constant C is specified and at least three sets of values of X or Y are entered and the data are plotted on rectangular coordinate paper, a curve may be passed through those data points.

However, if the equation is transformed to $\log(X) + \log(Y) = \log(C)$, straight lines may be plotted on graph paper by solving the new equation twice for one "curve" and once for any other value of C since all the straight lines will have the same slope and be parallel. If "log-log" graph paper is utilized, the effort will be minimized because only two data points for one value of C are required for the first solution and thereafter only one data point is needed for other values of C.

---

*   This is a very well-written article that illustrates the practical simplicity of graphical solutions of circuit design problems.
†   This is a very interesting and useful article describing graphical solutions to complicated reflector designs.

Appendix C: EIC Antenna Directivity

When a model was mounted upon the antenna radiation pattern measurement tower, rotation about the horizontal axis was equivalent to rotation about a real world vertical (azimuth) axis. An elevation angle would be set by rotating the tower about its vertical axis. The model would be set arbitrarily at zero degrees azimuth, and the power that the model's antenna received during 360 degrees of rotation would be plotted as an antenna radiation pattern, and also sent through the variable ratio transformer to an amplifier that drove the Earth Induction Compass (EIC) indicator.

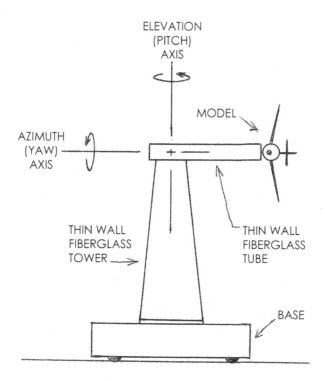

Antenna Radiation Pattern Measurement Tower

The indicator pointer would move off zero and stop at the end of model rotation. The total angular rotation, in degrees, was read and listed. Then the model tower would be turned to the next elevation angle and the process was repeated until all thirty-eight patterns were recorded. The EIC pointer would move further by the new amount and hold. By the end of the 360-degree rotation, the EIC would have summed all of the radial values contained on the radiation pattern.

After making a note of the sum for that elevation, the tower angle would be changed to a new elevation angle and the process would be repeated through all of the desired increments of elevation angle. Each data point added to the sum of the angles on the EIC.

I tested the compass indicator to be sure that the amount of its pointer rotation was linearly proportional to the voltage applied to the amplifier that drove it, which, in turn, was linearly proportional to the power extracted from the antennas in the models.

The resultant total rotation read from the EIC, in degrees, was linearly proportional to the integral of the signal from the model antennas so that all we had to do was calibrate the system by adjusting the amplifier gain to obtain a convenient amount of rotation of the compass indicator for a complete set of radiation patterns characteristic of a standard antenna whose directive gain was known and already calculated.

$$Directivity(dB) = 10log\left[\frac{(360N)+D}{(360n)+d}\right]$$

Where:

- N = the number of complete revolutions for the model antenna;
- n = the number of complete revolutions for the reference antenna;
- D = the number of degrees of revolution more than zero but less than 360 for the model antenna; and
- d = the number of degrees of revolution more than zero but less than 360 for the reference antenna.

Our standard antenna for calibration usually was a wire one quarter of a wavelength long perpendicular to a large-in-wavelengths circular metal image plane.

Sometimes we used slotted cylinders because they easily were mounted and easily were tuned by adjusting their slot length. Their radiation patterns as well as their directivity easily were calculated.[96]

The final step in the process was to record nineteen radiation patterns and the resultant total rotation, in degrees, for each polarization and then do whatever data processing was desired. Frequently we used the data to estimate the performance of aircraft systems, for instance, the range of performance of a communications antenna.

Appendix D: Military Radar Frequency Bands

S-Band was a World War II code expression meaning any frequency greater than 2 GHz and less than 4 GHz. Later the code was changed to E-Band for frequencies between 2 GHz and 3 GHz. F-Band means frequencies between 3 GHz and 4GHz. Old habits die hard. Many of us "Old Crows" still use the old S-Band terminology.

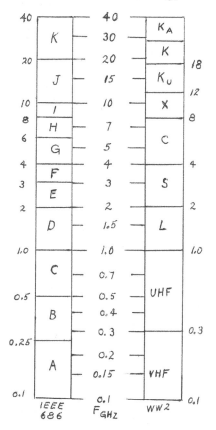

Military Radar Frequency Band Definitions

Appendix E: Outside U-2 Historical Studies

Recently I have read several books that address some of the earliest U-2 treatment attempts.

According to Bill Sweetman, the beginning of attempts to reduce the radar detectability of U-2 aircraft occurred in 1956. In his book *Lockheed Stealth*[97] he showed pictures on page 11 of a strange arrangement of wires on the fuselage, fin, and rudder of a U-2 aircraft. His description on page 13 does not agree with my experiences beginning in 1957 and seems quite muddled.

The CIA group may have attempted to use a crude analog of a Salisbury Screen utilizing wires supported several inches away from an aircraft's skin, with ferrite beads to provide attenuation, to reduce the Soviet Union radars' ability to detect and track the U-2 aircraft with little or no success.

That may be why Kelly Johnson looked internally of Lockheed and ultimately, selected me.

Curtis Peebles, in his book *Shadow Flights* (pages 164 and 165) described the "Dirty Bird" U-2 configurations that were said to have been flown over or near Soviet Union territory. There are several descriptions of anti-radar treatments that are incorrect. It seems that information was so scattered and distorted by security measures that much of it may be incorrect.

Perhaps their efforts failed because the ferrite beads were inert for high frequencies. The wires were too close to the aircraft's surfaces to cause any significant réduction of the low-frequency RCS.

Even if the arrangements had been effective in reducing the radar reflections, they would not have been useable because of the large aerodynamic drag they would cause and that, in turn, would result in serious loss of range and a dangerous loss of cruising altitude.

Appendix F: Salisbury Screen Design

The theoretical basis for the Salisbury screen seems very simple. It takes advantage of a portion of transmission line theory that says that the impedance at the terminals of a lossless transmission line one quarter of a wavelength long carrying the simplest distribution of electric and magnetic fields (the fundamental mode) and terminated by a short circuit is infinite.

Since the characteristic impedance of a lossless transmission line is purely resistive, the infinite impedance also is purely resistive and so elementary electric circuit theory can be employed to approximate the effect of adding a pure resistance element across the transmission line terminals. The result will be that the effective resistance will equal the added resistance applied to the transmission line terminals.

In its purest theoretical form, a Salisbury Screen consists of a thin plane membrane having electrical resistivity parallel to, and spaced away from, a perfectly conducting plane surface by one quarter of the free space wavelength of the incident electromagnetic wave. This assumes normal incidence. Normal means "perpendicular to" so that the waves strike the membrane and conducting surface perpendicularly.

We described the resistivity of the membrane in terms of ohms per square.

"Ohms per square" means the resistance that would be measured to current flowing from one edge of a square sample to an opposite edge if the thickness of the sample is extremely small compared to the size of the square.

Some energy would be extracted from the incident wave by the resistive membrane during the initial penetration but a considerable amount would reach the conducting surface. The wave then would be reversed in polarity and reflected to arrive at the membrane in time to allow some energy to penetrate the membrane and oppose the electric field of the next incoming wave. In the steady state, most of the incident wave energy would be consumed in the resistive membrane so that reflected waves from the outside surface of the membrane could be extremely small.

If "a" equals the decimal fraction of the magnitude of the power of an incoming wave that is absorbed by the lossy membrane alone, it can be shown that the attenuation caused by a Salisbury Screen can be calculated fairly accurately by

$$dB = 10 \log(1-a^2)$$

Note that if "a" equals one, the membrane absorbs all of the incoming wave power and the attenuation should become infinite. Conversely, if "a" equals zero, the attenuation becomes zero. However, if "a" equals one, no energy can pass through the membrane to generate the fields necessary to cause the effect of infinite impedance at the location of the membrane, and therefore the attenuation can not become infinite. Under carefully controlled conditions, the net reflected wave power may be less than 1 percent of the incident power. In other words, the reflected power may be reduced by more than 20 decibels.

This expression does not take into account the reverberations inside the screen and the decreasing amount of energy that leaks out due to each reverberation. Experience indicates that the formula is adequate for initial specification of parameters that can be refined after physical testing.

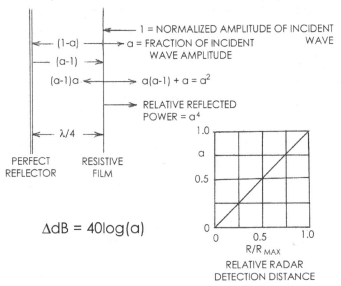

Simplified Version of a Salisbury Screen

For an example of how difficult it is to obtain a given result, if it were desired to utilize a Salisbury Screen absorber to reduce radar detection distance by 90 percent, 40 dB of attenuation would be required. To attain that amount "a" would equal 0.999949998 (approximately!).

If only a 50 percent reduction were required 12 dB of attenuation would be needed.

$R/R_{max} = 10^{(-dB/40)} = 10^{(-12/40)} = 0.5$.

For this case "a" would equal 0.9679381517 (again, approximately!).

Because the maximum effect depends upon time coincidence at the "outer" surface of the membrane of the incoming and reflected waves, the Salisbury Screen is sensitive to changes of frequency.

If "A" is the relative amplitude of the reflected wave compared to that of an incident wave, the following equation describes the results to be expected as a function of the ratio of the frequency of the incident wave to that of the designed frequency at which the greatest attenuation will occur.

$dB = 20 \log \{ 1 + A \cos [180 \cdot (F/F_0)] \}$, where

- $A \geq$ zero, with complete cancellation when $A = 1$; and
- F_0 = Frequency at which cancellation occurs.

This simple equation embodies the essence of the Salisbury Screen. Considerable information may be obtained by varying A, the relative amplitude parameter, and/or the argument of the cosine function. $A = 1$ corresponds to complete cancellation at the design frequency. Any value of A less than 1 will result in less than complete cancellation at any frequency.

An intrinsic property of such an energy-absorbing system is that similar electrical conditions occur for frequencies that are odd multiples of the lowest design frequency so that absorption bands occur that are odd harmonically related. Note that a Salisbury Screen is in effect a "comb" filter because it has multiple harmonically related absorption frequencies. This may not necessarily be true for a compact version of a Salisbury Screen.

Setting $A = 1$ allows one to determine the effectiveness of the lossy membrane by relating the bandwidth for given attenuation levels to the maximum amount of attenuation at the design frequency, even if it is obscured by measurement equipment noise. We used this information to overcome our measurement equipment's limitations.

The next figure shows the percentage bandwidth for various levels of attenuation assuming complete cancellation at a particular frequency (A = 1).

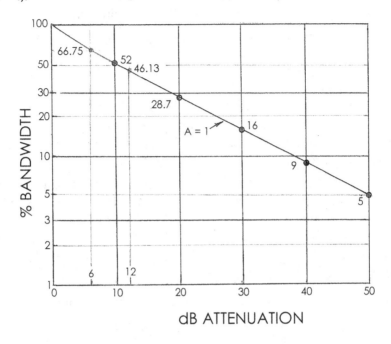

Percent Bandwidth as a Function of Attenuation

The following figure reveals the effect upon the relative radar detection distance that can occur.

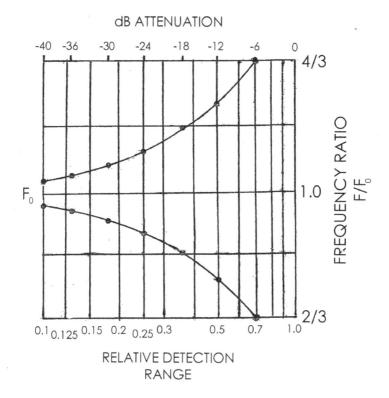

Best Possible Performance of a Salisbury Screen

As an example, the reduction of radar detection distance due to 12 dB of attenuation is 50 percent. The figures indicate that this result can be expected within a deviation of plus or minus 19.275 percent from the frequency at which cancellation occurs. If the design frequency is 3 GHz, this reduction can be attained for any radar frequency between 2.42 GHz and 3.58 GHZ.

Appendix G: Magic Tee

A reflectometer is a device that detects the presence of and/or facilitates measurement of the strength or intensity of energy reflected by a material body.

A reflectometer built using rectangular waveguides depends upon the directional properties of a hybrid junction. This type of junction consists of four waveguides joined together in a special way.

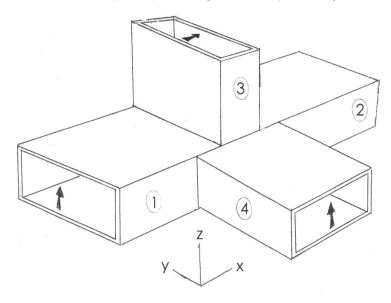

A Waveguide Hybrid Junction

If the two co-linear branches, 1 and 2 in the figure, suitably were terminated so that their reflection coefficients were equal and the reflected electric field amplitudes were equal and oppositely polarized at the center of the junction, no energy would be transferred between the branches 3 and 4. A hybrid junction operated in this way is called a "Magic Tee."[98][99]

The equipment that we used most frequently employed a single antenna for both transmitting and receiving electromagnetic energy and, therefore, required separation of the transmitted energy from the reflected energy. The Magic Tee junction was used to prevent the transmitted energy from entering the receiver.

When one of its co-linear branches was equipped to provide an adjustable reflection it was possible to nearly cancel the energy that otherwise would enter one of the side branches and the receiver.

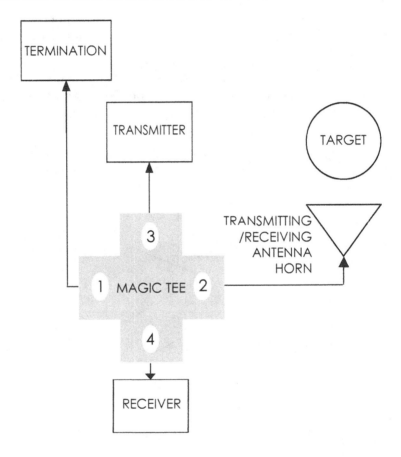

Reflectometer Using a Waveguide Magic Tee

In our use of this type of junction one of the branches 1 or 2 was terminated by a very well impedance matched horn antenna that was exposed to a region of extremely small reflectivity (anechoic chamber or open sky). The other co-linear branch was terminated by an absorbing device (load) and an adjustable reflecting device (tuner). Proper adjustment of the tuner element resulted in almost complete decoupling of the E arm (branch 3) and the H arm (branch 4). Then the transmitter power, introduced into one side branch (No. 3, for example), would divide almost equally between branches 1 and 2 so that nearly half the power would be radiated by the horn antenna and only an extremely small part of it would enter the receiver via the other side branch (No. 4).

Since the activity involved in reducing the transfer of energy resembled the adjustment of a simple Wheatstone "bridge" to result in a null indication, there seemed to be an analogous relationship and so the Magic Tee equipped reflectometer arrangement often was called a "bridge."

Energy carried by a wave reflected from a target entering the horn antenna would be divided almost equally between one co-linear branch (No. 1, for example) and the other side branch (No. 4) to enter the receiver. This resulted in a loss of three quarters of the available power and was serious in the early days before higher powered transmitters and more sensitive receivers were available.

Appendix H: Resistivity Measurements

To provide means for correlating DC resistivity measurements with waveguide attenuation and backscatter results, we used stepped-up in diameter coaxial fixtures to accommodate enlarged thin film specimens for direct current and high frequency resistivity measurements to improve measurement accuracy.

The steps in the coaxial transmission lines that were used for high frequency measurements were designed as analogs of lumped element impedance matching networks. The discontinuity capacitances were combined with the inductive effect of the smaller center conductor to preserve the characteristic impedance of the entire transmission line.[100] The increase in size at each step is arbitrary, but the ratio of the diameters of the conductors must be the same throughout the fixture. The only important source of reflection was the specimen under test.

The Figure shows a schematic of the general arrangement of the stepped coaxial conductors. Any number of steps may be used. We preferred to use three because that allowed us to use convenient size specimens.

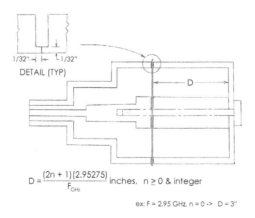

$$D = \frac{(2n + 1)(2.95275)}{F_{GHz}} \text{ inches, } n \geq 0 \text{ \& integer}$$

ex: F = 2.95 GHz, n = 0 -> D = 3"

Stepped-up Coaxial HF Test Fixture

The distance D measured from the short circuit must equal an odd number of quarter wavelengths.

D was made three inches so that measurements could be made using frequencies near 1GHz and 3 GHz.

The measurement procedure was based upon simple transmission line theory. If a loss-less transmission line is short circuited the reflected waves combine with incoming waves to cause an infinite impedance to occur every odd multiple of a quarter wavelength back from the short circuit toward the source (generator). The effect is as though the transmission line has been cut off at each location.

Impedance in the form of a thin resistive sheet placed at such locations will terminate the line and allow its resistivity to be determined by measurement of the resulting VSWR and the change in the position of a voltage minimum. The data may be plotted upon a Smith Chart to reveal the film resistivity.

We were interested in making films that were purely resistive and whose resistivity would agree with direct current measurements. Purely resistive films whose resistivity is greater than the characteristic impedance cause no voltage minimum shift. A quarter wavelength shift will occur if the resistivity is less than the characteristic impedance of the transmission line.

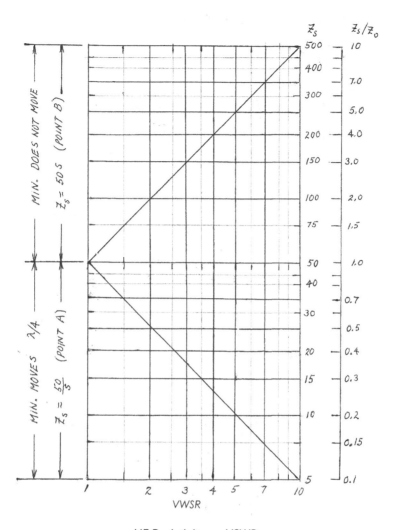

HF Resistivity vs. VSWR

The lower half of the chart (Point A) represents a resistance less than the characteristic impedance of the transmission line. The upper half (Point B) represents a resistance greater than the characteristic impedance of the transmission line. The point at the center indicates equality of film resistivity with the equivalent of the transmission line characteristic impedance.

The measurement procedure involved the following steps if the film impedances were purely resistive:

- With the test chamber empty, an appropriate frequency was selected;
- A voltage minimum was located;
- A sample resistive film was inserted and we read the resulting VSWR and the location of a voltage minimum;
- The film resistivity was determined from the chart.

We developed a portable version of a stepped-up coaxial resistivity device for DC surface resistivity measurements. The DC measurements supplemented the high-frequency data and were used for quality control measurements of mockup and flyable parts.

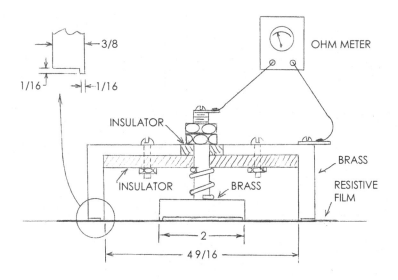

Stepped-up Coaxial DC Test Fixture

Thin film resistivity, expressed as "ohms per square" was measured by two different direct current arrangements. If the thin films were purely resistive, microwave measurements should agree with DC measurements.

One, using coaxial electrodes, yielded an answer that was compared to another that utilized two parallel electrodes on opposite sides of a rectangular sample. Very high conductivity silver paint was used to connect to test specimens.

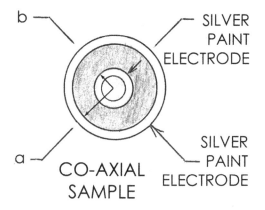

b —   — SILVER PAINT ELECTRODE

a — CO-AXIAL SAMPLE

SILVER PAINT ELECTRODE

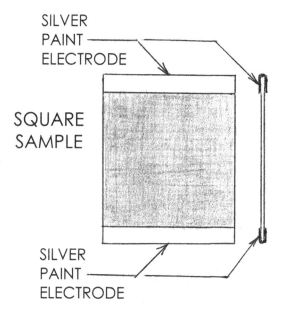

SILVER PAINT ELECTRODE

SQUARE SAMPLE

SILVER PAINT ELECTRODE

Two DC Resistivity Measurement Configurations

The thin film resistivity was calculated from direct current coaxial measurements:

$$R = \int_{a}^{b} \frac{R_s da}{2\pi a} = \frac{R_s}{2\pi} ln(\frac{b}{a})$$

or

$$R_s = \frac{2\pi R}{ln(\frac{b}{a})}$$

Where:

- R = DC resistance measured between the coaxial electrodes;
- R_s = film resistivity in ohms per square;
- ln = "natural" (base "e") logarithm;
- b/a = ratio of the inner and outer diameters of the conductors of the coaxial transmission line.

We made (b/a) equal to 2.303 to correspond to that for 50 ohm air insulated coaxial transmission lines. Then the thin film resistivity was 7.532 times the DC resistance.

High frequency measurement of resistivity, expressed in ohms per square, was accomplished by measuring the VSWR caused by very thin specimens mounted in our coaxial test fixtures.

- R_s = (Z_o/S) if a voltage minimum moved a quarter wavelength;
- R_s = (Z_oS) if the voltage minimum did not move;
- S = voltage standing wave ratio;
- Z_o = characteristic impedance of the coaxial line.

If Z_o = 50 ohms, the simple formula results in R_s = (50/S) or (50S) ohms per square. We used Z_o = 50 ohms because that was characteristic of all our coaxial slotted line test equipment.

When waveguide slotted line test equipment was used, the simple formula used for coaxial transmission lines did not apply because the waveguide characteristic impedance (always resistive) is more difficult to define. Also, it varies with frequency. It was necessary to calibrate each waveguide for several frequencies by utilizing thin film samples of known resistivity.

Calculated values of the characteristic impedance of rectangular waveguides, based upon information published by S. A. Schelkunoff,[101] are displayed in the figure. The data presented here were not verified by measurements utilizing resistive films in waveguides and are intended only to emphasize the fact that waveguide characteristic impedance varies with changes of frequency.

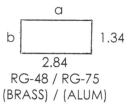

RG-48 / RG-75
(BRASS) / (ALUM)

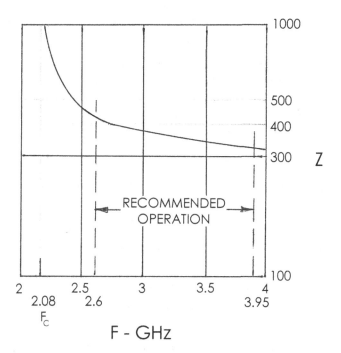

Waveguide Characteristic Impedance

Most of the waveguide resistivity measurements were performed using RG-48 sized S-Band waveguide slotted line equipment.

Before measurements of the thin films with resistive coating were performed, it was necessary to match the waveguide characteristic impedance using a "slide-screw tuner" and a resistive termination to minimize the reflections from the termination. Then, by utilizing a resistive film of known DC resistivity held perpendicular to the waveguide axis and measuring the resulting VSWR, the waveguide characteristic impedance could be calculated by using a formula similar to that used for coaxial measurements. This procedure, repeated for each frequency of interest, made the waveguide tell us its true characteristic impedance.

Schelkunoff derived three equations differing only by multiplier factors to describe the characteristic impedance of rectangular waveguides carrying the fundamental mode. The calibration procedure was designed to determine the correct multiplier for use in calculating waveguide characteristic impedance. It was based upon the same theory as that used in the coaxial measurements, shunting the resistive waveguide characteristic impedance by a thin film of known resistivity and measuring the resulting VSWR.

For greatest accuracy, the thin film resistivity should be approximately equal to the estimated waveguide characteristic impedance. An estimate of the waveguide characteristic impedance multiplier that should be used in Schelkunoff's equation may be obtained by:

$K = [(240\,\pi)(60\,\pi^2)(15\,\pi^3)]^{1/3}$

$= [(754)(592)(465)]^{1/3} = 592.$

The procedure began by assembling a waveguide resistive termination, a "slide-screw" tuner, an empty thin film holder, a waveguide slotted line and detector, a signal generator, and a VSWR indicator.

Then the slide-screw tuner was adjusted to obtain the lowest VSWR, as near to unity as possible.

The next step was to insert a thin film of known DC resistivity into the holder between the slide-screw tuner and the slotted line section and then measure the VSWR.

The waveguide characteristic impedance then could be calculated from:

$$Z_o = \frac{b(S-1)R_s}{a\sqrt{1-(\frac{F_c}{F})^2}}$$

Where:

- Z_0 = True characteristic impedance;
- R_s = thin film resistivity, ohms per square;

- S = VSWR;
- F_c = waveguide cut-off frequency;
- F_c = (5.904/a) GHz;
- F = test frequency;
- a = waveguide cross section width, inches;
- b = waveguide cross section height, inches;

The calibration procedure was performed using more than one thin film resistivity for each of several frequencies within the range of 1.3 to 2 times the cut-off frequency.

Index

Lovick, Ronald 227
Lovick, Sherre (nee Lilley) v, xiii, xiv, 9,
   10, 37, 145, 212, 213, 227, 228
Lulu Belle, Lockheed P-80 39

M

MacDonald, Luther Duncan 'Mac'
   xvii, 27, 28, 30, 32, 73, 81, 84,
   87, 88, 90, 92, 93, 107, 108,
   116, 125, 127, 134, 135, 141,
   158, 178, 277
Magic Tee 89, 94, 120
Marine Corps Logistics Base Barstow
   110
Martin, Edward 'Ed' 44, 83, 88, 182,
   185, 186, 188, 189, 190, 205
Martin, William R. 'Bill' 60, 65, 67, 72,
   76, 81, 88, 96
Massachusetts Institute of Technol-
   ogy 53, 85, 110, 132
McDonnell-Douglas 191, 218
Morita, Tetsu 75, 76
Moule, Bill 178, 224
Myers, Grace 19

N

Naval Air Weapons Station, China
   Lake, California 35, 37, 127,
   216, 227
Naval Ordnance Test Station, Inyok-
   ern, California 34, 35, 37, 38,
   39, 42, 47, 53, 127
Naval Research Laboratory, Washing-
   ton, DC 82, 218
Nelson, Norman 'Norm' 213
Nethken, Harley 132

O

Oshiro, Frederick 'Fred' 193
Oughtred, William 26
Overholser, Denys 178, 187, 188, 191,
   198, 199

P

P-38 International Association 228
Paradise Ranch 1, 83
Park, Bill 200
Patino, Ed 224
Pendelton, Wayne 157
Phantastron 53, 274
Pioneers of Stealth 185, 228
Plott, Robert 164, 165
Plumer, J. Anderson 'Andy' 199
Powelson, Nolan 227
Powelson, Patricia (nee Lovick) 227
Powers, Francis Gary 84, 115, 180,
   277
Pratt and Whitney 131, 132, 152, 154,
   155

R

Ramsey, John 108
Randolph, Lisa Brey xiv, 213
RATSCAT (RAdar Target SCATter) 190,
   191, 192, 193, 195, 196, 198,
   205, 206, 221, 225
Rawlins, Jr., Robert E. 'Bob' 31, 53, 54,
   76
Rawson, E. 110, 111
Reciprocity 61
Reedy, Perry Merlin 'Merlin' 83, 84,
   87, 88, 90, 92, 116, 195
Reichert, James 'Jim' 199, 217
Rempt, Henry 79
Rich, Ben 116, 188, 190, 202, 219
Richter, Elvin O. 'E.O.' 53, 76, 82
Riggs, Gordon 75
Roadrunners International 228
Robert E. Gross Award 202, 203
Rockford, Illinois 45, 47
Rodgers, Frank 127, 128
Rodgers, Franklin 'Frank' 107
Rogers, Phillip 'Phil' 206, 207, 208,
   209
Rohlfs, Albert 163

References

1. Robert L. Weber, Kenneth V. Manning, Marsh W. White, "Maria Goeppert Mayer," *College Physics 4th Ed.* (New York: McGraw-Hill Book Co., 1947), 661.
2. Susan Quinn, *Marie Curie: A Life* (New York: Simon & Schuster, McGraw Hill Book Co., 1995).
3. Ruth Lewin Sime, *Lise Meitner, A Life in Physics* (Berkeley: University of California Press, 1997).
4. David Bodanis, *Ada, Countess of Lovelace* (North Branch, MN: Electric Universe, Crown Publishers Random House, 2004), 68.
5. Mario Livio, *The Golden Ratio* (New York: Broadway Books, a Division of Random House, Inc., 2002).
6. Edward Lovick, Jr., "Frequency 'Wobblers' For Service Oscillators," *Radio Craft* (November 1937): 273.
7. Austin V. Eastman, *Fundamentals of Vacuum Tubes 2nd Ed.* (New York: McGraw-Hill Book Company, Inc., 1941), 13–14.
8. Herbert J. Reich, "Thermionic Emission," in *Theory and Applications of Electron Tubes, 1st Ed.* (New York: McGraw-Hill Book Company, Inc., 1939).
9. Raymond W. Dull, *Mathematics for Engineers* (New York: McGraw-Hill Book Company, Inc., 1941).
10. Edward Lovick, Jr., "Determination of Directional Characteristics of Aircraft Antennas," *Aero Digest* (July 1943): 259–260.
11. Barrett Tillman, *Vought F4U Corsair Warbird Tech Series* (North Branch, MN: Specialty Press, 2001), 46.
12. John T. Hayward and C.W. Borklund, *Bluejacket Admiral: The Career of Chick Hayward* (Annapolis: Naval Institute Press, 2000).
13. Captain William Crawford Eddy, USN and Ronald K. Jurgen, "Captain Eddy: the Man Who Launched a Thousand EEs," *IEEE Spectrum* (December 1975): 53–56.

14. Clarence Leonard "Kelly" Johnson with Maggie Smith, *KELLY More Than My Share of It All* (Washington, D.C.: Smithsonian Institution Press, 1985).

15. D. Van Nostrand, "Cyclotron," *Van Nostrand's Scientific Encyclopedia 3ʳᵈ Ed.* (Princeton: D. Van Nostrand Co. Inc., 1958), 472.

16. James R. McDade, "Phantastron Control Circuit," *Electrical Engineering* (October 1948): 974–977.

17. Tom Kitaguchi, "Transistorize a One-Shot Phantastron Circuit," *Electronic Design* (9 December 1959): 152.

18. Author unknown, "Circuit Classics," *Electronic Equipment Engineering* (July 1962): 59.

19. Ronald W. Foster, "Directive Diagrams of Antenna Arrays," *Bell System Technical Journal* (April 1926).

20. G.H. Brown, "Directional Antennas," *Proceedings of the Institute of Radio Engineers* 25 No. 1 (1937): 78–145.

21. Harry F. Olson, *Dynamical Analogies* (New York: D. Van Nostrand Company, Inc., 1943).

22. Sander Bais, *The Equations: Icons of Knowledge* (Cambridge: Harvard University Press, 2005), 18.

23. Harold I. Sharlin, "From Maxwell to Marconi," in *The Making of the Electrical Age* (New York: Abelard-Schuman, 1963), 82.

24. Irving M. Gottlieb, "Make Graphs Work for You," *Radio-Electronics* (May 1976): 60.

25. J. Tykocinski Tykociner, "Investigation of Antennae by means of Models," *Bulletin of the Illinois Engineering Experiment Station* (May 1925).

26. Frederick E. Terman, *Radio Engineers' Handbook 3ʳᵈ Ed.* (New York: McGraw-Hill Book Company, 1943), 786–787.

27. George Sinclair, "Theory of Models of Electro Magnetic Systems," *Proceedings of the Institute of Radio Engineers* 36 (November 1948): 1364–70.

28. Raymond E. Davis, Francis S. Foote, and W.H. Rayner, "Figure 170: Polar Planimeter," in *Surveying Theory and Practice* (New York: McGraw-Hill Book Company, Inc., 1928), 240–241.

29. Author unknown, *Radar System Fundamentals* (Washington, D.C.: Navships 900,017 (Unclassified), Bureau of Ships, Navy Department, April 1944), 316–317.

30. Don Lancaster, "Synchros and Selsyns and Accelerometers— Oh, My!," *Poptronics* (May 2000): 61–62 and 64.

31. Winfield W. Salisbury, 11 May 1943, "Absorbent Body for Electromagnetic Waves," *U.S. Patent 2,599,944* (sequestered for security; issued 10 June 1952).

32. David Bodanis, *Electric Universe* (New York: Crown Publishers, Random House, 2004), 87, 164 and 180.

33. Arthur Beiser, *Physics* (Reading, MA: Addison-Wesley Publishing Company Inc., 1986), 174–178.

34. John L. Heilbron, ed., "Newton's Cradle," in *OXFORD Illustrated Companion to The History of MODERN SCIENCE* (New York: Tess Press, 2008).

35. Author unknown, "Electronics WAR REPORT: SCR-584 Radar," *Electronics* XVIII (1945) and XIX (1946): 110–117.

36. Louie N. Ridenour, ed., "SCR-584 Autotrack Radar," *MIT Radiation Laboratory Series, Vol. 1* (New York: McGraw-Hill Book Company, Inc., 1948), 207–210, 228, and 284–286.

37. R.V. Jones, *The Wizard War, British Scientific Intelligence 1939–1945* (New York: Coward, McCann & Geoghegan, Inc., 1978), 347, 349, and 431, map on 368.

38. William H. Nebergall, Frederic C. Schmidt, and Henry F. Holtzclaw, *College Chemistry* (Boston: D.C. Heath and Company, 1963), 411–425.

39. John C. Bailar, Jr., Therald Moeller, and Jacob Kleinberg, *University Chemistry* (Boston: D. C. Heath and Company, 1966), 462–475.

40. Cornelia T. Snell and Foster Dee Snell, *Chemistry Made Easy* (New York: Chemical Publishing Company, 1959), 44–49.

41. Joel H. Hildebrand and Richard E. Powell, "Principals of Chemistry," in *Reference Book of Inorganic Chemistry 6th Ed.* (New York: The MacMillan Company, 1957), 218–220.

42. Edward Lovick, Jr., "A New Type of Radar Search Antenna" (Lockheed Aircraft Corporation Report LR 11308, LAC 242931, 3 March 1956): 22–26.

43. Robin Beach, "Electrostatic Ills and Cures of Aircraft, Part I, Electrification of Airplanes and How It Causes Radio Interference," *Electrical Engineering* (April 1947): 325–334.

44. Robin Beach, "Electrostatic Ills and Cures of Aircraft, Part II, Radio Interference and Its Control," *Electrical Engineering* (May 1947): 453–462.

45. Willard H. Bennett, "Snow Static on Aircraft," *Electrical Engineering* (October 1948): 947–954.

46. Ross Gunn, "The Electrical Charge on Precipitation at Various Altitudes and Its Relation to Thunderstorms," *Proceedings of the American Physical Society, Physical Review* 71 No. 2 (15 January 1947).

47. R.L. Tanner and J.E. Nanevicz, "Precipitation Charging and Corona-generated Interference in Aircraft," *Stanford Research Institute Report* 73 (April 1961): 57–61.

48. M. Newman and A.O. Kemppainen, "High-Voltage Installation of the Precipitation-Static Project," *Proceedings of the Institute of Radio Engineers* 34 No. 5 (May 1946): 247–254, Figures 4 and 8.

49. S.A. Schelkunoff, "The Impedance Concept and its Application to Problems of Reflection, Refraction, Shielding, and Power Absorption," *Bell System Technical Journal* 17 Issue 1 (1938): 17.

50. S.A. Schelkunoff, *Electromagnetic Waves* (New York: D. Van Nostrand Co. Inc., 1943), 319, Equation 21-21.

51. R.A. Smith, F.E. Jones, and R.P. Chasmar, *The Detection and Measurement of Infra-red Radiation* Oxford (London: University Press, Amen House, 1958).

52. "Black Bodies," (Van Nostrand 1958), 196.

53. J.C. Toler, et al., "Hooded Antenna for Measurement of Electromagnetic Radiation in a Shielded Enclosure," in *Contract to Marshall Space Flight Center (MFS-21240)* (Pasadena: California Institute of Technology, 1976).

54. M. Abraham, "Die elektrischen schwingungen um einen Stabformigen leiter, behandelt nach der Maxwellschen theorie," *Ann. der Phys.* 66 (1898): 435–472.

55. M. Abraham, "Ein satze uber modelle von antennen," *Jahr. der Dracht. Tele.* 16 (1920): 6–70.

56. J. Tykocinski Tykociner, "Investigation of Antennae by means of Models," *Bulletin of the Illinois Engineering Experiment Station* (May 1925).

57. George Sinclair, "Theory of Models of Electromagnetic Systems," *Proceedings of the Institute of Radio Engineers* 36 No. 11 (1948): 1362–1370.
58. Ed Lovick, Jr., "Effect of Scaling on Attenuator Conductivity" (Memorandum to C.L. Johnson, 15 February, 1960).
59. J.B. Johnson, "Thermal Agitation of Electricity in Conductors," *Physical Review* 32 (July 1928): 97.
60. Frederick Emmons Terman, "Johnson Noise," in *Radio Engineers' Handbook 1ˢᵗ Ed.* (New York: McGraw-Hill Book Company, Inc., 1943), 476.
61. A.E. Adam and J.D. Whitehead, "Measuring the Mean Square Amplitude of Fading Signals Using a Selected Quantile Output Device (SQUOD)," *Proceedings of the Institute of Radio Engineers* (June 1960): 1172–73.
62. William Schroeder, L. D. MacDonald, and C. L. Johnson, "The Probability of Radar Detection of Airborne Targets," (Lockheed Advanced Development Projects Report SP-119, 30 April 1958).
63. Edward L. Ginston and Arthur E. Harrison, "Reflex Klystron Oscillators," *Proceedings of the Institute of Radio Engineers* 34 No. 3 (March 1946): 97P–113P, Figure 1.
64. Francis A. Jenkins and Harvey E. White, *Fundamentals of Optics* (New York: McGraw-Hill Book Company, Inc., New York: 1957), 355–361.
65. Ed Lovick, Jr., "Source of Error in Full Scale Measurements," (Memorandum to C.L. Johnson, 11 January 1960).
66. C. L. Kelly Johnson, "Weight Performance Contract Attachment, Archangel Log", (Lockheed Aircraft Corporation Advanced Development Projects, Burbank, CA)
67. "Schlieren Windows," (Van Nostrand, 1958): 1462.
68. "Skin Effect," (Terman 1943), 28–37.
69. Paul Crickmore, *Lockheed SR-71: The Secret Missions Exposed* (Sterling Heights, MI: Osprey Publishing, 1993)
70. Francis Gary Powers and Curt Gentry, *Operation Overflight* (New York: Holt, Rinehart & Winston, 1970).
71. Curtis Peebles, *Shadow Flights, America's Secret War Against the Soviet Union* (Novato, CA: Presidio Press Inc., 2002). 164, 165

72. R.L. Sproull and E.G. Linder, "Resonant Cavity Measurements," *Proceedings of the Institute of Radio Engineers* 34 No. 5 (1946): 305–312.

73. "Q," (Terman 1943), 135–172.

74. "Sharpness of Resonance," (Van Nostrand 1958) 1336 and 1492.

75. Charles L. Optiz, "Metal Detecting Radar Rejects Clutter Naturally," *Microwaves* (August 1976): 12–14.

76. David C. Aronstein and Albert C. Piccirillo, *Have Blue and the F-117A* (Restin, VA: AIAA, 2002), 24.

77. H.C. Marlow, D.C. Watson, C.H. Van Hoozer, and C.C. Freeny, "The RATSCAT Cross Section Facility," *Proceedings of the IEEE* 53 No. 8 (1965): 946–953.

78. T.B.A. Senior, M.A. Plonus, and E.F. Knott, "Designing Foamed Plastic Target Supports," *Microwaves* (December 1964): 38–43.

79. Charles J. Michaels, "Horizontal Antennas and the Compound Reflection Coefficient," *The ARRL Antenna Compendium, The American Radio Relay League* 3 (1998): 175–184.

80. "Notice of Availability for Donation of the Test Craft Ex-SEA SHADOW (IX-529) and Hughes Mining Barge (HMB-1)," *Federal Register* 71 No. 178 (Thursday, September 14, 2006): Notices.

81. T. Moreno, "Microwave Transmission Design Data," in Publication No. 23-80 (Great Neck, NY: Sperry Gyroscope Company, Inc., 1944), 132.

82. Thomas T. Taylor, PhD., "Advanced Antenna Theory," (UCLA course X136 notes, circa 1952).

83. Phillip H. Smith, "Transmission Line Calculator," *Electronics.* 12 (1939): 29–31.

84. Phillip H. Smith, "An Improved Transmission Line Calculator," *Electronics* 17 (1944): 130.

85. Christopher Horme, "Smith Chart Fundamentals," *Nuts & Volts* (August 2004): 75.

86. "Smith Chart," (Van Nostrand 1958), 1515.

87. John Derbyshire, *Unknown Quantity* (New York: Penguin Group (USA) Inc., 2006), 7–12.

88. E.C. Jordan and K.G. Balmain, *Electromagnetic Waves and Radiating Systems* (Englewood Cliffs, NJ: Prentice-Hall, Inc., 1968), 232–235.

89. Bronwell, A.B. and Beam, R.E., *Theory and Applications of Microwaves* (New York: McGraw-Hill Book Company, Inc., 1947), 164–175.

90. "Slide Rules," (Dull 1941), 392–405.

91. P. S. Carter, "Charts For Transmission Line Measurements and Calculations," *RCA Review* 3 (January 1939): 355–368.

92. Robert L. Peters, *Nomographs for Electronics* (Boston: Cahners Books, 1973).

93. R.P. Hoelscher, J.N. Arnold, and S.H. Pierce, *Graphic Aids in Engineering Computations* (Champaign, IL: The Garrard Press, 1942).

94. Henry K. Bradford, "High-Speed Analysis of Electronic Circuits by Geometry," *Electronic Buyers' Guide* (20 July 1961): 50–64.

95. J.W. Downs, "Geometric Design of Compound Reflectors," *Microwave Journal* 28 No. 5 (1985): 187–201.

96. George Sinclair, "Patterns of Slotted-Cylinder Antennas," *Proceedings of the Institute of Radio Engineers* 36 (December 1948): 1487–92.

97. Bill Sweetman, *Lockheed Stealth* (St. Paul: MDI Publishing Company, 2001), 11 and 13.

98. C.G. Montgomery, R.H. Dicke, and E.M. Purcell, "Principles of Microwave Circuits," in *M.I.T. Radiation Laboratory Series Volume 8* (New York: The McGraw-Hill Book Co., Inc., 1948), 306–308.

99. "Magic Tee," (Van Nostrand 1958), 1003.

100. J.R. Whinnery and H.W. Jamieson, "Equivalent Circuits in Transmission Lines" *Proceedings of the Institute of Radio Engineers* 32 (February 1944): 98–114.

101. "Electromagnetic Waves," (Schelkunoff 1943), 319.